Exile Cinema

THE SUNY SERIES

HORIZONS OF CINEMA

MURRAY POMERANCE | EDITOR

Also in the series

William Rothman, editor, *Cavell on Film*

J. David Slocum, editor, *Rebel Without a Cause*

Joe McElhaney, *The Death of Classical Cinema*

Kirsten Thompson, *Apocalyptic Dread*

Frances Gateward, editor, *Seoul Searching*

Exile Cinema

Filmmakers at Work beyond Hollywood

Michael Atkinson, editor

STATE UNIVERSITY OF NEW YORK PRESS

Cover photo: Kyle McCulloch as Grigorss in *Careful* (1992, dir. Guy Maddin).

Published by
State University of New York Press, Albany

Printed in the United States of America

For information, contact State University of New York Press, Albany, NY
www.sunypress.edu

Production by Marilyn P. Semerad
Marketing by Anne M. Valentine

Library of Congress Cataloging-in-Publication Data

Exile cinema : filmmakers at work beyond Hollywood / edited by Michael Atkinson.
p. cm. — (SUNY series, horizons of cinema)
Includes bibliographical references and index.
ISBN 978-0-7914-7377-1 (hardcover : alk. paper)
ISBN 978-0-7914-7378-8 (pbk. : alk. paper)
1. Motion pictures—Developing countries. 2. Motion pictures—Europe. 3. Experimental films—History and criticism. I. Atkinson, Michael, 1962–

PN1993.5.D44E97 2008
791.43'7—dc22 2007025405

10 9 8 7 6 5 4 3 2 1

Contents

Acknowledgments

SOME OF THE CHAPTERS IN THIS BOOK previously appeared—often in substantially different form—in the following publications, to which grateful acknowledgment is made:

The Believer (Dennis Lim's "Kuala *L'Impure*: The Cinema of Amir Muhammad"); *Chicago Reader* (Jonathan Rosenbaum's "Bullet Ballet: Seijun Suzuki"); *Cinema Scope* (B. Kite's "A Kurosawa Kiyoshi Kit," and Ed Park's "The Bong Show: Bong Joon-ho"); *City Pages* (Mark Peranson's "Guy Maddin"); *Film Comment* (Michael Atkinson's "Blunt Force Trauma: Andrzej Zulawski," Godfrey Cheshire's "Ross McElwee," Howard Hampton's "Double Trouble: Tsui Hark & Ching Siu-Tung," and Maitland McDonagh's "*Dellamorte Dellamore* and Michele Soavi," Chuck Stephens's "Moebius Dragstrip: Monte Hellman Circles Back," and David Thompson's "Pleasures of the Flesh: Walerian Borowczyk"); *Senses of Cinema* (Geoff Andrew's "Beyond the Clouds: The Films of Nuri Bilge Ceylan"); and *Sight & Sound* (Jonathan Romney's "Bela Tarr").

Introduction

Michael Atkinson

This book could be considered a manifesto. Then again, virtually anything written by the essayists, critics, and scholars represented herein on the subject of film could be as well. Manifestos can be defined as such by their contexts, and any writing about cinema as an art form—not a commercial project or thoughtless distraction or an academically theorizable cultural phenomena—has by this late date acquired an insurrectionary character. What the writers collected in this volume are struggling to do—in my view—is insist on a cinephile's view of movies, as a matter of bedazzlement, profundity, tangible cultural intercourse, and rampaging pleasure. It is not glamour-drunk sycophancy. It is not speculative, jargon-drenched "research," performed for the benefit of tenure. It is an exaultation of film critics (to co-opt the group name for larks), exercising allegiance to their frantic medium's neglected territories.

This is a necessary stance precisely because our perception of cinema today is shaped almost entirely by publicity. Ninety-nine percent of all culture "journalism" in this country—print, radio, TV, and Web—is performed at the behest of public relation firms. Celebrity profiles and cross-pollinating cable-marketings dominate, while too many workaday reviewers know little or nothing about cinema culture (editors blithely transferring them from a newspaper's dance or restaurant or real estate desk is common), and are content in co-publicizing the profitable product of the week, regardless of its value. DVDs are routinely marketed as being "supplemented" by their own advertising; consumer-targeted Web sites offer commercials as entertainment. Books published about film, primarily from small and university presses, are many and varied in their content, but those chosen to stock the scant "Film, TV & Radio" shelf in most of the nation's "big box" bookstores are dominated by alphabetical video guides, coffee-table photo collections and unauthorized biographies. (Serious works of critical scholarship, such as J. Hoberman's history of Yiddish cinema *Bridge of Light*, go unreviewed, unsold and unread.) What films get made, what films we see, and what filmmakers we know about are all matters largely predetermined by the cataract of marketing, advertising, and media exposure. Thus, a film's importance is largely predetermined for us by those who will profit from it and who are willing to manufacture metric tons of marketing discourse toward that end.

For the average filmgoer, for whom cinema once meant human drama, empathic involvement, and catapulting adventure (if not always, as it was in the post–World War II decades of imported film, poetic transcendence, and sociopolitical force), mainstream movies now ordinarily embody meaningless noise, visual patronization, and derivative retro-experience. Such American movies continue to rule the globe's box office and media stream, but at least in South Korea, or France, or Egypt there's a thriving local cinema offering up some resistance. We have little such luck, what with the absorption of independent film into the mainstream revenue stream, and the thorough neutering of the imported-film distribution marketplace. For a supremely testy autopsy on the entire phenomenon, see Jonathan Rosenbaum's book *Movie Wars: How Hollywood and the Media Limit What Movies We Can See*; for now, let's just note that the largest internationally grossing non–English-language film, Ang Lee's *Crouching Tiger, Hidden Dragon*, took in just a few more million ($128 million, give or take) in its entire theatrical revenue life than Sam Raimi's *Spider-Man* made in its first American weekend. The first weekend's grosses, let's remember, are not the results of word-of-mouth or any other expression of consumer satisfaction, but purely of marketing power. Sometimes willing reviewers can help to a marginal degree, but most of the time not.

It should go without saying—and it sometimes can for those of us lucky enough to live in or near cities where film distribution isn't limited to the three or four weekly releases produced in Los Angeles, and who have persevered in acquiring a certain hunger for, grasp on, and perspective about cinematic aesthetics—that there's more to the picture than we are ordinarily allowed to see. There is, in fact, a vast movie-crazed globe outside of the market kingdom, where madmen, geniuses, and apostates roam freely, subject to a relatively minimal degree, if at all, to corporate industry and spin control. These filmmakers battle the greatest odds a modern artist can face: the opposition of mass culture at large, in a medium that nonetheless requires enormous expenditures in every stage of production and distribution. Naturally, the average American moviehead rarely gets a chance to see these marginalized directors' work and often knows about them only through dazzled rumors and rhapsodic hearsay.

Ironically, the films by these artists and many, many others are available to us now to a heretofore unimaginable degree—anyone with an inexpensive all-region DVD player, an Internet connection, and a credit card can order otherwise-impossible-to-see discs from anywhere on Earth. But to do so, you'd have to know what you're looking for, and therefore have acquired the resilience and tenacity and acculturated sophistication to swim upstream against the very culture that surrounds you and strives to curb your options. Every dyed-in-the-wool cinema connoisseur is aware that to prefer the films of Hou Hsaio-hsien to those of Steven Spielberg is to place yourself decidedly outside the primary cultural discourse of American life. But Hou occupies the inner, most ballyhooed circle of non-Industry artistes, an elite selection that may be occupied by a half-dozen candidates these days (Lars Von Trier or Zhang Yimou one moment, and then not the next); what about the rest of moviemaking mankind? In cinema as in literature, music and even news, the rest of the world is of little importance to stateside profiteers and so, therefore, largely unknown to consumers. How many Americans know the names Bong Joon-ho or Nuri Bilge Ceylan or Chantal Ackerman? How many even go to a movie because of a filmmaker's unique reputation rather than because of its advertising?

You probably do, because you're holding this book, but you belong to a minority that, if it can be gleaned from the movie tickets bought and DVDs sold annually, may be as small as 2 percent of the cinema-consuming public. Which, marketwise, makes you and I fish far too small to fry—if we depend on the businesses that run culture to do the cooking. Our tribe seeks out alternatives, not merely for the sake of iconoclasm but because the movies exiled from the deal table are usually exiled for fabulous reasons that are hard to sell: profound truth, formal rigor, idiosyncratic style, personal expression, fresh narrative engineering, outright experimentation, thematic substance, unorthodox (or culturally specific) visual syntax, political radicalism. In fact, this exile is more than just the result of difficult saleability: Modern, post–Reagan-era Hollywood homogeneity is a carefully calibrated, deliberately contrived system of visual syntax that, like television advertising, seeks to inculcate us to its ad-fast rhythms and sensations and thereby, in the longer run, make us less capable of wanting more—more sophistication, ambiguity, originality, depth. One could make the case that filmmakers like Michelangelo Antonioni, Jean-Luc Godard, and Luis Bunuel could find sizable and attentive audiences in the 1960s because our visual-narrative training was at that point nominal, and the Walter Lippmann-Edward Bernays-formulated industrial science devoted to controlling our view of life was still in its adolescent stages. Thus, an entire generation, liberated by postwar affluence and social progressiveness, was allowed to receive movies then in mutable, unpredictable, even confounding ways; the challenge of cinema was still viewed, to an open social mind, as a stimulus.

Today, you must have the resources and instincts of a bounty hunter, prepared to step outside of the common dialogue and shirk your market conditioning. Small battles are won all the time by the true cinephiles every time someone buys a film festival ticket, subscribes to *Film Comment* or *Sight & Sound*, purchases a Criterion Collection DVD, or gets lost online at *Senses of Cinema*. These alternative-seekers are naturally a discontented lot, and this book is theirs, a salute, totem, hornbook, starting gun, and mission statement for the serious cinephile in a world of pulverizing thought control and megaplex homogeneity. At best, the interested reader here will have multiple windows thrown open for them and will be compelled to launch into cultural landscapes they might not have known existed.

The writers included herein were selected first, and the individual subjects were their choice. Underappreciated European giant, brand-new Asian wunderkind, psychotronic mini-master, American undergrounder—the writers made the call. The only guidelines imposed on the critics pertained to their subjects' mortality—they must be alive and at least potentially productive—as well as their subjects' visibility in the English-speaking world's media eye. As in, they should have as little as possible. The filmmakers' work could be distributed in the United States, but only sparsely, or badly, or invisibly. (Several have had no stateside exhibition to speak of, while others have had decades of shoddy or low-rent distribution.) Roughly speaking, if the directors had been profiled in *The New Yorker* or *Vanity Fair* or *Premiere*—welcomed to the machine, so to speak—then they were hardly eligible.

The resulting collection of viewpoints and celebrations is nothing if not whimsical and deeply subjective—being dedicated film lovers, each of the critics had baskets of candidates, and I sense that many final selections, either of new pieces written especially for the book or recently published essays rescued from the periodical abyss, were made out of the impulse to exact justice on an unfair world. But since the process was entirely personal, the book should not be taken as some kind of hierarchal statement—essays on *the best* international directors. The field is too monstrous and too rich for that. Indeed, additional volumes could come out annually, perpetually *in futuro*, without ever crisscrossing the same terrain twice. In 2006, employing the same parameters, we could've just as easily surveyed the work of Jacques Rivette, Peter Watkins, Abderrahmane Sissako, Wojciech Has, Karoly Makk, Jan Nemec, Craig Baldwin, Juraj Jakubisko, Claude Faraldo, Artavazd Peleshian, Elia Suleiman, Fred Kelemen, Apichatpong Weerasethakul, Miklos Jancso, Alain Resnais, Hur Jin-ho, Stanley Kwan, Soulyemane Cisse, Yvonne Rainer, Jan Jakob Kolski, Jean-Marie Straub/Danièlle Huillet, Bruce Conner, Otar Iosseliani, Shinji Aoyama, Manuela Viegas, Gianluigi Toccafondo, Michael Snow, Alex de la Iglesias, Zeki Demirkubuz, Jem Cohen, Darius Mehrjui, Faouzi Bensaidi, Jean Rouch, Tian Zhuangzhuang, Helke Sander, Alexei German Sr. and Alexei German Jr., Jaime Humberto Hermosillo, Fernando Solanas, Hong Sang-soo, Jan Lenica, Youri Nourstein, Hans-Jurgen Syberberg, Jean Rollin, Lee Chang-dong, Roy Andersson, Ann Hui, Youssef Chahine, Yim Ho, Peter Solan, Lewis Klahr, Nils Malmros, Kazuo Hara, Andrew Kotting, Rakhshan Bani-Etemad, Nonzee Nimibutr, Pjer Zalica, Goran Paskaljevic, Vera Chytilova, Harun Farocki, Werner Schroeter, Lisandro Alonso, Vitali Kanevsky, Teresa Villaverde, Park Kwang-su, Jang Sun-woo, Marta Meszaros, Wisit Sasanatieng, William Greaves . . . and scores of others.

The vital artists ignored and kept to the distribution-exhibition margins are legion, and if aging cinephiles such as Richard Schickel and the late Susan Sontag have kvetched loudly in the last years about the "death" and "decay" of cinema (as compared to the new-wave heyday of the 1960s), this might very well be because they only saw what the present-day distribution channels would allow them to see. Beyond that, cinema thrives without our attention—indeed, one could argue that success within the American system for any or all of the above-listed directors, or any of the filmmakers written about herein, could spell disaster or at least summon hurdles, for their visions and integrity. Perhaps—but the implicit argument of this book is not taken from the artists' perspective, but from the viewers' only. Filmgoers are the last stop, the lions on the food chain of movie culture; the filmmakers can fend for themselves, and probably will. As devotees, we can only be concerned with why the zebras are so spindly, and the wildebeest so few. And with meaty prey that takes a little more hunting to find and enjoy. To which end the present volume of cinephiliac evangelisms, testaments from the frontier, is pressed upon you by a healthy wedge of the English-speaking world's best film essayists—not, I reaffirm, academics "reading signs" and employing post-Freudian theory that's as useless and enjoyable to digest as ground glass, but film-loving writers unafraid of aesthetics and movie-love and canonical thinking. As such, the book is also something of a paean to movie critics themselves. Lumped into this demographic are festival reporters, devoted editors, programmers who write and passionate cineastes who may not have regular weekly columns anywhere but who make it a career-and-lifestyle choice to attend the fests, hunt for the DVDs, pay to see the gone-in-a-blink-of-the-eye imports and write for the handful of periodicals that are authentically concerned with cinema.

Generally, professional American film criticism is a beleaguered, betrodden profession, glutted with illiterates, shysters, and camera hogs, and yet only these obsessives see enough movies to claim with validity any knowledge about the state of the art. Only they report from the ramparts of new film releases without the agendas of marketing. It is the critic's job, performed well or not or not at all, to embrace the visual text in question as a totality—as an expression, a creation, a consummable product, a market agent, a social symptom—but as a totality with intent. That intent is to be viewed, by people, for enjoyment, stimulation, and/or satisfaction, and so the critic is the cultural pointman, the reconnoiterer for his fellow citizens for whom a movie is an experience to be had, enjoyed, contemplated, and argued over, nothing less and often little more. Their responsibilities begin and end in the seat, in the dark, watching, with their readers. Perhaps only 20 percent of them can, in the end, write an interesting sentence, but from that subgroup (substantially represented here) comes our culture's only dependable exegesis on this most mysterious and commerce-corrupted art form. Consider what their absence would mean, and at the same time—since film critics do not, ostensibly, suck at the marketing teat and therefore are a force to be neutered one way or another—how substantially disempowered they've become, in import, currency, and page space, since the wild west of Pauline Kael, Andrew Sarris, Judith Crist, Parker Tyler, Manny Farber, John Simon, Vincent Canby, et al.

A naturally occurring bugbear that should be addressed in the process is the relative paucity of women filmmakers represented (two out of twenty-three) and women critics engaged (four out of twenty-three). There are several, dovetailing circumstances reflected in this happenstance—hardly a conscious editorial choice—and they should all come as no suprise. On one hand, the international filmmaking community, as well as the community of film writers, remains disproportionately male, due to the typical and familiar nexus of socioeconomic reasons. On the other hand, while insightful film critics are difficult to find in any gender, female filmmakers are hardly scarce, and I would have loved to procure essays about, say, Samira Makhmalbaf, Lucrecia Martel, Kira Muratova, Nadir Mokneche, Keren Yedaya, Barbara Hammer, and Judit Elek, just as I would have loved to include exhortations on dozens of additional artists in general. That said, many other notable women working in the field at the moment—Agnes Jaoui, Claire Denis, Catherine Breillat, Lea Pool, Lynne Ramsay, Liv Ullmann, Brigitte Roüan, Suzanne Bier, Allison Anders, Nancy Savoca, Jane Campion, and so on—often do find American distribution at least partially on the strength of their marketable feminism, and, having had a measure of success, wouldn't be quite eligible in any case. There is, perhaps, another book waiting to be assembled on women filmmakers marginalized in American culture.

In fact, many books—and articles and symposiums and DVD entrepreneurships and art-house programs—could be summoned onto the cultural stage addressing the contemporary cinema that the current American business model keeps us from experiencing. It does seem to be, in the end, largely a matter of economic resistance, and counter-publicizing that which is not easily sellable to stateside filmgoers. Let's hope, then, that I am, or at least could be, wailing to a substantial choir, and that the audience for off-radar cinema might be more of a robust minority than I sense on my darker days. In which case, *Exile Cinema* could serve as a salve for the cineaste's lonesome fury. Not that such ire isn't useful—cultural rebellion can be a sweet thing, and the sooner a national community forms around the idea of rescuing film from the soulless shill of consent manufacture, the better. As a ferocious short film by Canadian filmmaker Guy Maddin, represented here both as subject and author, once cried in exuberance, *kino! Kino! KINO!*

PART 1

Rockets from East Asia

1

Howard Hampton

Double Trouble

Tsui Hark & Ching Sui-tung

In the tumultuous, gloriously disreputable movie era that transpired between by the arrival of Hong Kong cinema's New Wave circa 1979 and the long-dreaded "reunification" with China 1997, Tsui Hark and Ching Sui-tung came to define its outlandish, shoot-from-the-id pop sensibilities. Tsui was instrumental in Hong Kong's resurgence as an alternate movie universe (producing John Woo's breakthrough works *A Better Tomorrow I/II* and *The Killer*, directing *Zu: Warriors from the Magic Mountain*, *Peking Opera Blues*, and *Once Upon a Time in China*), while Ching would direct/co-direct/action-direct a host of oneiric movies that might have sprung fully (de)formed from cinema's collective unconscious (*A Chinese Ghost Story*, *Swordsman II*, *The East is Red*, all produced by Tsui). Bringing out the audacious best in each other, the pair developed a film vocabulary dedicated to "the excavation of evocative detail," as Ackbar Abbas described HK cinema's genrefied space: a simultaneously manic and contemplative aesthetic of "the incredible as real."

Though he worked with Tsui on the New Wave kick in the head *Dangerous Encounter of the First Kind* (1980; sociopath-finding urban alienation and paranoia delivered with the sucker-punch of a Lydia Lunch b-side), it was on the celebrated *Zu: Warriors from the Magic Mountain* (1983) where Ching's aerial martial arts displays paved the way for the modern HK fantasy mode. He would serve as Tsui's right-hand man and alter ego, as influential action director on *ABT II* (1987) and *The Killer* (1988) as well as *Peking Opera Blues* (1986) and Tsui's own *A Better Tomorrow III*. Ching's floating, mythic air wafts through the violence in them, but it is on the dazzling *A Chinese Ghost Story* (1987; he also did the 1990 and 1991 sequels) where it fully comes into its own, though producer Tsui often winds up cited as the principal auteur. The question of who directed what on any given Tsui-associated film can be difficult to untangle (on *Swordsman*, King Hu was credited as director though fired as shooting began, and at least five other directors including Tsui and Ching seem to have worked on the film), but there is a lunatic vision that is distinctly recognizable as pure Ching. Diaphanous nocturnal shots of silken veils and enchanted forests, fleeting images fusing slow-motion with quick, nearly subliminal cuts, boy-meets-ghost romance soaring up into the trees and off into uncharted Busby Berkeley realms, a singing ghostbuster, a tree demon with a hundred-foot tongue, and an Orpheus-like rescue mission to hell and back are strictly poetic par for the Ching Sui-tung course.

Tsui's own oeuvre runs the gamut from grimly radical to the cloyingly inane, brutalist to zany—there is scarcely a genre Tsui hasn't dabbled in. Though he's understandably identified as HK's answer to Steven Spielberg, in practical terms Tsui's rangy off-the-cuff output is more an anarchic and/or synthetic fusion of Hawksian bravura (good) with the contrasting pop archetypes of Lucas (mostly bad) and sped-up Leone (the ugly-beautiful). A master fabulist who often sells his own work short, Tsui displays this schizophrenic quality most conspicuously in the immensely popular *Once Upon a Time in China* (1991), a film that has thus far spawned five sequels. Equal parts epic anti-imperialist tract, gleeful exploration of melodramatic violence, wholesome comic folk tale, and wistful quest for spiritual unity, it encapsulates a cinema of multiple artistic personalities and irreconcilable differences. *Peking Opera Blues* offered a new synthesis of screwball entertainment and cinematic vision: plunging a gender-inverted Hawks ensemble into slapstick Brechtian politics amid the trappings of traditional Chinese theater, with dulcet echoes of Leone-Peckinpah gunplay exploding like firecrackers off in the middle distance: wave after wave of ecstatic invention, one wondrously sustained climax on top of another.

Narratively unrelated, both *Shanghai Blues* (1984) and *Peking Opera Blues* broke new but backward-looking ground. Each viewed the past through the prism of movie history, joining nostalgia and modernism in an allusive, punning pop style, rendering life as near-incessant montage. Directing *A Better Tomorrow III* (1989; depending on whom you believe, a project either inherited or hijacked from Woo), Tsui took the HK gangster mythos to Vietnam, shooting on location in Saigon. It's his second-greatest achievement, but he insists "that film was out of control": it translates excess into dream-time, effectively occupying the no-man's-land between *Jules et Jim* and *Bullet in the Head*. Then there is the autistic loveliness of his one-from-the-heart fiasco *Green Snake* (1993), as well as high-concept outings like the time-travel farce *Love in the Time of Twilight* (1995): restless, peripatetic, uneasy stabs at rapprochement between mass taste and idiosyncrasy. But the latter film had a pensive, enigmatic tone that caught what pre-*Donnie Darko* back-to-the-futurism missed: the weight of the past upon present, the sense of loss as fate.

For all Tsui's sheer gutbucket virtuosity—mixing expressionist angles, ravishing tableaux, archaic wipes, shock cuts, elegant pans, and lunging, disoriented POV shots—there remains a persistent lack of core sensibility, or at least continuity, to his work. That missing "personal" touch, and the attendant haphazard quality of much of his later work, exposed a penchant for the impractical, the grandiose, and the mechanically formalist. While his Film Workshop succeeded (for a time), he acquired a dictatorial reputation (allegedly ghost-directing or recutting a fair portion of the films that list him as producer). His ambitions and designs generally kept one eye squarely on the bottom line, reverting to the path of least resistance as easily as *The Chinese Feast* (1995) served up mildly pleasant stupefaction. Disastrously attempting to follow Woo's path out of Hong Kong, he took his crack at directing Eurotrash action-hulk Jean-Claude Van Damme in the disjointedly mannerist, ultra-vapid *Double Team* (1997). Shooting the mannequin-on-steroids trio of Van Damme, Dennis Rodman, and Mickey Rourke as beefcake sculpture, Tsui dropped hints of a Mapplethorpe photo session slipped into a bad, mildly outré sixties spy caper. Surely there and in the marginally less awful *Knock Off* (1998), Van Damme must have expected something closer to slambang Tsui productions like the visually exciting *Wicked City* (1992, a live-action remake of a popular anime feature) or the sleek Jet Li vehicle *Black Mask* (1996).

Tsui has rarely seemed particularly invested in action for action's sake, with a general ambivalence about physical expression in his films, and a tendency for violence and motion to be dispersed into kinetic abstraction. After the failure of his punk/B-flick black hole *Dangerous Encounter* (aka *Play With Fire*, notable for its zip gun portrait of a hilariously sullen, "crazy bitch" sociopath), he made an 180-degree turn to broad, scatterbrained slapstick and hit it big with the 1981 spoof *All the Wrong Clues . . . for the Right Solution*. (Often cited as early evidence of Tsui's "sellout," it nonetheless contains a classic tasteless gag involving a Volkswagen, a couple of nuns, an orphan who asks "How do we get to heaven, sister?," and a very sudden answer.) From the cannibal-house gross-out comedy *We're Going to Eat You* (1983) to the unfortunately innocuous *Working Class*, there's a strain of depersonalization in his work that lends itself as easily to blatant schlock and rote dumbness as it does to lurid, intellectualized hyperbole like *Dangerous Encounter* or the sparse, beguiling Borges multiplied by *A Touch of Zen* labyrinths of *Butterfly Murders*. With *Time and Tide* (2000) and the ill-fated remake *The Legend of Zu* (2001), the rapid-fire impersonal has taken over completely—commercial enterprises given over to senseless bursts of energy, random patterns, prettified tics, and an unrelenting flashiness so insular and airless it might almost be a new mode of deconstructionism.

His purest, most successful forays into conventional action movie territory have been as producer for Woo, naturally (a devout aesthete caught up in the glamorous and sacramental aspects of screen bloodshed), but also Kirk Wong's *Gunmen* (1988) as well as Johnny To and Andrew Kam's *The Big Heat*. Where *Gunmen* is a blistering, much-improved-upon version of *The Untouchables* (the frantic reworking of De Palma's baby-carriage routine is one of the most rococo set pieces in the history of HK mayhem), *The Big Heat* remains the *ne plus ultra*violence of Hong Kong cinema. With the look of a training film for coroners, it has a clinical eye for nihilistic detail that would do Cronenberg proud, turning cops and robbers into *Crash* test dummies. But in Tsui's own *A Better Tomorrow III*, the action is voluptuously stylized: Anita Mui fires a pair of automatic rifles in such super-slo-mo you can count the expended shells, and bodies seem to fall like snowflakes in a paperweight reverie. The urgency here is emotional, wildly romantic, but barely physical at all. In its contemplative sense of arrested time—the speed of life and death reduced to a painterly crawl—*ABT III* anticipates Wong Kar-wai's atmospheric developments as it carries Woo-derived tropes to the point of rapt stasis. The fall of Vietnam becomes the backdrop against which intertwined film/social/personal histories are projected, all collapsed into a tight allegorical space where the tanks of Tiananmen Square patrol the streets of Casablanca, and Mui irresistibly embodies the mythos of Bogart's Rick and Jeanne Moreau's Catherine rolled into one trenchcoated figure.

The closest Tsui has come to unrelenting, action-purist intensity is in *The Blade* (1995), in which he borrows the classic *One-Armed Swordsman* premise only to turn it into a perverse and exhaustively ferocious answer to Wong's *Ashes of Time*. Narrated in perfect mock-*Ashes* fashion by a not-very-bright young woman, it undermines Wong's languorous philosophizing and romantic alienation by representing life as appetite and savagery: animals and humans alike emblematically tempted into the steel jaws of waiting traps. But in its magisterial bleakness, *The Blade* avoids violence-as-release: in its universe, amputation leads to survival but not regeneration—the mutilated hero rises only to discover resurrection's a form of living death. More jarring slice of existential horror than martial artistry, the film manages to be every bit as abstract in its spasmodic hyperrealism as *Ashes of Time* is in lyric opacity. They're antithetical twins, joined at the hip: each contains what the other denies. Human feeling in *The Blade* recedes into the same opium haze of memory, which strangely enough helps us recall how *Butterfly Murders* opens the door for Wong's prismatic imponderability.

The clotted, glistening homoeroticism of *The Blade* extends Tsui's customary erotic ambiguity to the male body. Typically, he cast gender-identity elements in terms of women negotiating a man's world, most remarkably launching Brigitte Lin as a peerless icon of bisexual heroism. *The Blade*'s violence is seen through the girl's eyes, flushed with voyeurism: there's a classic scene where she watches naked men being flogged that suggests a flipped-out Zhang Yimou. The brutality amounts to an elaborate system of displacement in which sexual tensions are disastrously played out in a bloody pantomime of lust and sublimation: the action concurrently sexualized, spiritualized, and ironically detached. Tsui's earlier work offers a more elusive composite of the carnal and the ethereal (in *The Blade*, the latter is interchangeable with the delusional)—an unstable mix best displayed in the riotous role-playground of *Peking Opera Blues*, the fatalistic passion of *Better Tomorrow III*, and the proto-*Blade* paroxysms that take up the last third of *Once Upon a Time in China*.

In that film, one chastity symbol (the ascetically handsome Jet Li) strives to save another (the primly Westernized Rosamund Kwan)—and indeed China itself—from a fate worse than death. Tsui seems to be reaching all the way back to the silent era for this melodramatic bric-a-brac. Yet below the spectacle of innocence, a darker fairy tale is taking shape amid the close, dungeon-like quarters: the blood smeared so brazenly on Kwan's bare shoulders, the sadomasochistic purity of Li (who might be channeling Lillian Gish as well as Douglas Fairbanks), and the captive women who push their tormentor into an open furnace. What silent age is this stuff from—the one where Artaud directed cathartic swashbucklers in lieu of descending into madness? As *The Blade* sustains such extremity for its entire length while renouncing morality-play heroics in favor of fistful-of-cruelty annihilation, it lacks the reassuring foundation that made the *Once Upon a Time in China* series a success: too arty for the popcorn crowd and too unyieldingly feral for arthouse-sitters.

Fusing pop and art in ways bound to dismay low-, middle-, and highbrow tastes alike, Tsui's prime work opted for a polymorphous semiotics, nowhere more pointedly than in the gaga fairy tale *Green Snake*.

Evoking the childish delirium of Indian musicals and picture-book Chinese mythology, it features a pair of beguilingly incestuous serpent-demons (Maggie Cheung and Joey Wong) who can assume Eve-like human form. Zao Wen-zhou's fanatical monk reaps destruction of the human world when he tries to expel them from it, making this just as feverish an allegory of sexual repression as *The Blade* under its campy, Willy Wonka veneer. Man's capacity to reject pleasure in the name of socialization is explored through laughable special snake-effects, indecorous shifts in tone and content (we're not accustomed to seeing our little mermaids reach under a monk's robe and feel him up), and intermittent spells of erotic wonder always verging on scarcely intended Pythonesque silliness. *Green Snake* makes the process of human socialization seem like a war on enchantment itself—an ancient wish to drive sex out of the world pitted against the eternal right-to-return of the repressed. These beatifically amoral creatures find earthly morality means suffering and loss, as though the capacity for emotion were merely the precondition for the puritanical need to extinguish it.

Unconflicted and uninhibited, Ching Sui-tung's body of work has been a film sensualist's delight. Besides the *Chinese Ghost Story* series (1987/1990/1991), he would direct or co-direct many of Film Workshop's best productions, including *The Terracotta Warrior* (1990; co-starring Gong Li and Ching's future employer Zhang Yimou as the marvelously stony-faced, dashing hero), *Swordsman* (1990), *Dragon Inn* (1992; redoing King Hu as a cross-dressing neo-*Rio Bravo*), his masterpiece *Swordsman II* (1992), and its still more astonishing (if uneven) continuation, *The East Is Red* (1993). Bathing rooms in blue light and streaming it through bullet holes, making bald sexual metaphors into rousing action sequences (trains crashing through walls, dreamers flying through the night, a belltower taking off like a rocket, or a water tower exploding like a pornographic piñata), he might have been illustrating critic Paul Coates' assertion: "Film alone reveals the extent to which reality yearns for another world which is not itself." This skewed inner landscape of Tinker Toy sets and vertiginous desire makes the viewer experience his images as if they were flashbacks to some unaccountable primal trauma/thrill, in a place where Hitchcock and *Batman* intersect.

Ching's comic-book sensibility links him to Tim Burton and Sam Raimi, as attested by the catwomen-galore triumph *The Heroic Trio* (1993), which he produced and co-directed (sometimes uncredited) with Johnny To, and its sequel *Executioners* (1994, though shot back-to-back). But there he takes that sensibility much further, into areas of unrest and profane illumination, until it becomes a surrealist impulse that devours the boundaries of the possible like a magician's tapeworm. His quest for exquisite incongruities can lead to something as airy as the battle scene in the amusing Indiana Jones rip-off *The Raid*, with full-size biplane replicas maneuvered on wires inside a soundstage so they strafe the heroes while soldiers leap from their wings and join in the attack. He assembles bewitched forests in the studio and creates playgrounds that can suggest both deep spaciousness and claustrophobic density—expanding and contracting the frame, a world opening up and closing in on the audience at the same time. Ching's extravagant excess is shaded, nuanced: wonder and the sinister go hand in hand, or hand on throat, the archaic future and anarchic past collide, while *The Heroic Trio* exterminates the children who have been inducted into an army of darkness.

There's a throwaway scene in *Executioners* that catches Ching's emotive essence. It's Christmas Eve in the near, post-1997 future, martial law is in effect, and weary military policemen are resting in a crowded corridor at headquarters. Suddenly an anonymous, grief-stricken woman bursts in, dragging a body past them. They order her to halt and she whirls, firing an automatic rifle and mowing down the soldiers. She kicks in the door to the captain's office and hurls the body at the officer's feet. Sobbing that the authorities murdered her husband, she kneels beside his corpse and swiftly turns the rifle on herself. The sequence is one sweeping, panoramic gesture that serves no purpose but to instill itself like a desperate cry that echoes in the heart like an aria.

Ching is a true primitive who grew up on movie sets and seemingly knows nothing else, yet he has a bold and complex visual sense that orchestrates movement with visceral grace, imagery full of the wish to transcend itself. First coming to prominence as martial arts director on Patrick Tam's *The Sword*, he made his directorial debut in 1982 with the fine *Duel to the Death*—a spare, quite formalist work that felt both detached and unhinged, like a stripped-down/spaced-out gloss on the King Hu aesthetic. Ching goes for flow almost in spite of characterization; his interest is in the particularity of the dream and not the dreamers per se. *Swordsman II* is Ching's greatest showcase, but in recasting the main roles (with Jet Li, Rosamund Kwan, and Michelle Reis), and featuring Brigitte Lin in probably her most emblematic role as the transsexual Asia the Invincible, he also achieves a triumph of pop iconography. Straightaway heading into the sexually ambiguous mystic, it treats the convoluted courtship rites of Lin and Li with a lucidly bemused romanticism: Ching's ode to mutability gives us a world that is constantly turning itself inside out. (During one clash, the ground rolls up like a giant carpet.) The most feverishly expansive of his movies, its violence moves with such uncanny swiftness it takes on the horrifying comic grandeur of a Gotterdammerung battle staged as an epic practical joke on mankind. Instead of being restored, order is scattered to the winds and power harnesses disorder. Fatalism is taken even further in the story's final installment, *The East Is Red*. The title comes a famous Maoist anthem—"He shall be China's saving star"—so it is with wicked irony that the film has Lin's character come back from the dead to take revenge on the authoritarian doomsday cults that have sprung up in Invincible Asia's name. What follows is a blasphemous fable of total destruction, dislocated sexual identity (my favorite gambit: the skin is pulled off a woman to reveal an albino ninja within), and swoon-fed passion. It burrows into the chthonic recesses/excesses of religion, its roots in fantasy, charismatic ceremony, and erotic trance, perhaps because Ching understands that myth and the movies tap the same universal, primeval impulses.

Next to such dark flights of fancy, Tsui's *Peking Opera Blues* seems almost down-to-earth, yet there too is Brigitte Lin as a more human revolutionary, suspended in midair by Ching's invisible wires forever. The film is fast and mellifluous, while managing to linger on so many textures of life commingled with old movies: Lin's sorrow when she has to betray her corrupt father, the flush across Cherie Chung's face when a jewel box lands in her lap, Sally Yeh's shy, awkward resolve to break into the all-male opera. What the film ultimately captures is that elusive and so often falsified quality in film—hope. (Lin's heroic, melancholy intransigence suggests a fantasy precursor of student rebellion leader Chai Ling.)

Despite the title, *A Better Tomorrow III* is about the death of that hope, the fears of Hong Kong in the then-immediate shadow of Tiananmen Square, projected back onto the last days before Saigon's fall. Presented as a blue-tinted nightmare, it's a city administered by an roving army of gangsters, but where resistance erupts in bursts of fantastic bravado and reckless absurdism. All of which culminates in the perfect moral gesture enacted by Chow Yun-fat, carrying his mortally wounded lover to her other love's side so she can close the dead man's eyes, a sublimely operatic moment. It is as if the film passes from the reality of our suppressed lives into the history we dream of making, and back again—left in ruins, our dreams haunt us like memories of an imaginary homeland that has disappeared from the map.

Certainly the Hong Kong that Ching Sui-tung and Tsui Hark once defined is history—the industry has survived, but the singularity has migrated elsewhere. Tsui has spent the new decade mired in hack work when he as been visible at all. One can only hope *Seven Swords* (2005) will be a return to form; at least echoing Kurosawa more than *Star Wars* or *Mighty Morphin Power Rangers*. Ching's career, after floundering for years in uninspired swill like *Naked Weapon* (a 2002 blot on the good name of Clarence Fok's trash classic *Naked Killer*), has taken an ironic turn:

reunited with Zhang Yimou as action choreographer on *Hero* (2002) and *House of Flying Daggers* (2004). More importantly, on the former he is brought together with cinematographer Chris Doyle, which in this case is a little like Stan Kenton hiring Eric Dolphy and Charlie Mingus for his elephantine big band. *Hero* is an epic distillation of the entire *wuxia pien* genre, wherein Ching and Doyle get to pay homage to themselves, just as Maggie Cheung's Flying Snow pays tribute to Brigitte Lin. Mobilizing massive armies of stately composition, color-coordinated acrobatics, pointed glances, sharp-shooting leaf-blowers, and reverential lyricism, it is a panoply of magical moments frozen in ostentatious tragedy: too perfect, too sane. The flying dagger of respectability strikes again; there's no place here for crazed, invigorating gesticulations of *The East Is Red*, which belong to a century whose passions have passed into classicism, nostalgia, or worse.

2

Jonathan Rosenbaum

Bullet Ballet

Seijun Suzuki

Can I call a film a masterpiece without being sure that I understand it? I think so, since understanding is always relative and less than clear-cut. Look long enough at the apparent meaning of any conventional work—past the illusion of narrative continuity that persuades us to overlook anomalies, breaks, fissures, and other distractions we can't process—and it usually becomes elusive. Yet it's also true that we have different ways of comprehending meaning. I once watched some children listen to passages from James Joyce's *Finnegans Wake*, possibly the most impenetrable book in the English language, and saw them burst into giggles, plainly understanding better than the adults that this was exactly the way grown-ups talked, only funnier.

I first saw Seijun Suzuki's *Pistol Opera* (2001) in early 2002, and half a year later I served on a jury at an Australian film festival that awarded the movie its top prize, calling it "a highly personal blend of traditional and experimental cinema." I can't think of another film I've seen since that has afforded me more unbridled sensual pleasure—which may explain how I could dip into an unsubtitled DVD any number of times and never worry about not understanding it. (I should note, however, that this film, starting with the eye-popping graphics of the opening credits, needs the big screen to achieve its optimal impact.)

I couldn't give a fully coherent synopsis of *Pistol Opera* if my life depended on it, but it's still the most fun new movie I've seen since *Mulholland Drive* and *Waking Life* (both also 2001). Yet I have to admit it must not be everybody's idea of a good time; even in Japan it seems to be strictly a cult item and a head-scratcher. Having recently seen the movie again with subtitles and read a few rundowns of the plot, I'm only more confused about its meaning. The gist of the narrative is that a beautiful young hit woman known as Stray Cat (Makiko Esumi)—"No. 3" in the pecking order of the Guild, the unfathomable, invisible organization she works for—aspires to be No. 1 and proceeds to bump off most of her male colleagues.

They include Hundred Eyes, aka Dark Horse, a young dandy with chronic sinus problems who's currently No. 1; Goro Hanada (a character revived from Suzuki's 1967 *Branded to Kill*), who's middle-aged and walks with a crutch, answers to the name of "The Champ," and used to be No. 1; the Teacher, No. 4, who's middle-aged and gets around in a wheelchair; Dr. Painless (Jan Woudstra), No. 5, a Westerner who's built like a Viking and periodically speaks English; and, apparently, Lazy Man, No. 2, who's referred to many times and cited in the credits but whom I seem to have missed. To complicate matters further, many of these men are killed by No. 3 not once but repeatedly, springing back to life like Wile E. Coyote in a Road Runner cartoon—and some of them kill Stray Cat repeatedly as well.

In between these deadly encounters, Stray Cat has scenes with females from at least four generations, including a grandmotherly rustic woman who takes care of her; the former No. 11, who sells her a Springfield rifle; a middle-aged agent with a bright purple scarf mask who sends her on missions and periodically flirts with her; and a little girl named Sayoko who speaks more English than Dr. Painless (reading or reciting, among other things, "Humpty Dumpty" and Wordsworth's "Daffodils") and clearly wants to grow up to be a hit woman herself.

The scenes with the rustic woman and Sayoko tend to register like relaxed family get-togethers. The other meetings with men and women often start as Guild assignments and wind up, at least symbolically, as sexual assignations, full of taunts, teases, and gestures that drip with innuendo. They also come across like children's games: the blade of Dr. Painless's knife is collapsible, all the guns are bandied about like phallic toys or fetish objects, and any pain is clearly make-believe. (As Godard once said of his *Pierrot le Fou*, the operative word is "red," not "blood.")

Static poses are often struck; the story unravels more like a ballet than an opera (the movements of actors and camera as well as the cuts are synchronized to pop music, much of it performed on trumpet by a Miles Davis clone); and the action shifts between industrial, rural, or urban locations that are used theatrically and studio sets that often take the form of theatrical stages used for Kabuki, butoh, and Greek or Roman drama (we see columns suggesting a Mediterranean amphitheater). Other scenes appear to be set in some lava-lamp version of an afterlife, with an otherworldly lime-colored dock and a shimmering gold river over which ghostlike figures in white hover.

I don't subscribe to notions of "pure cinema" or "pure style," because even abstraction has content—color, shape, movement. But this free-form and deeply personal movie suggests purity more than any other recent film that comes to mind. It's often as abstract and as stringently codified as Cuban cartoonist Antonio Prohias's "Spy vs. Spy" comic strip in *Mad* magazine, though the color of most of the kimonos is too gorgeously lush to evoke Prohias's minimalism. And the feeling of sacred passion conveyed by many of the compositions—the sense that many of the characters, costumes, props, and settings are the objects of Suzuki's unreasoning worship, as carefully placed and juxtaposed as totems in a Joseph Cornell box—imbues the whole film with some of the aura of ecstatic religious art, even if it's cast in the profanely riotous pop colors of a Frank Tashlin.

Suzuki, who turned eighty last May, directed at least forty quickie features at the Nikkatsu studio between 1956 and 1967—practically all of them B films in the original sense of that term, meaning features designed to accompany A pictures. I've seen half a dozen of these, ranging from the 40-minute *Love Letter* (1959), a black-and-white 'Scope film with a ski-lodge setting, to the 91-minute *Branded to Kill* (1967), a baroque hit-man thriller (also in black-and-white 'Scope) that remains his best-known work—and was, along with Jean-Pierre Melville's *Le Samouraï*, the major inspiration for Jim Jarmusch's *Ghost Dog*. *Branded to Kill* so enraged the president of Nikkatsu that he fired Suzuki for making "incomprehensible" films. A Suzuki support group was duly formed, and Suzuki sued the studio, as he later put it, "to protect my dignity." A full decade would pass before he directed another theatrical feature, and he never returned to Nikkatsu. His output became sporadic, much of it consisting of TV commissions, and eight years of silence preceded *Pistol Opera*. Before *Pistol Opera* I wasn't one of Suzuki's most ardent fans. Frankly, I didn't know what to make of him, even as a cult figure. According to my favorite Japanese film critic, Shigehiko Hasumi, "Suzuki is appreciated in the West, but essentially he's a traditional Japanese man who regards Western people as barbarians, in the traditional Japanese meaning of that term." This implies that one can't adequately (or accurately) rationalize his craziness by calling him a Japanese Sam Fuller, and one can't palm him off as an old pro churning out entertainments, though that's how he represents himself, at least in part.

In a 1997 interview in Los Angeles included on the DVD of *Branded to Kill*, Suzuki, after insisting that he just wants to make films that are "fun and entertaining," goes on to argue that there's no "grammar" for cinema—at least for his kind of cinema—because he doesn't mind defying the usual rules respecting the cinematic coordinates of time and space: "In my films, spaces and places change [and] time is cheated in the editing. I guess that's the strength of entertainment movies: you can do anything you want, as long as these elements make the movie interesting. That's my theory of the grammar of cinema."

This may sound like a recipe for formalism—especially given that the film's subtitle is *Killing With Style*—but there's far too much content in *Pistol Opera* to make its dream patterns feel arbitrary or reducible to a simple theme-and-variations format. Indeed, one of the reasons I find the film so exhausting is that it doesn't take time out for anything. Whatever it's after, it always feels on-target.

Suzuki's protracted hiatus from filmmaking may be partly responsible for the sense of manic overdrive. Orson Welles once speculated that the hyperbolic style of his *Touch of Evil* was the consequence of feeling bottled up creatively for much too long, and considering all the striking and even stunning locations used in *Pistol Opera*, I'd like to imagine that Suzuki spent years discovering them, saving them for whenever he'd be able to show them off in a film.

Obviously the movie has a lot to do with gender. There's the dominance and aggression of the women (not counting the country grandmother, who seems to belong to a different era), combined with Stray Cat's phallic preoccupations ("I think it's OK to lead my life as a pistol," she says at one point; elsewhere she addresses her gun as "my man") and the pronounced disability of the men (not counting Dr. Painless, who appears to signify "America")—all of which seems like a precise inversion of the structure of Japanese society. The other themes are no less Japanese. There's the obsession with hierarchy, competition, and professional identity. There's the surrealist view of death as lyrical expression: according to the Champ, "Killing blooms into an artwork," and a steam shovel turns up at the door of a rural cottage with rose petals dropping from its jaws. More subtle and profound is the memory of military defeat, made explicit in one of the masked agent's late soliloquies and in a vision of a mushroom cloud that suddenly appears on a rotating stage. Most of these themes seem to come together in the former No. 11's climactic speech about a dream she had in which a headless Yukio Mishima appears and she tries without success to sew his head back on using all sorts of string and wire.

In fact, *Pistol Opera* registers as so prototypically Japanese in both style and content that the preponderance of English dialogue is notable mainly for the sense of foreignness it conveys. My favorite howler in the dialogue—"I didn't mean to kill each other, really"—sounds like the way adult Americans talk, only funnier. It also perfectly conveys the Japanese language's conflation of singular and plural and all the ambiguous crossovers between self and society that seem to derive from this.

The absence—or rather sublimation—of sex is equally operative. "I don't really like sex," Suzuki declared in a 1969 interview. "It's such a hassle." He then responded to the question "In which period would you have liked to be born?" with the equally defeatist "Well, not as a human, in any case." At first it may be difficult to reconcile this negativity with the film's sense of joyful discovery, but the dream logic whereby opposite attitudes produce each other seems central to *Pistol Opera*—an ambivalence that's conveyed even by its title.

3

DENNIS LIM

Kuala *L'Impure*

The Cinema of Amir Muhammad

> The Malay had been a fearful enemy for months. I have been every night, through his means, transported into Asiatic scenes. . . . Southern Asia, in general, is the seat of awful images and associations.
>
> —Thomas de Quincey, *Confessions of an English Opium-Eater*

The Wrath of Mugatu

IN ORIENTALIST LITERATURE, THE Southeast Asian nation of Malaysia—previously Malaya, the Federated Malay States, and the Malay Archipelago—was the land of Conrad's noble savages and Maugham's oblivious colonials. Today, its tourist-board image hinges on more mundane exotica: nice beaches, good food, a friendly multicultural population. I was born and raised in Malaysia, but have not lived there for more than a dozen years, returning infrequently during that time. The longtime expatriate is susceptible to identity slippage, one of the stranger forms of which arises from the gap between how he remembers his homeland and how others perceive it—or, as the case may be, how others don't. Even among the well-read and well-traveled in cosmopolitan cities like London, where I lived in the early 1990s, and New York, where I have lived since the mid-nineties, Malaysia is routinely confused with one of its neighbors: Indonesia, which trumps it for unambiguous distinctions (world's largest archipelago and most populous Muslim nation), or Singapore, which was once part of Malaysia and is more flamboyant in its nanny-state tyranny: the chewing-gum ban, the caning of the American kid, the totalizing corporate-park sterility that prompted William Gibson to dub it "Disneyland with the death penalty." Absent such honorifics, mention of Malaysia, in my experience, prompts faint recognition at best, and that dim spark tends to be connected to one of four things, which collectively suggest that nearly two centuries after De Quincey's laudanum freakout, Malaysia still exists in the Western consciousness as a shadow realm of "awful images and associations":

- Mahathir Mohamad, the country's prime minister from 1981 to 2003. One of a dying breed of Asian strongmen, a quasi-despot who outlasted China's Deng Xiaoping, Indonesia's Suharto and Singapore's Lee Kuan Yew, he was for years a reliable fount of anti-Western (and anti-Semitic) rhetoric. These inflammatory pronouncements were usually blurted, almost Tourette's-style, in the vicinity of news microphones and other heads of state.
- The tallest buildings in the world, built between April 1996 and October 2003. The eighty-eight-story Petronas Twin Towers, which protrude like silver ears of corn from the chaotic skyline of the capital Kuala Lumpur, are the work of architect Cesar Pelli (who also designed Manhattan's World Financial Center) and featured prominently in the 1999 Sean Connery–Catherine Zeta-Jones heist caper *Entrapment*. The Malaysian government considered banning the movie because of sneaky editing that suggested the buildings were adjacent to "slums" (in reality they are surrounded by manicured gardens; the actual slums are many miles away).
- Terrorism. Two of the 9/11 hijackers attended what was thought to be a meeting of al Qaeda associates in Kuala Lumpur in January 2000. Malaysian members of Jemaah Islamiyah have been linked to terrorist attacks in Indonesia, including the most recent Bali bombing in October 2005. Bush's war on terror has actually improved relations between the United States and Malaysia, which

Washington quickly identified as a modern, moderate Islamic state, and as such useful strategically. Mahathir, while criticizing the U.S. invasions of Afghanistan and Iraq, was quick to target Islamic militancy, which conveniently also meant cracking down on his chief political threat: the Islamic opposition party.

- *Zoolander* (2001), Ben Stiller's splendid absurdist farce, in which evil fashion designer Mugatu (Will Ferrell) attempts to brainwash supermodel Derek Zoolander (Stiller) into assassinating the prime minister of Malaysia—duly mistaken at one point for Micronesia—so as to keep child sweatshops in operation. *Zoolander* was banned in Malaysia.

Amnesia Nation

> The imagination lingers here gratefully, for in the Federated Malay States the only past is within the memory for the most part of the fathers of living men.
>
> —W. Somerset Maugham,"Footprints in the Jungle"

It's no wonder the outside world knows so little about Malaysia—Malaysians themselves are not predisposed to knowing very much about Malaysia. The country has been continuously governed by the same political party, in much the same repressive manner, since it gained independence from the British in 1957. Malaysia Tourism's website proclaims it "the longest serving freely elected government in the world."[1] Opportunities for reform, few and far between, have been quickly squashed and remain largely forgotten. What Malaysian leaders like to think of as stability is more a case of self-perpetuating inertia and instilled amnesia. Malaysians abroad have an even easier time forgetting. Since leaving, I have not been the most avid consumer of news from home. In my line of work, editing and writing film reviews, Malaysia is not something that comes up. I was, therefore, a little startled to hear talk a few years ago of a Malaysian film movement. Would these movies seem foreign to me? Was I supposed to feel nationalist pride? Did they require a cultural perspective that I had (perhaps willingly) lost? I was even more startled when I finally saw one of these movies, *The Big Durian* (2003), the first Malaysian feature ever to screen at Sundance, and realized that my reluctance to remember was precisely the subject of the film.

Some facts and statistics: Malaysia consists of West Malaysia, an equatorial peninsula south of Thailand, and—across the South China

Sea—two states in northern Borneo that make up East Malaysia.[2] The population of twenty-six million lives in an area that is, per the CIA's *World Factbook*, "slightly larger than New Mexico." Per capita income is the fifth-highest in Asia. But the "Freedom in the World" index, which weighs political rights and civil liberties in all countries and rates them on a scale of 1 for most free to 7 for least, awarded Malaysia a 4.5 last year (worse than Indonesia and the same as Singapore). As of September 2005, 112 people were being held under Malaysia's draconian Internal Security Act (ISA), which allows for arbitrary detention without trial and prohibits the judicial review of these cases. A very small sampling of the very many cultural products and publications that have been banned at some point in Malaysia: *Schindler's List*, *The Passion of the Christ*, an indigenous-dialect translation of the Bible, all newspapers from Singapore, various episodes of *Friends*. We can trace Malaysia's most maddening contradictions to the peculiar position that ethnicity occupies in this multiethnic society: race is both foundational principle and primal taboo, at once enshrined in government policy and not up for public discussion. According to 2004 estimates, the population is roughly 50 percent Malay, 25 percent Chinese, and 7 percent Indian; most of the rest are indigenous groups in sparsely populated East Malaysia. Kuala Lumpur (commonly called KL) and most of the cities are on the west coast of West Malaysia; many of them have Chinese majorities. The Malays are Muslim (Islam is the official religion) and speak Malay (also the official language); the Chinese are mainly Buddhist and Taoist and speak any of a half-dozen Chinese dialects (in KL, usually Cantonese); the Indians are mainly Hindu and speak Tamil. It's common to hear Malaysians veering, within the space of a sentence, from national language to native dialect to English—or more precisely, a mutant form of English, stripped of grammatical niceties, richly seasoned with the saltier bits of local vernacular, and evocatively called Manglish.

Multiculturalism is a big part of the country's official narrative, framed as the happy by-product of trade routes and colonial rule. The early Malay kingdoms, based in Java and Sumatra, were Hindu and Buddhist. Islam, brought by fourteenth-century Arab merchants, became the dominant religion in the Indo-Malay archipelago with the ascendancy of Malacca, a Muslim-ruled port a hundred miles south of what is now Kuala Lumpur. The colonial era began with the sixteenth-century Portuguese conquest of Malacca. The Dutch wrested power in the seventeenth century and ceded it in 1824 to the British, who wasted little time expanding into the rest of the Malay peninsula. The Chinese and Indians, a presence since the Malaccan trade heyday, arrived en masse during British rule to fill increased labor demands—the Chinese usually as tin miners and merchants, the Indians on rubber plantations.

What's generally left out of textbooks and travel brochures is the fraught history of ethnopolitics. Malaysian industry, as the British conceived it, depended on an ethnic division of labor, which bred lasting stereotypes about the nature and economic function of each race, not to mention a pervasive mutual mistrust. The colonial game of divide and conquer was so effective at subjugating the natives that as the country transitioned to self-governance, the new Malaysian ruling class decided to adopt it too. From the very inception of the Federation of Malaya on August 31, 1957 (Malaysia was formed six years later with the addition of Singapore and East Malaysia), the national myth of multiculturalism has coexisted with official endorsements of racial disparity. The constitution safeguards the "special position" of the majority Malays, in vague terms that government policies have since taken to mean preferential treatment in virtually all aspects of educational and economic life. It further loads the issue by linking race and religion, defining all Malays as Muslim. Malaysian race relations, as played out in the halls of government, have long been plagued by entrenched hierarchies and a dubious logic of score-settling. UMNO (United Malays National Organization) is the biggest party in the Barisan Nasional (National Front) ruling coalition, followed by the Chinese and Indian parties. It has always been understood that the political dominance of the Malays exists in part to redress the disproportionate economic might of the Chinese. Frictions were present from the start, and in 1965, Chinese-majority Singapore opted to go it alone. On May 13, 1969, three days after a general election that saw the ruling coalition lose ground to the opposition parties, riots broke out when a Chinese victory march passed through the predominantly Malay KL neighborhood of Kampung Baru. Hundreds died; a state of emergency was called; the government suspended the press for a few days and parliament for nearly two years.[3] As a Malaysian Chinese born in 1973, I absorbed the sense of "May 13" as a forbidden topic at an early age. I grasped what it signified before I learned what had transpired: it was the great repressed, forever threatening to return.

In 1987, it nearly did. Ethnic tensions were on the rise, though this time it was less clear why. There were power tussles within UMNO, disputes over Chinese language schools, a shooting in a KL Chinese neighborhood, and on October 27, the arrest under the ISA of more than a hundred dissidents allegedly harmful to national stability—most of them activists, writers, and opposition leaders. All the average Malaysian could do in the pre-Internet age was connect the dots with the occasional help of a largely progovernment press that reported the news with almost no context and analysis. Several papers, not sufficiently slavish in their coverage of the detentions, had their publishing licenses revoked. Despite having obviously bruised the national psyche, the events of 1987 and

1969 remain curiously murky—it doesn't help that a colonial relic called the Sedition Act is still brandished from time to time as a reminder that some things are not to be talked about. The crazy notion that such fresh national traumas can be so easily occluded is key to understanding not just how Malaysia is run but how its population has been conditioned to think. Which brings us back to *The Big Durian*, a brash wake-up call for a society that keeps hitting the snooze button. This personal essay-cum-semiscripted documentary braids the quizzical ruminations of its Malay Muslim director, thirty-two-year-old Amir Muhammad, with testimonials, real and acted, on the free-floating anxiety of 1987 and the obscured horrors of 1969. The film exposes prejudices, punctures taboos, savors urban legends, cracks ethnic jokes, ventures conspiracy theories; it's a scathing, well-argued attack on racial politics and a wry, impertinent love letter to the Malaysian people that won't excuse them their apathy. Uninitiated viewers could not ask for a crisper snapshot of the national temperament. For Malaysians of a certain generation, the effect is tantamount to unearthing a real alternate history—one that we lived through but never could corroborate. I'm about the same age as Amir, and *The Big Durian*, named for the most intensely pungent of local fruits, triggered powerful sense memories: it took me back to a moment that I now recognize as a bleary political awakening—an uneasy realization that where I was from was not necessarily where I belonged. But it also had another, somewhat unexpected effect: it made me homesick.

Running Amok

> I've tried bribes, I've tried gifts. I even sent him some pet oxen. I mean, they love that crap in Malaysia.
>
> —Mugatu in *Zoolander*

The durian, a creamy-fleshed delicacy native to Southeast Asia, is notorious for its overpowering aroma and thick husk, which is both hazardously thorny and very tough to crack. The "Big Durian" is also a sobriquet for KL, and the hybrid confusion and polyglot cacophony of Amir's film are endearingly true to life in the Malaysian capital. Kuala Lumpur literally means "muddy estuary"; Jean Cocteau supposedly once called the city Kuala *L'impure.*

The Big Durian spirals outward from the October 1987 rampage of a Malay soldier named Adam, who ran amok with an M16 in Chow Kit, a Chinese section of KL, killing two people. The film's structure is both dense and digressive, inserting asides within asides. *Amok*, the narrator-director points out, is one of two Malay words used in the English language (the other being *orangutan*). A young interviewee who remembers nothing of 1987 instead shares his memories of a childhood electrocution. The viewer is asked to ponder the baffling popularity in eighties Malaysia of teen-pop pinup Tommy Page and Eurodisco duo Modern Talking.

Fittingly for a filmmaker whose favorite Orson Welles movie is *F for Fake*, some of the subjects are really being interviewed, while others are actors improvising or working off a script. The mockumentary elements, apart from their usual deconstructive purpose, have a larger in-joke resonance: not knowing what to believe is a big part of being Malaysian. That doesn't stop most people from having an opinion, though. As one subject puts it, "Anything happens in Malaysia and you speculate, because the truth never comes out." Churning up a paranoid storm of conjecture, *The Big Durian* demonstrates that, in a culture of secrecy and disinformation, rumor is the same as memory is the same as history.

Even as he amusingly evokes the Malaysian government's Ministry of Truth evasiveness, Amir, a sometime newspaper columnist with a law degree from the University of East Anglia, mounts a damning case against its heedless hypocrisy. The Mahathir regime in particular did not hesitate to stir up racial tensions for political gain and was equally quick to silence any challenges in the name of racial harmony. Needless to say, this is how any autocratically inclined administration—not least the current American one—deploys whatever instrument of fear is at its disposal. In Malaysia, it works every time. The 1987 detentions and media clampdown, code-named *Operasi Lalang* (Weeding Operation), had the desired result of stifling dissent. In 1998, at odds over responses to the Asian financial crisis, Mahathir fired his deputy and ex-protégé, Anwar Ibrahim, and had him arrested on charges of corruption and—for extra tabloid value—sodomy. The blatant outrageousness of this particular maneuver sparked *reformasi*, a multiethnic movement inspired by the Indonesian revolution that brought down Suharto. Facing massive demonstrations for the first time, the authorities cracked down, citing the ISA and an unlawful-assembly law that prohibits gatherings of more than three people without a police license. The new opposition alliance, the closest thing to a meaningful political alternative in the country's history, eventually crumbled due to differences between the two main parties—one Islamic and Malay, the other secular and mainly Chinese. Yet again, the threats to the status quo were successfully weeded out.

The Big Durian, which recaps this recent history, is angriest and most poignant as a study of political inaction—that is, when it's wondering what makes a society so averse to risk, so afraid of change. Is indifference culturally conditioned? Can it be legislated into existence?[4] Amir, to his credit, finds this all deeply exasperating and—when he steps back for a contextual irony or zooms in on a ridiculous detail—quite funny. His sense of outrage, impassioned but never self-righteous, is equaled by a taste for the absurd. This instinctive poise is perhaps best captured in his fifteen-minute short, *Kamunting*, which records a road trip to the titular ISA detention center where a friend is being held. Its quiet indignation peaks with the placid recitation of a series of detainee testimonies. What makes the film uniquely Amir's are the deadpan jabs at prison administration and the doomed comic attempt to smuggle a camera into the facility.

Kamunting is part of a cycle of six films made in 2002 and 2003, collectively titled *6horts*. Almost all are intimate first-person meditations on the pricklier aspects of identity (whether national, racial, religious, or sexual). *Checkpoint* recounts experiences of post–9/11 racial profiling at the Malaysia-Singapore border. *Lost* is an existential reverie prompted by a stolen identity card and the ensuing bureaucratic nightmare.[5] *Friday* is a not entirely reverent rumination on being a modern Muslim, gently riffing on compulsory prayer attendance and footwear theft at mosques.

Boldest of all, *Pangyau*, a dreamy confessional set to a smeared video tour of KL's mainly Chinese Petaling Street night market, is a three-in-one taboo-buster, filtering racial, religious, and sexual difference through the fond memory of a teenage more-than-friendship. Exquisite and even erotic in its threading of the delicate and the vulgar, *Pangyau* (*friend* in Cantonese) reflects on otherness, forbidden fruit, and the knotty Malay-Chinese relationship, drawing provocative connections with breathtaking aplomb. Just before the Malay narrator recalls the loss of his virginity to a high-school friend—a same-sex, interracial encounter, on a Muslim holy day no less—he remembers his first illicit mouthful of pork, and the voice-over dizzyingly echoes an earlier description of a porno blowjob: "I took it in slowly. I thought I might gag."

Division of Leisure

> The Malaysian film industry was founded on Chinese money, Indian imagination, and Malay labor.
>
> —Malaysian film historian Hamzah Hussin

Marginal at home, Malaysian film is barely a blip on the world-cinema map. As the local press likes to remind its readers, there are well-known Malaysian-*born* movie personalities: Hong Kong star Michelle Yeoh; Tsai Ming-liang, the master of psychosexual Taiwanese minimalism; James Wan, the Australian-based director of the torture-chamber thriller *Saw.* But Malaysian productions are not generally considered exportable, and until a year or two ago, they almost never popped up at international film festivals.[6]

William van der Heide's historical survey *Malaysian Cinema, Asian Film* (Amsterdam University Press, 2002), which predates the indie boom by a matter of months, now reads even more like an excavation of a lost culture—in the sense that the best new Malaysian films have little or nothing to do with their supposed forerunners. The first Malaysian movie, 1933's *Laila Majnun* (directed by B. S. Rajhans, a recent arrival from India), was a song-and-dance romance based on an ancient Persian-Arabic legend about doomed lovers. Shaw Brothers, the Chinese powerhouse studio, swooped in soon after, setting up shop in Singapore. Many early productions were slapdash remakes of Indian or Chinese hits; the main genres were melodrama and folklore. For Malaysians of any race, the idea of old local movies conjures only one name: P. Ramlee, a beloved Malay actor-director-singer, often called the Malaysian Chaplin (though Bob Hope maybe a more apt comparison), who starred in dozens of musical melodramas and the comic *Bujang Lapok* ("old bachelor") series in the fifties and sixties.

The push-pull between racial exclusion and inclusion is acutely reflected in the national cinema. The moviegoing market remains largely segregated (the Chinese favoring HK imports and the Indians sticking with Bollywood, though Hollywood blockbusters cut across racial lines), so it's no surprise that Malaysian films, for economic and political reasons, have always been overwhelmingly Malay, in both theme and language.

Singapore was home to the Shaw and Cathay studios, and its departure from the federation hastened the decline of the industry. Despite the 1981 creation of FINAS, the National Film Development Corporation, to boost production and ensure Malay involvement, the official Malaysian film industry never fully recovered. The current uptick in activity, like Chinese film's impressive post-Tiananmen groundswell, is squarely rooted outside the official system. Festival programmers, well aware of neighboring Thailand's recently elevated art-house profile, are eager to herald a Malaysian new wave.[7]

These up-and-comers—spearheaded by Amir, James Lee (*The Beautiful Washing Machine*), and Ho Yuhang (*Sanctuary*)—are a close-knit, multiracial, KL-based group, most in their late twenties and early thirties, who work quickly and prolifically, helping out on each other's films in various capacities. Digital technology was a key factor in their emergence, and so were the bootleggers who have made available an abundance of foreign movies since the eighties.[8] The new generation adds diversity to a local cinema scene that has been a Malay stronghold for decades, even as their individual films suggest wider diasporic connections. Lee's and Ho's ironic, oblique, unfailingly patient portraits of estrangement extend the bloodlines of Taiwan's Tsai Ming-liang and Hou Hsiao-hsien; Deepak Kumaran Menon, director of *The Gravel Road,* a Tamil-language film set on a rubber plantation, acknowledges the influence of Indian master Satyajit Ray's Apu trilogy.

Predictably, the new non-Malay Malaysian films make the cultural gatekeepers slightly uneasy. When *Sanctuary* was offered prestigious competition slots at the Pusan and Rotterdam festivals, Ho, a minor celebrity at home for his comic turns in TV commercials, went to FINAS for help with the cost of conversion from digital to film, but he was denied on the grounds that his movie, about a Chinese brother and sister, wasn't sufficiently multicultural. (Ironically, the titular protagonist of his previous feature, *Min,* was a young Chinese woman adopted by Malay parents.) *The Gravel Road,* meanwhile, was deemed ineligible for a tax rebate because it was not made in the national language. But as some filmmakers are finding out, international acclaim is the first step to national exposure: *Sanctuary* won jury citations at Pusan and Rotterdam, prompting the Culture Minister to publicly question FINAS's decision. Lee's *The Beautiful Washing Machine* won the Southeast Asian competition at the Bangkok Film Festival in January.[9] Three months later, *Washing Machine* finally opened domestically. Most Malaysian indies are still confined to movie-club screenings and VCD sales; some—Amir's insolently tossed grenades, most notably—could never hope to get past the censorship board that infamously deemed *Schindler's List* overly sympathetic to Jews, and is even more scissor-happy with local and regional fare, which must conform to "Asian values," an all-purpose catchphrase of the Mahathirera. Malaysian censorship often makes such outlandish demands that it practically constitutes a form of conceptual art, along the lines of Dogme 95's "Vow of Chastity." Supernatural themes, deemed un-Islamic, are often propped up with tortured quasiscientific rationales. It was suggested that a KL production of *The Vagina Monologues* be revamped to avoid the word *vagina.* Recently, confronted with the sweetly utopian color blindness of Yasmin Ahmad's interracial teen romance *Sepet,* film censors complained that the Malay heroine had failed to ask her Chinese boyfriend to convert to Islam.

The Big Pomelo

Making art in Malaysia could drive you mad. But Amir Muhammad has the requisite resilience and adaptability: in his brief career he has already reinvented himself several times. Following his debut, *Lips to Lips* (2000), a raunchy, talky, no-budget comedy often identified as ground zero of the Malaysian indie scene, he was inspired to try his hand at cine-essays after, of all things, reading about them, in Phillip Lopate's "In Search of the Centaur: the Essay Film." Which is not as random as it sounds: The salient quality of Amir's work is its wide-open intellectual curiosity—an awareness that, especially in a culture as porous and polymorphous as Malaysia's, ideas can come from anywhere and exist to be borrowed and bastardized. Steeped in Western references but unquestionably local in outlook, he's something of a kindred spirit to Thailand's Apichatpong Weerasethakul, whose fiction films have the flavor of hallucinated documentary, and whose debut doc, *Mysterious Object at Noon*, adapted its methodology from Breton's exquisite corpse. Dense with text and narration, Amir's film essays are a logical extension of his journalistic persona. In the late nineties he wrote a lively literary column in an English-language daily: titled "Perforated Sheets," after the first chapter of Salman Rushdie's *Midnight's Children*, it was canned in 1999 for espousing a few too many antiestablishment views. *6horts* and *The Big Durian* suggested he'd found a niche in sardonic political commentary, but after Mahathir stepped down in 2003, replaced by his bland, handpicked successor Abdullah Badawi, Amir headed to Japan and Indonesia. He returned with a pair of films that could not be more different from his early work. While on a Nippon Foundation grant, he discovered experimental filmmakers like Stan Brakhage and Michael Snow and proved a quick study. From a single line of inspiration—Lebanese writer Jalal Toufic's observation that "All love affairs take place in foreign cities"—he crafted an avant-garde tone poem, *Tokyo Magic Hour*, fusing processed digital imagery with traditional Malay verse. Shot against the backdrop of Indonesia's first direct elections, on the Jakarta set of Riri Riza's *Gie*, a biopic about the late Indonesian-Chinese student activist Soe Hock Gie, *The Year of Living Vicariously* is an essay on rebellion and nationalism in the guise of a making-of doc. The implicit question is, as suggested in the title: *Why did the irreform movement succeed and ours fail?* Back home in KL, he's balancing another pair of projects. He's set to start shooting his first mainstream movie, *Susuk*, a horror flick titled for a black-magic implant procedure that grants eternal youth—a sort of witch-doctor Botox. He's also editing a new quasi-nonfiction, *The Last Communist*, a musical-documentary-biopic on Chin Peng, the former secretary-general of the Communist Party of Malaya who now lives in exile in southern Thailand. I sent Amir an email recently asking for a status report. His excited reply suggests he's back in *Big Durian* mode: mash-up mystification, local fruit-as-metaphor, and yet another slice of Malaysian history that his countrymen will never think about the same way again. Or perhaps think about for the first time:

> It travels from place to place based on the chronology of Chin Peng's life from birth to Independence. There is written text, like a potted bio, randomly interspersed with interviews with people who are somehow connected to some aspect of his story. (For example, a bicycle seller[,] after we find out that CP's family owned a bicycle shop.) Some of these connections are more tenuous than others. They talk about their jobs, their towns, their beliefs, in various languages. We then cut to cheesily choreographed music videos, with seven girls, on topics like How to Conduct Jungle Warfare. The longest sequence takes place in Betong, Thailand, home of many exiled members of the Malayan Communist Party. It ends in KL on the stroke of Independence, where we interview the people who maintain the bell that strikes at midnight. Actually if I were to sum it up in one word, the documentary is about landscape. If I were to sum it up in more than one word, it's about counter-hegemonic discursive terrains. We think the poster will just have a big pile of pomelo fruit in the middle of a highway. We interviewed a hilarious pomelo seller.

Notes

1. What is essentially a one-party system coexists, ironically, with a revolving monarchy, wherein each state sultan (the traditional Malay ruler) has a five-year stint in the mostly ceremonial role of *Agong*, or king.

2. The rest of Borneo, not counting the tiny, oil-rich kingdom of Brunei, belongs to Indonesia and is known as Kalimantan.

3. In response to the riot, the government instituted the New Economic Policy in 1971. The stated objective of this exercise in socioeconomic engineering was the redistribution of wealth via quotas and subsidies—from non-Malays to the *bumiputra* ("sons of the soil," a classification for Malays and some but not all indigenous groups), who then controlled only 2.4 percent of the economy. More than half remained in foreign hands, and while the Chinese were generally better off than the Malays, the Indians were not. While the NEP has reduced poverty and increased bumiputra ownership, this discriminatory system also paved the way for corruption and cronyism among politically powerful Malays.

4. Political apathy is especially pronounced on the part of the non-Malays, who not only accept but embrace their position on the margins of national politics. The idea of knowing one's place in what is still a patriarchal society translates to an instinctive self-exclusion. The Indians are not expected to weigh in on

Malay-Chinese conflicts; the Chinese stay out of debates between moderate and hardline-Islamist Malays. I recognize that on some level, my decision to live halfway around the world is merely an active form of this fundamental passivity.

5. The Malaysian Mykade insists on religion as an identifying category.

6. A notable exception, U-Wei bin Hajisaari's *Khaki Bakar*, which transposed William Faulkner's short story "Barn Burning" to rural Malaysia, screened at Cannes in 1995. (The film had been commissioned—and rejected—by a local televison network.) The first Malaysian movie I saw outside the country was the comic youth flick *From Jemapoh to Manchester*, directed by the writer and veteran activist Hishamuddin Rais, at the Rotterdam Film Festival in 1999. The filmmaker was recently detained for two years under the ISA and is the friend Amir was visiting in Kamunting prison.

7. In January 2005, the Rotterdam Film Festival included seven Malaysian features in an expanded Southeast Asian program. A few months later, the San Francisco Film Festival devoted an ample sidebar to Malaysia. In addition, I helped arrange the New York premiere of *The Big Durian* and four Amir Muhammad shorts at a *Village Voice* series at BAM in the summer of 2005.

8. It's impossible to understate the cultural importance of piracy in the region, and I do not state this glibly. My early pop education consisted strictly of illegal product, and even today, much foreign or nonmainstream film and music is available only on bootleg. There's a scene in Chinese director Jia Zhangke's 2002 *Unknown Pleasures* where someone tries to buy pirated copies of Jia's earlier films *Platform* and *Xiao Wu*. The bootleggers' tastes have apparently gotten more rarefied, too—many Criterion Collection titles can be obtained for a fraction of the U.S. retail price in night markets throughout Asia.

9. It beat out fourteen other films, including the most expensive Malaysian movie ever produced, music-video director Saw Teong Hin's *Princess of Mount Ledang*, a lumbering romantic epic set in fifteenth-century Malacca that cost four hundred times as much as *The Beautiful Washing Machine*.

4

B. KITE

A Kurosawa Kiyoshi Kit

> There is an infinity of rational numbers, that is, numbers thatcan be written as the ratio of two whole numbers. There is also an infinity of irrational numbers, numbers that cannot be expressed as any such ratio. But their two orders of infinity are not comparable. The infinity of irrationals is "greater" than the infinity of rationals. In particular, between any two rationals, no matter how close, lies a cluster of irrationals. Stepping from one rational to the next, as we do every day, is . . . like crossing a bridge whose piers are joined by something that does not "really" exist.
>
> —J. M. Coetzee, "Robert Musil's Stories of Women"

I SAW THIS ON TV: THE TRANSFIXING horror of a stage hypnotist running a volunteer through a variety of roles—drunk, in love, an opera singer, an animal—each of which the victim enters with an utterly unselfconscious wholeheartedness. Before sending him back to his table, the hypnotist warns: Watch out for the strings, indicating an imaginary grid running along the floor, below knee-level, every couple of feet. The victim, restored to himself, takes his bow, then high-steps back to his seat. "Why are you walking like that?" the hypnotist asks. "Because of the strings," the man replies, as if it's a stupid question.

Rules of the Game: Both formally and thematically, Kurosawa Kiyoshi's films are a series of fluctuations between rigid and chaotic elements, grids in which emphasis is placed variously on the lines and the spaces. The lines: the hard angles of his long-take long shots, sectioning the screen in balanced but asymmetric compositions; the confines of genre; the habitual codes of consensual reality. The spaces: unexpected activations of seemingly static planes or elements within those strict compositions; pushing generic considerations to a larger, allegoric frame of reference, then beyond to ambiguous apocalypse in which an old order/means of perception is abolished in an act of either nihilism triumphant or possibility affirmed—or maybe both, an affirmative nihilism.

Lineage: If the box compositions suggest a mutant family tree whose branches include Ozu, Lang, and Antonioni (and the shift from generic to metaphysical concerns makes him seem an unlikely hybrid of the latter pair in particular), the way in which apparently dead areas of the frame become saturated with possibility suggests another sinister magician—Méliès—with the Frenchman's explosions, leaping devils, fantastic transformations shifted to the sphere of the mundane world, possessing its objects. In conjunction with such tableaux, lines laid down by the camera: tidy lateral tracking shots, often of a character walking parallel to a wall or a road—then symmetrical backwards movement as the character reverses direction or another character crosses the trajectory and redirects the focus. Chains of action and reaction.

In opposition to these grids, set in place or drawn through space, sudden eruptions of shaky handheld camerawork for moments of violence or intensity—though violence can also figure in the cool remove of the boxshots, the sounds of a gunshot or a body struck by a mallet or a pipe horribly blunted, without any of the aural foregrounding that draws attention to the central event in mainstream cinema practice. A scene near the end of *Charisma* (1999), of heads being smashed with a mallet ("smashed" is too lively a word for the affect—it's a heavy, hollow thump) is reminiscent of the desultory atrocities in the last section of Godard's *Week-End*.

In interviews, Kurosawa affirms his cinephile cred but points particularly to directors such as Don Siegel and Robert Aldrich, two others who push past the perimeters of genre into the multivalent mythic. Think of the pod people of *Invasion of the Body Snatchers*, readable, should one desire, as either embodiment of Communist threat or American groupthink, or the mass of association that gets packed into the Pandora's box of *Kiss Me Deadly*.

These are my initial associations. Kurosawa himself is more likely to refer to *Dirty Harry* or *Emperor of the North Pole*. *Dirty Harry* seems to hold particular pride of place in Kurosawa's imagination, judging by how frequently he refers to the character in interviews. Harry Calahan is, in Kurosawa's telling, a figure uncontaminated by psychological motivation, an urge (anger) in action. This helps to clarify some of the uses to which Kurosawa applies genre—he is drawn to its patterns while resisting the simplified psychologies that set the action in motion (since even Harry's anger is assigned perfunctory cause in Siegel's film). This resistance allows him to thin his characters toward allegory or thicken them beyond the range of concise explanation by suggesting untapped depths of conflicted will, according to his needs of the moment. And these uses are not contradictory, they coexist as aspects of personality (examine for a moment the various narratives with which you explain yourself to yourself), even if the sometimes-rapid focal shifts between them in Kurosawa's films may create a certain metaphysical vertigo.

This attraction to primal motivation paired with a tendency to complicate (or obfuscate) psychology wreaks havoc on the narrative arc of cause and effect, warping genre structures into unending spirals, serial repetitions, Piranesi prisons. Miyashita, the protagonist of Kurosawa's 1998 V-film *Serpent's Path* (scripted by Takahashi Hiroshi, who also wrote the *Ringu* screenplay) is driven by vengeance—his young daughter was raped and killed, so he and his cryptic friend Nijima kidnap and torture the Yakuza member believed to be responsible. Yet the object of revenge endlessly recedes: one syndicate member after another passes the buck, crowding the torture chamber with new candidates. Miyashita's determination pushes him along a straight line, which twists in serpentine convolutions before leading back to himself. His fixed trajectory is finally the death of him. Nijima, whose role is unassigned, proves the better player.

Spaces: The territory between the lines or on the margins is the position of power in Kurosawa's work. Consider the prime mover in *Cure* (1997), a young man whose refusal of fixed identity allows him privileged access to the psyche of others, individuals who have allowed themselves to be defined by their roles rather than undertaking the perpetually fluctuating work of self-definition. The stultified habit that presumptuously calls itself reality is rigid yet brittle; violation sets off a chain reaction in which all walls tumble. So, here, a serial killer who never, himself, kills. Instead, he unlocks reservoirs of rage in the people he encounters, triggering murderous breaks unremembered afterwards—and initiating a cycle that continues after his death. (Freedom is a virus in Kurosawa's films, and it's often birthed in blood. KK, in an *Acid Logic* interview: "I think that most humans live with deeply repressed rage and hate. We are repressed by such things as conventions and morality."

Reverse the field so the figure/ground relation shifts, the lines become cracks. Through them (initially through the deceptive gray-on-gray planes of Kurosawa's much-loved concrete bunkers, then through the phone lines) the dead return in *Pulse* (2001). One character explains the cyber-infestation as the result of overcrowding in the afterlife: leakage is occurring. Like *Cure*'s master hypnotist, the dead bring the curse of self-knowledge, which in this case is knowledge of the empty, isolated self. Their loneliness survives the victims as stains on the architecture.

Border Crossings: Horror films, like the paranormal in general, seem always to carry a taint of the disreputable—Kurosawa's films doubly so, because they take the paranormal seriously enough to use it to move beyond metaphor, to literalize, in their exploration of existential concerns. In so doing, they frustrate genre expectations and threaten to degenerate into chaos.

A number of critics and viewers seem to think the threat is fulfilled, that Kurosawa perversely abandons control at some point in his films and allows promising setups to dribble away to incoherence. I think the aim is somewhere else: combining traditional elements in unexpected ways to transcend habitual response to the ocean of conflicted and unnamed thought/feeling that lies beyond. (Kurosawa, in a *Midnight Eye* interview, on the bouncy musical theme that crops up at unexpected moments in *Charisma*: "The direction that I gave my composer was that I wanted him to compose folk music that belonged to no country anywhere in the world, that sounded oldish but might actually be new, sound newish but actually be old.")

Pulse begins as a ghost story before reversing its terms. Its horror is death-in-life; its zombies are respectable citizens ("Who are they?" asks one victim-to-be, gesturing at a bank of monitors, each of which traps a lonely soul sitting in front of another monitor. "Are they really alive?"). Though the film has been tagged "*Ring* on the Net," the function that the Web serves is distinct from *Ring*'s haunted videotape. It becomes instead another of Kurosawa's figures for illusory connection, lines that isolate even as they draw together, no more or less virtual for him than any other form of community. He isn't shy about laying his themes out, here in the form of a computer simulation of human interactions, white blobs floating in black space: "If two dots get too close, they die. But if they get too far apart, they're drawn closer." Such scenes in Kurosawa's films (*Serpent's Path* and 2003's *Bright Future* offer similar examples) are best regarded as embedded emblems—not answers to a problem but a condensed expression of it.

A television news program reports that a message in a bottle dropped into the ocean has finally been discovered after ten years. Yoshi, the protagonist of *License to Live* (1998), emerges from a ten-year coma at age twenty-four to find his family dispersed. He asks: "If only for a moment, can't we all be together again?" Twice, he virtually succeeds, though the father is present only televisually the first time and Yoshi himself is absent the second. Dropped back into life only to be yanked out again by a tragedy timed like slapstick, his being is almost as intermittent as the young man in *Barren Illusion* (1999) who, like a transmission received and occluded, fades in and out of existence in front of a window on a bright, blank summer day. Yoshi's dying moments may represent the affirmative limit point of human connection for Kurosawa: "Am I dreaming? Did I really exist?" Yes, he is told, you absolutely existed. It's not nothing.

> Like Ulrich, the hero of The Man Without Qualities, we can maintain a certain reserve toward the real world, a living sense of alternative possibilities. This reserve defines one as what Ulrich calls a "possibilitarian," someone prepared to exist in "a web of haze, imaginings, fantasy, and the subjunctive mood," to live a "hovering life" without ideological commitment, to be "without qualities," someone whose natural mode will be the mode of irony ("With me," said Musil in an interview, "irony is not a gesture of condescension but a form of struggle").
>
> —J. M. Coetzee

The World as Will: Once off the main roads, the ground becomes slippy underfoot, as Detective Yabuiki, on mandatory vacation, discovers in *Charisma*. A parable with continually shifting frames of reference, the film seems initially a sort of murder mystery, with the culprit (possibly) or victim (maybe) the tree of the title. (Kurosawa says he intended "an Indiana Jones/two-teams-vying-for-a-treasure" story but it became something "much more complex.")

The sickly Charisma bears its own scaffold, set up as life support by one of the contending forces surrounding it. Is it a rare botanical treasure under assault or a vegetative monster intent on destroying the countryside to maintain itself? What to do, when given a choice between saving the unique specimen or the forest as a whole? Characteristically, when confronted with a binary "either/or" Kurosawa opts for an impossible both. The ecological conundrum appears uprooted with Charisma itself when one team finally gains possession of the tree and burns it.

But having pulled the rug out, Kurosawa restates the quandary in more abstract terms. Yabuiki (played by Kurosawa favorite Koji Yakusho—"He is the same age as me. So our points of view are alike. We're on the same level as human beings," from the *Midnight Eye* interview) locates a huge, dead trunk and improbably identifies it, on the basis of no evidence whatsoever, as "another Charisma." No member of the opposing teams agrees, but nevertheless the force of his attention sets it in play as the new counter in the game, which soon dissolves into chaos. "You are Charisma," Yabuiki is told by a former player as he leaves the field. At the end Yabuiki returns to a city in flames—another of Kurosawa's exterminating angels?—as the ecological metaphor is seen to cover in turn the relation of the individual to society, the self to the world.

Fill in the Blank Generation: A similar miracle of applied will forms the crux of his latest film, *Bright Future*: acclimatizing a jellyfish to fresh water in order to release it in Tokyo's aqueducts. It too emerges from the margins—dumped from its tank in a fit of rage, it survives beneath the floorboards, appears again below a boiler in a derelict factory, then at last into the open waterways en masse, and headed to the city.

An electric current of violence buzzes close beneath the surface of the film—"Could be there's a storm coming," says Mamoru, another of Kurosawa's easygoing enigmas, looking through the rectangle window of a bourgeois home, where the nuclear family swims fishlike in yellow light. His younger friend Yuji is the main conduit, pitched on the verge of explosion, waiting only for Mamoru's signal (thumb towards the chest: wait; index finger out: go ahead).

As always, Kurosawa's style carries its own charge of lingering immanence, here subtly altered through his engagement with digital and high-definition video. The long takes register a slight handheld tremble, colors are sometimes hallucinogenically saturated (an aquatic bowling alley of rich blues and greens, then the roll of a shiny red gutter ball), sometimes fuzzed over in a lowlight grain. Characteristically confined to the outskirts (even the fish never make it downtown), the film's cityscapes are bleached into photocopier imprints and otherwise stretched and twisted into treacherous configurations. Overhead shots web the streets in phone lines and power cables. A telephoto squeeze renders a jog across an overpass into the Zeno marathon.

Favorite themes reemerge. The generation gap is a chasm for Kurosawa and he generally places himself on the side of youth (he hesitated over casting Tatsuya Fuji, best known for his role in Oshima's *In the Realm of the Senses*, claiming he had never worked with an actor older than himself). Here it's tentatively, touchingly, bridged for a moment, in Yuji's relation with Mamoru's father (Fuji). The connection is (apparently) terminated, plans and agendas once more set adrift to arrive on unknown shores. Even the jellyfish invasion is diverted, as the creatures leave the poisoned canals and head back to sea.

But the ramifications of any act are never predictable; the invasion may succeed in ways unsuspected. The film returns at the end to a gang of teens, earlier rhymed with the fish through an overhead shot of the group drifting through the city streets at night, illumined by their glowing walkie-talkie headsets. Their aimlessness and matching uniforms (black pants and white Oxfords over matching Che Guevara T-shirts) might not suggest anything spectacularly promising, but Kurosawa places the title under them as a caption—Bright Future—and has insisted he means it. Why not? Like the fish, they're adaptable and perched on the point of transition. Even the Che shirts resonate on indeterminate frequencies: revolutionary sympathy or commodification of rebellion? Or maybe something that moves beyond these dichotomies, a mutant strain in the culture stream. (Richard Hell: "People misread what I meant by 'Blank Generation.' To me, 'blank' is a line where you can fill in anything. It's positive. It's the idea that you have the option of making yourself anything you want, filling in the blank.")

Between Freedom and Form: Ambivalent Future (2002), the fascinating documentary made during the film's shooting, shows the extent to which indeterminacy is a guiding force at every stage of Kurosawa's artistic process. He expresses an almost Bressonian refusal to either create psychologically defined figures ("I can't invent a character . . . with a reason for everything") or help the actors find their way into a role ("I'm terrified that the more we talk, we'll clarify motivations, which I hate."). He shoots quickly (two weeks for *Ambivalent Future*), making compositional decisions in response to the environment—and in one instance, indecisive himself, turning the choice over to an assistant.

Assumptions that works like *Barren Illusion*, *License to Live*, and *Bright Future* itself are more personal for lacking bloody generic hooks receive no support from the filmmaker. He searches, he says, for the proper balance "between freedom and form," so it's easier for him to make films "in and out of the conventions of genre." The producer's insistence on a film "comprehensible and cool . . . based on the characters' experiences" left him "flummoxed—because that means anything goes. My point of view as a filmmaker could get very hazy. It's so easy for the film to devolve into a real mess."

He reaffirms his preference for physical rather than psychological confrontation ("that's very Aldrich"): "So in the editing, I really tried to eliminate the psychological drama. But it's still there." Perhaps this was one impetus for the film's gradual shrinkage: the original 115-minute cut sliced down to 92 minutes for Cannes. Unfortunately, the shorter cut is the only version widely available in the United States. Though the director has said he stands behind both versions, and indeed finds the 92-minute edit "tougher," it strikes me as both much less powerful and much more sentimental, largely due to the way the omissions soften Yuji's character.

Smudging the Lines: Pitched between the habitual order of the comfortably normal and the creeping void of *Cure*'s hypnotist, Kurosawa's heroes move fluidly between positions. Likewise the films: Much to the irritation of viewers expecting contained variations on familiar formulas, they refuse to treat actions as blocks in a prefabricated narrative architecture. Instead, as curator Mark McElhatten notes, any given occurrence functions as a pivot, opening new directions for movement: "Events which would often signal final or longlasting resolutions prove to be temporary and just another turning point in a vast, unforeseeable relay."

For the character and for the viewer, the ground keeps shifting; agility is required. Signals pass through unexpected mediums, their meaning often coming unfixed in transit. Mamoru's final "go ahead" (to what?) is relayed postmortem through his father (he had hardwired his finger into position before hanging himself). Yabuike's odyssey in *Charisma* begins with an ambiguous instruction to "Restore the Rules of the World" (but maybe the rules are determined by the player). A young woman flirtatiously slips an uninscribed picture postcard into Yoshi's book in *License to Live*. It's discovered only after his death and resonates with possibilities unknown. Kurosawa's films often end on abrupt ambiguities that overturn assumptions and leave the viewer to rethread the film in the mind. Definitive resolution may not be possible or desirable. The glowing red jellyfish is as good an emblem as any for freedom, Kurosawa-style: deadly, diaphanous, and mutable.

5

Ed Park

The Bong Show

Bong Joon-ho

Allegorical and intimate, terrifying and wry, South Korean director Bong Joon-ho's films are black comedies written with invisible ink, or suspense pictures that neatly derail into hip-deep melancholy, composed with something like the acid eye of Billy Wilder. Bong navigates disparate environments with equal ease: a gargantuan Seoul apartment complex in *Barking Dogs Never Bite* (2000), a weatherbeaten hamlet with far too many unprotected arteries in *Memories of Murder* (2003). Though the films differ in tone and atmosphere, they share a capacity for narrative and visual surprise, a serious philosophical bent (*Dog*'s alternate English title is *A Higher Animal*), and not least a social critique as subtle as it is penetrating, teasing out the eroded borders where culture ends and greed, madness, even atavism surface. Add to these virtues Bong's considerable storytelling chops and you have a thirty-four-year-old director of eye-popping originality and voracious range.

Near the start of his assured debut, *Barking Dogs Never Bite*, two bored-at-work young women languidly attack a crossword puzzle over the phone—15 across, to be specific, with spaces for four syllables. "Reciprocal?" asks Hyeon-nam (Bae Du-Na), an employee in the maintenance office of the stolid mega-apartments where most of the movie transpires. "No, it's *reciprocate*," says her plump friend, a convenience store worker, and chides Hyeon-nam for not knowing what it means.

To reciprocate, of course, is to return in kind; the verb suggests a mirroring corollary to the golden rule: Do unto others. As it happens, Hyeon-nam knows the meaning well enough. Inspired by television news footage of a petite bank teller thwarting a robber, she's a heroine-in-waiting, doing good deeds and looking for her moment to shine. She certainly understands the word better than the picture's well-educated male protagonist, Yun-ju (Lee Sung-jae), does; he will spend the film learning. *Dogs* opens with him despairing over the difficulties of landing an academic post. His pregnant wife brings home the bacon, emasculating him further with capricious demands; his seemingly useless degree is in human behavior. Hearing a dog, he suddenly goes bonkers, and soon he's scooped up the offender and tried to hang the poor creature in the basement of one of the buildings. He catches a glimpse of himself in the mirrored door of a busted armoire, suffers an attack of scruples, and secretes the dog inside the furniture for some enforced quiet time.

With that one misguided act, Yun-ju slips into a moral twilight zone, localized as the topsy-turvy domain of the basement. Bong, playing on the knife edge of farce and nightmare, has a field day showing how even a seemingly minor transgression can send out devastating ripples, with tragic consequences for the culprit as well. Yun-ju sees a little girl's poster: her missing dog can't bark because its vocal cords have been removed. Hightailing it to the basement to free his innocent quarry, he finds the armoire empty—until he has to jump in himself, as footsteps sound.

As in a Poe tale, he watches in terror as the janitor butchers the dog for stew meat, then—hearing a noise from Yun-ju's vicinity—approaches, blade in hand. Is the universe reciprocating—putting him in the now-dead dog's place, sending an executioner in response to his brazen dognapping? Another custodian provides a distraction, and the canine-consuming janitor, still rattled by the mysterious subterranean noise, regales him with the story of Boiler Kim. With spartan effects, Bong presents this as the ultimate campfire tale—a real-estate ghost story, told over a cooking fire, no less. Forgotten for the moment, Yun-ju is out of immediate danger, and there's something Shakespearean in his concealed, privileged eavesdropping and this attention to the mechanicals' talk.

Soon after the apartment was slapped together in 1988 (i.e., the time of the Seoul Olympics-driven building boom), chronic heating problems led the owners to summon the legendary Boiler Kim, who could solve any maintenance dilemma. But when his job was complete, to everyone's satisfaction, he raged at his employers ("How much did you steal?"), knowing that such shoddy construction meant that funds earmarked for the proper building materials must have been embezzled. In the ensuing fracas, he hit his head on a nail in the wall and died. His body was covered with cement, and every night an eerie "spinning" sound can be heard. Despite Koreans' protestations to finger-wagging Westerners that the eating of dog meat (always only a delicacy) is a thing of the past, no doubt the cuisine has its holdouts. Bong reveals his objections by showing how the dog's absence crushes its owner, a first grader who tells the concerned Hyeon-nam, with utter resolution, "If I don't find him I'll starve myself to death." Someone's fancy feast will mean her own private famine.

Dogs also exposes another "traditional" practice: bribery. Palm-greasing exists everywhere, of course, but the practice seems particularly ingrained in Korean society. (My father recounts how men he served with in the army regular bribed their way out of service after three years, instead of fulfilling the required five—as, alas, he did. South Korean president Kim Dae-jung, it is said, even bribed his way to a Nobel Peace Prize. His "Sunshine" policy, viewed at the time as a progressive development in North-South relations, was actually facilitated by the millions he paid Pyongyang to show up for the requisite meetings and photo ops.) The heads of some Korean university departments are widely known to bestow favor on job candidates willing to make it worth their while. Yun-ju's friend advises him that a gift of about 10 grand should do the trick. Yun-ju vows that if he ever becomes a professor, he will never accept a bribe, but despite his distaste, he realizes that this is how one gets ahead in Korea—and to hold out is to commit career suicide. Bong artfully complicates this view with two secondhand stories—the cautionary tale of Boiler Kim (whistle-blower turned ghost) and the heroic tale of the bank teller (rewarded for stopping a theft of money that wasn't even hers). In the end, one must choose how to act.

Yun-ju's gnawing career dilemma and his tensions with his wife leave him feeling powerless. The one thing he can control is the volume level. After emerging at last from the chamber of horrors (locked in the basement, he climbs out through a window, slowly sprawling backward onto the grass as though being born), he abducts another dog—the real yapping culprit—and this time goes not below but above. Once resigned to God's will when it came to his professional career, he now makes an unconscious blood offering by flinging the dog over the edge of the roof.

This second death mortally affects the dog's owner (an old woman). God (let's say) returns in kind. First, Yun-ju's wife brings home a newly purchased, ludicrously coiffed poodle, on whom she dotes. Then the dog disappear while Yun-ju grumblingly walks it, his sight and mind obscured as they pass through a blinding, ever expanding fumigation cloud. He crosses paths with Hyeong-nam, ever the do-gooder. She finally has the chance to play the hero, rescuing the poodle from its captor (an insane homeless man with a taste for canine flesh). Her act saves Yun-ju's marriage and, it turns out, his career (his wife converts her severance pay into the bribe money).

Whether the subsequent life, thus attained, will be of any value is a different matter. "Close the curtains, please," says Yun-ju at the film's close, a professor at last. His lecture is about to begin, complete with "charts on modern behaviorism." The light is blocked, window by window. Is it the beginning of the lecture, or the end of the show? As darkness swallows the new professor, Bong cuts to Hyeon-nam and her friend, walking in the woods in glorious daylight.

Drawing from a real-life serial-killer case in rural South Korea, circa 1986, *Memories of Murder* is a grimmer, more ambitious, and superficially dissimilar affair: a *policier* manqué, crime and punishment losing their definitions somewhere in the garden of forking paths. *Dogs*, for all its muttophagia and marital-strife dissection, has an ineffable charm—the passages buoyed by antic, bass-propelled jazz, and the affectionate friendship of the two young women. It is dead serious but somehow jaunty; the work of an optimist, it ends on a beautiful sunlit day. In *Memories*, the weather leaves something to be desired (the rapist-killer strikes during downpours), music becomes an instrument of terror (the culprit, it is discovered, always requests that a radio station play a certain song before he strikes), and you fear for every woman who wanders onscreen—in this open-ended menace, there will be no final girl.

Bong refrains from dramatizing the killings, and the gruesomely dispatched bodies are even more disturbing for their mysterious morbidity: bound and gagged with their own underwear, sometimes invaded with foreign objects. But *Memories* has more than its share of onscreen violence, committed by inspectors Park (*Joint Security Area*'s Song Kang-ho), Jo (Kim Ro-hae), and Suh (Kim Sang-kyung)-upon the ever changing cast of suspects. Local men Park and Jo's m.o. is to beat first, ask questions later, then try to put words in the perps' mouths. Though they're fans of a television crime drama (*Inspector Chief*), they're untrained in the complicated psych-out known as good cop/bad cop, and simply resort to bad cop/worse cop, with Jo always willing to deliver a flying kick across an interrogation desk. Unlike the real-estate developers and academics in *Dogs*, these cops are free of avarice. Nevertheless, they're thoroughly corrupt in their brutal pursuit of justice. (Set in 1986, six years after the Kwangju massacre and two years before the modernized face of the Seoul Olympics, *Memories* offers an elliptical commentary on Korea's history of repression by the state.)

That Bong's unheroic trio is anything less than monstrous is thanks mostly to their bare-bones operation (a semen sample needs to be sent to the United States for analysis) and thorough incompetence. Park devises hare-brained hypotheses—for example, since no pubic hair was found on one victim, he deduces that the rapist-murderer must have shaved nether regions (perhaps a monk is involved?) and scopes out the population at the public baths. They can't even sweat out a confession from a retarded man who knew one of the victims ("So you didn't not kill only Hyung-sook, correct?"). The more principled Suh, a Seoul transplant, initially rejects their uncouth lines of inquiry and torture tactics but by the end has become the hardest hitter of the three, a burnt-out case.

When nongenre artists deign to appropriate the crime story, they (or their non–genre-consuming critics) often note that the work in question isn't so much a whodunit but a *whydunit*, as if a well-plotted thriller wasn't rewarding enough on its own terms. Perversely, *Memories* isn't even a whydunit-indeed, it's a whodunit all over again, except we never find out who. (It's occasionally also a whendoit or wheredoit, as the cops scramble to anticipate the next murder's coordinates.) Bong fulfills the requirements of the serial-killer flick—increasingly brutal crimes, flashlights cutting through the dampness—but as the murders continue and the investigation turns down one dead end after another, it's the silence that is most chilling. Emblems of muteness appear in *Dogs*—the non-barking first victim, Sun-ju's wife balancing a walnut on his mouth while he dozes, his enforced speechlessness while concealed in the basement. In *Memories* all the victims have been gagged; the suspects won't talk, and when they do, their words have already been distorted beyond utility by mental handicap, police pressure, personal fantasy.

The title suggests both the unreliable accounts of the suspects as well as a look backward on the whole wrenching time. And here we note that a pair of girls—they may even be played by the same young actress—bookend Bong's two films to date: the girl postering for her missing pet in *Dogs*, who will not eat until she finds him, and the inquisitive girl who greets the former inspector Park in *Memories*' epilogue. Though their cumulative screen time is probably less than five minutes, they figure as palindrome angels, floating on either side of innocence. Seventeen years have passed; Park, a bottled water sales rep now living in Seoul, takes a business trip that leads him through the field where he first encountered the killer's handiwork—a body in a covered ditch. When he was there in 1986, he was distracted by a young boy who parroted every word out of his mouth. ("Get out of here, kid." "Get out of here, kid.") This time, a young girl asks what he's doing. His reply is vague. She reports that she recently saw another man peering into the same opening. "He remembered doing something here long ago," she says, "so he came back for a look." Startled, he asks her to describe what he looked like, the girl replies. "Just . . . ordinary," she says. For Bong the past is a sentence that trails off but never ends, a devastating ellipses in the mind.

PART 2

On the European Outskirts

6

GEOFF ANDREW

Beyond the Clouds

The Films of Nuri Bilge Ceylan

IF SUCH A THING MAY BE SAID WITH regard to a filmmaker with just three features (and one short) to his name, I came a little late to the work of Nuri Bilge Ceylan; my first encounter with the young Turk's work was at the 2003 Cannes Film Festival, at the press screening of *Distant* (*Uzak*). I was very impressed by the film, and was later very pleased when it picked up a couple of major prizes, but it was really only some months later, when I was preparing for an interview with Ceylan, that I fully realized what a remarkable filmmaker he is. My appreciation of his achievements was deepened not only by the discovery of his unusually modest working methods, but—more importantly—by my then having had the opportunity to catch up with his first two features, *The Small Town* (*Kasaba*, 1998) and *Clouds in May* (*Mayis Sikintisi*, 2000). To watch these two films and *Distant* in the order of their making is not merely to witness a filmmaker developing his already considerable skills and refining his art; since the second and third films reflect back on and develop upon their predecessors in various ways, it is also a question of seeing a kind of organic enlargement occurring from film to film, so that while each film succeeds perfectly well in its own right, each acquires even greater resonance by being part of an ongoing series that is the step-by-step progress of Ceylan's career.

At this point, it is probably useful to provide some idea of what the films are about. *The Small Town* has a gentle, even meandering, narrative, the first half of which focuses on the seemingly inconsequential experiences of a teenage girl and her younger brother as they go to school and play about in the fields and forests around their small Anatolian town; the second half has the children listening in to what becomes a slightly heated discussion between different generations as their family camps out for the night during a harvest festival. Little happens, but Ceylan subtly ensures that we become acutely aware not only of the children's perceptions of the world around them—the weather, the pace of life, the places where they can feel free—but of the social, economic, and historical factors that have shaped this family and its experience of life: most notably the seductive but to some extent false allure of a better or, at least, more profitable and less provincial life in the city.

Clouds in May, set in the same provincial town, centers on a filmmaker (Muzaffer Ozdemir) now living in Istanbul who returns to visit his parents and, it transpires, to make a film in which he eventually persuades them to play the leads. Again, not a great deal happens: the filmmaker mopes around, his father worries about his orchard, a cousin (Emin Toprak), bored with life in the provinces, helps out on the movie and asks the filmmaker to try and find him work in Istanbul. But what is so interesting is that the filmmaker's parents (Emin and Fatma Ceylan)—besides being Nuri Bilge Ceylan's own parents—are the same people we saw playing the grandparents in *The Small Town*; that the cousin also played a dissatisfied youth in the earlier film; and that we now see a recreation of the shooting of the night-picnic scene from that movie. The effect is in some respects not unlike that in Kiarostami's *Through the Olive Trees* when we see (a fictional recreation of) the filming of a scene from his earlier *And Life Goes On . . .* ; also reminiscent of the Iranian's work (most notably *The Wind Will Carry Us*) is Ceylan's less than flattering (self-) portrait of the filmmaker, who quite happily exploits all around him to further his film while barely registering that they too have needs and concerns of their own.

Though *Clouds in May* boasts a slightly tighter narrative than its predecessor and is shot not in black and white but in color, it clearly inhabits the same world as *The Small Town*. On the surface, then, *Distant* would seem to entail something of a change in tack. Set mostly in a wintry Istanbul (except for its opening shot of a young man—Toprak—crossing snow-covered fields to catch a bus), it charts the growing tensions in the relationship between a clearly disenchanted Istanbul photographer (Ozdemir) and the country cousin who comes to stay in his apartment while he looks for work on the ships that might enable him to go abroad. Save, then, that the city sophisticate is now a commercial photographer rather than a filmmaker, the film might be seen to some extent as a sequel to *Clouds in May*—and, indeed, given that the restless cousin is in all instances played by Toprak, to have originated in *The Small Town*, too. But we are not simply talking linear progression here: precisely because the films *cannot* quite be reduced to being a series of films that follow on one from another in straightforward narrative terms, there is a resonance which not only echoes some of the self-reflexive and formal concerns of Kiarostami but which also gives the films a certain universality. Precisely because he could be but isn't quite playing the same character in every film, Toprak (who was indeed Ceylan's cousin and who died, tragically, in a car accident shortly after *Distant* was completed) to some degree takes on a near-archetypal status as a figure representing all those country cousins who were left behind by their peers to get bored at home and who, when they eventually made it to the city, didn't fit in that well anyway. Likewise with Ozdemir (who appears only very briefly in the prologue to *The Small Town*—as a village idiot!); his characters eloquently evoke the disappointments of all those who had no small talent but who for one reason or another never lived up to their initial promise or fulfilled their dreams, instead—almost without noticing—selling their souls to Mammon.

Ceylan achieves this universality of reference and resonance in several ways. First, in his own unusually quiet, laconic, understated way, he does confront the big questions: what are we doing with our lives and why, how does the past influence the present and future, how may we reconcile our needs and ideals with the disappointments of reality, and how can our relationships with family and friends survive when the world is changing so quickly and people are forever being encouraged to move on in search of something better than what they already have? In this respect he has rather more in common with the great masters of art-house cinema than with most of his contemporaries. But he also does it by an extreme (and, of course, in many ways deceptive) simplicity of narrative, and by focusing closely on specifics. It is frequently the case that the stories that resound most widely are those firmly rooted in the particularities of a filmmaker's environment and experience. Ceylan takes this to an extreme, using narratives clearly inspired in part by his own experiences, casting family and friends, using unusually small crews of a mere handful of people, and producing, writing, shooting, directing, editing, and even selling all his films himself. It's clear from Ceylan's work that he knows exactly what he's talking about, because he has rich personal experience of such people, places, and situations (which is rather more than can be said of most filmmakers and their subjects), and since that knowledge is so profound and precise, he's able to communicate it to us in such a way that we feel we know them too.

Not that Ceylan's work could adequately be described as in any way realist. Agreed, there is an honesty, an authenticity, that serves as a wonderfully sturdy foundation for the artifice he creates, but as with Kiarostami's beguiling blends of reality and fiction, Ceylan's methods are essentially poetic. Both his narrative and his visual style might be termed "impressionistic"; he favors ellipsis, discreet metaphor, repetition, rhyme, and rhythmic flexibility; he is acutely alert to place and time, as expressed by the seasons, by changes in sound and light, and to how they affect our moods. (It's fascinating to see his fine short *Koza*, also made with his parents and his then-teenaged cousin; with its wordless, fragmented "narrative," its complex, comparatively rapid montage and its shots deeply suggestive of symbolism, it's an even more obviously "poetic" affair, and feels rather self-conscious next to the more assured features; as with many early works, one is left with the impression that he was perhaps trying to do a little too much with the film given its brief running time.) And besides Kiarostami—and Chekhov, to whose influence Ceylan readily admits—there are two other points of comparison I'd like to suggest. Ceylan's awareness of how the experience of individuals is affected by changes in the world around them recalls the work of Edward Yang; and then there is the humor, so droll, so deliciously deadpan, so inextricably tied up with a view of life as darkly absurd, maybe even tragic, that one can't but think of Keaton. My advice, if and when you have an opportunity to catch up with his films, is twofold. First: do try to see them in the order in which they were made. Second: remember that, while they are serious, they are also often very funny and most definitely meant to be *enjoyed*.

Postscript

Since writing the above, the author was fortunate enough to catch Ceylan's new film, *Climates* (*Iklimler*), when it premiered in the Official Competition at the 2006 Cannes Film Festival. Unlike its immediate predecessor, it won no prizes; perhaps the Jury found it a little too modest (it "only" concerns the breakup of a relationship) or an insufficient advance upon the achievements of *Distant*. Whatever; for this writer *Climates* was one of the triumphs of the Festival, providing still further evidence of Ceylan's considerable talents as a filmmaker.

Essentially a story told in three acts, the film begins with a couple—Isa, a photographer approaching middle age (played by Ceylan himself) and his rather younger girlfriend Bahar (the director's wife Ebru, who had a small role in *Distant*)—holidaying on the coast. It's clear from the first couple of scenes that neither is entirely happy with their relationship, and soon Isa is suggesting they take a break from one another for a while. Bahar, aware of his fickleness, sees his proposition as more permanent in intent than he makes out, and returns to Istanbul alone. Some months later, Isa, by then also back in the city, visits a friend's lover, with whom he's had a fling before; though she responds to his seduction, she too knows his lack of commitment, and mentions somewhat deliberately in passing that Bahar has taken a job in Eastern Turkey. In the film's final act, Isa travels to the snowy provincial town where Bahar's television crew is filming, and attempts to win her back; against her better judgement, she is tempted, but after one long night of weary discussion together, both backtrack from what for a while seemed an agreement to get together again, and Isa returns to Istanbul.

In scale, tone, and concerns, *Climates* is wholly in keeping with its predecessors. Ceylan did deploy a slightly larger crew than previously for shooting, not only because someone was needed to operate the HD camera while he was acting but also because some scenes were shot with a Steadicam; as it transpired, he didn't like the results and included none of the Steadicam footage in the finished film. In most other respects, however, *Climates* resembles the earlier films: in its (deceptive) narrative simplicity, its aura of semi-autobiographical intimacy, its mordant wit (the surprisingly robust scene of Isa having sex with his friend's lover is both unsettling and frequently very funny), and its emotional honesty. Most notably, Isa is not a particularly sympathetic protagonist: his self-serving (and self-deluding) attempts to persuade Bahar, toward the end of the film, that he is a changed man have a painful authenticity that suggests Ceylan himself may have been in such a situation himself at some point in the past. It's this unsentimental, sophisticated understanding of human motivation, coupled with a means of expression that is at once delicate, subtle, and unusually direct, that takes the film way beyond most cinematic explorations of the games men and women play with one another.

Finally, if the Cannes jury failed to respond to that rare and special quality in the film, even they must surely have noticed its visual splendor. Ceylan is one of very few filmmakers so far to have really made fruitfully innovative use of the possibilities now afforded by high-definition video. There are numerous shots in the film of quite astonishing detail and breathtaking beauty, as, for example, when we see Isa seated on a beach in the foreground of one side of the screen, Bahar further away down by the water on the other, and between them the sea, with a boat passing by at a point about halfway to the distant horizon—with every element of the eloquently framed composition in perfectly sharp focus. Ceylan's background as a photographer stands him in good stead, though it must be said that the film's visual splendor is never merely decorative; as with his telling but judiciously restrained use of summery, autumnal, and wintry climates to enhance tone and meaning, the meticulous images remain as poetically resonant as in his earlier films. For Ceylan, it really is the case that *every* picture tells a story.

7

Jessica Winter

Pawel Pawlikowski

Dreaming All My Life

Having made a relatively recent transition from documentaries to fiction features, the Polish-born, British-based director Pawel Pawlikowski has staked out a fertile borderline territory between uncanny verisimilitude and oneiric abstraction. Strongly attuned to landscape, Pawlikowski's movies transpire in dazing liminal spaces: the Russian mother-and-son refugees in *Last Resort* (2000) idle in bureaucratic limbo and temporary housing, while the mercurial, romantically yearning teenagers of *Twockers* (1998) and *My Summer of Love* (2004) hover on the threshold between childhood and adulthood. Achieving an extraordinary spontaneity of incident and performance—the words uttered in a Pawlikowski movie never seem scripted, but raw and new, fresh off the tongue—his films are marvels of lean lyricism, each as compact and determined as a sonnet.

The thrill of discovery owes much to Pawlikowski's partiality for unknown actors and to his ingenious adaptations of documentary methods to his fiction films, which he "sculpts"[1]—a favored term—from impromptu combinations of spare scripting (the screenplay for the eighty-six-minute *My Summer of Love* was thirty-seven pages long; he wrote just ten pages for the forty-minute *Twockers*), improvisatory workshops, and last-second revisions. During shooting, Pawlikowski will even feed lines to his performers as they occur to him. Always thinking on his feet, he has developed a flexible method—one he describes as "a balance between creative chaos and editorial austerity"—that allows the fibers of his narratives to generate themselves in real time, as the camera rolls.

A thematic through-line can also be drawn from his nonfiction to his recent work. Pawlikowski has encapsulated his documentaries as "surreal tales of small heroes caught up in the vortex of history,"[2] while the fiction films percolate with between-the-lines social commentary: *Last Resort* provides a mordant sidelong critique of contemporary Britain's treatment of its refugees, and *Twockers* and *My Summer of Love* are witheringly frank about the drudgering futures laid out for underclass Yorkshire teens. Yet only the faintest palimpsest traces of a Ken Loach–style social realism can be detected in *Twockers* and *Last Resort*, and they're completely effaced by *My Summer of Love*; furthermore, his landscapes are weirdly denuded of modern signposting (chain stores, advertising, etc). The director's viewing schedule during preproduction on *Summer* is instructive: Malick and early Kusturica—purveyors of the "mythic realism" that Pawlikowski says he strives for—as well as a sampler of Czech New Wave, a likely wellspring for his typical gentle absurdism and matter-of-fact anarchism. Startlingly real but decidedly distinct from verité, his films inhabit an enclosed, heightened reality, often evoking a timeless fairy tale. His characters are romantic wayfarers, proverbial strangers in a strange land. It's a condition familiar to the director, who emigrated to England in his teens—wilderness years even when you have the luxury of knowing the local language.

Amid the moribund "British film industry" (an oxymoron at best), Pawlikowski is an outsider by birth and, perhaps more significantly, by temperament. His inclusion in a book about marginalized filmmakers may strike some readers as slightly curious given his near-twenty-year association with the British Broadcasting Corporation, where he first established himself with off-kilter contributions to the network's "Bookmark" literary series: *From Moscow to Pietushki* (1990), a symposium on the poetics of extreme alcoholism starring the wrecked but enduring samizdat author Benedict Yurofeyev; *Dostoevsky's Travels* (1992), wherein the author's doleful great-grandson indifferently undertakes a European lecture tour to raise cash for a Mercedes; and the astonishing *Serbian Epics* (1992)—shot in the Bosnian countryside as Sarajevo smoldered in the valley below—which looked at fascist bloodlust through the prism of patriotic verse. Another document of rabid nationalism, *Tripping with Zhirinovsky* (1995) traveled down the Volga with ultra-right-wing candidate Vladimir Zhirinovsky: "Vote for us and you'll never have to vote again!" (The film provided raw material for Pawlikowski's first fiction feature, *The Stringer*, which premiered at Cannes in 1998 and then disappeared so decisively that Pawlikowski was able to win the BAFTA award for Most Promising Newcomer for *Last Resort.*)

Of his documentary period, Pawlikowski says:

> Making documentaries allowed me to rummage for authentic characters and situations in the historical landscapes of eastern and central Europe, in the Slavic world where collapsing Communism, renascent religion, and nationalism made a very strong context for stories. Strong characters at the mercy of history is a favorite paradigm of mine; *Ashes and Diamonds* marked me for life. Also, you could say Eastern Europe was unfinished business for me. [German poet, novelist, and essayist] Hans-Magnus Enzensberger, a great supporter, once pointed out to me that maybe I was exploring the situations I could have lived had I stayed on in that part of the world. Anyway, that's now changed. Globalization is unstoppable and my part of the world has become like everywhere else. People's behavior and choices are becoming uniform and the historical context is clear the world over.

Furthermore, by the mid-nineties, the much-laureled documentarian found it nearly impossible to get backing from an increasingly homogenous and ratings-fixated BBC for his nonfiction films. His choice of subjects didn't appeal to a mass audience, and his oblique storytelling mode, refusal of voice-over narration, painterly long-lens compositions, and dreaded use of subtitles were edged out by *Big Brother* descendants and artless, sensational DV docs. Once he'd made the switch to fiction (still under the aegis of BBC Films), Pawlikowski's solid preference for elliptical narratives, untried actors, and sketchy, mutable scripts restricted him to tiny budgets. The critical success of *Last Resort* did earn him the original director's spot for the Sylvia Plath–Ted Hughes biopic that eventually became *Sylvia*, but when it became clear that star Gwyneth Paltrow's schedule would accommodate neither extensive workshopping nor a lengthy search for a lead actor, Pawlikowski cordially bowed out, and returned to *Last Resort*'s no-stars, no-budget model for *My Summer of Love*. On the evidence of his diplomatic withdrawal from a "prestigious" but artistically untenable situation, Pawlikowski would appear to be stubbornly incorruptible: a conscientious objector, a true-blue dissident. "I try to be a bit documentary about everything . . . to create a situation where cinema can *happen*," he says. "It's not drama I'm talking about, or realism. I'm talking about a poetry of cinema."

Born in Warsaw in 1957 to a doctor and a former ballerina, Pawlikowski came to England in the early 1970s with his mother, who married a Brit and became a lecturer in English. (His parents eventually remarried and re-divorced in the West; their tumultuous relationship, Pawlikowski says, partly accounts for his attraction to the Plath-Hughes saga.) Of his first years in England, Pawlikowski recalls:

> It was a bit of a shock because I didn't know I was leaving for good; I never even said goodbye to my friends and almost-girlfriend. I was torn out of my world and I didn't speak a word of English. I was sent to some strange boarding school for Polish emigrés run by the Jesuits, and I had a horrible time and got kicked out. I found English society really weird, because no one ever spoke their mind—it's the opposite of Poland, where people are pretty direct and express their emotions. It was a traumatic, very confusing time . . . I didn't learn anything, I escaped a few times from school. It was not a happy time, but it left a mark—it couldn't get any worse than that, and it's good to reach that point early on in life.

Pawlikowski made an impressive recovery, studying German literature at Oxford and landing a job at the BBC's access-television wing, called the Community Programme Unit, set up so that members of the viewing public could request specific types of programming. There, Pawlikowski made his first documentary, *Lucifer Over Lancashire* (1986), about a Christian evangelist who intended to ward off local Satanic activity by erecting a twenty-meter cross on the hillside site of a seventeenth-century witch-hanging. (The Christian never pulled off his stunt, but Pawlikowski fulfills his wish by proxy in *My Summer of Love*, wherein the protagonist's born-again brother mounts a cross in the Yorkshire countryside.)

As early as *From Moscow to Pietushki* and, especially, *Dostoevsky's Travels*, Pawlikowski was molding his documentaries into firm narrative shapes ("I never just followed people around") and even introducing staged elements, such as the overhead shot of Dmitri Dostoevsky scribbling notes for a speech in a bathroom. From this constructed glimpse onward, we know that Dostoevsky, a breathtaking vacuum of charisma, is as much the director's actor-conspirator as his subject, even as this hangdog, Keatonesque hero stumbles ineptly through his interminable lectures and, penniless, seeks aid from a hirsute, shirtless-and-suspendered used-car dealer and a Russian hermit monk. *Serbian Epics* and *Tripping with Zhirinovsky* accessed the same bone-dry absurdism as *Dostoevsky's Travels* but drained it of any picaresque pleasures. Needless to say, Pawlikowski's encounters with fascist axioms Zhirinovsky and Radovan Karadjic—the latter named in an intertitle as

"Poet and psychiatrist / Leader of the Bosnian Serbs"—were far less collaborative projects, though the director did convince Karadjic to recite his verse and perform patriotic anthems on the droning *gusle* (a Balkan single-stringed instrument, played with a bow), and a couple of British Ministers of Parliament attempted to suppress *Serbian Epics*, mistaking its stunned gallows humor for sympathetic portraiture.

Twockers was the film that decisively marked a logical progression from the hybrid experimentation of *Dostoevsky's Travels*. (Pawlikowski shared a producer-director credit with Ian Duncan on *Twockers*.) More than just introducing fabricated components to documentary, here Pawlikowski fashioned fictional characters from real-life cloth. He cast local nonprofessionals, taped their conversations, and used the recordings as raw material for the final dialogue. Lead actor Trevor Wademan, a Yorkshire teenager with a daydreamy streak who dabbled in burglary and poetry, was chosen to play Trevor, a Yorkshire teenager with a daydreamy streak who dabbles in burglary and poetry. The film's emotional core is ginger-haired Trevor's unrequited ardor for a slightly older girl, Amie (Amie Oie), whose boyfriend abandoned her after she became pregnant with his child. Opening cold on Trevor's grim job interview at the chicken processing plant (a slight nod to the interrogation of Antoine Doinel toward the end of *The 400 Blows*), *Twockers* practices what might be broadly defined as an exaggerated realism. Its comical backdrop of bored kids on an unchecked loot-and-burn rampage through the Yorkshire dales visually underlines the catastrophic absenteeism of parents and constructive social services without a word of commentary. Allergic to stridency, Pawlikowski is a modern master of "show, don't tell."

Like the heroines of *Last Resort* and *My Summer of Love*, Trevor is a romantic who's not yet protected by scar tissue from the hard knocks he's already taken. Whether projecting fantasies of fatherhood onto a photo of Amie's ultrasound scan or composing his heartfelt doggerel (proving right Wilde's trusty dictum on whence bad poetry springs), Trevor longs for an illusion of love that his hopeful mind was too complicitous in conjuring. Likewise, in *Last Resort* (incidentally the first film for which Pawlikowski was credited as Pawel rather than "Paul"), the twice-divorced Tanya (Dina Korzun) allows herself to be deceived by a mirage of idealized romance. Traveling from her native Russia to England, she becomes what she calls a "refugee by accident" after her supposed husband-to-be fails to collect Tanya and her ten-year-old son, Artiom (Artiom Strelnikov), from the airport. Mother and child are thus marooned in tower-block housing in coastal "Stonehaven," aka Margate, a damp purgatorio of frigid-dishwater tides, cinder-block towers, and empty lots. This concrete-island prison, scored by a dirge of wailing seagulls, is as gray and bleak as any outpost of the former Eastern Bloc—an irony subtly inferred from the opening shot of the Russian newcomers moving backward through the airport tunnels, a study in reverse momentum. (Pawlikowski has called *Last Resort* "slightly" autobiographical, "because it's a mother and a child in a new country, and the mother is driven by bizarre romantic ideas of the world.")

Pawlikowski's spry, rapid-response filmmaking technique is evident in the camerawork: director of photography Ryszard Lenczewski switches nimbly back and forth from long-lens establishing shots (the barren, color-leached beach; low, inky skies; a debris-strewn asphalt "courtyard"), handheld hustle, meticulously composed medium shots, and the occasional, carefully dispensed close-up. A mordant document of Britain's dumping ground for its refugees and other undesirables, *Last Resort* is also an expressionist fresco of Tanya and Artiom's confusion and alienation, down to the blithely insulting sign above the dinky local arcade: "Dreamland Welcomes You." Stonehaven is a state of mind, a muted nightmare from which Tanya must awaken. (Aptly, the accordion, organ, and toylike keyboard of Max de Wardener's soundtrack evoke an abandoned seaside fairground in eternal winter.) The rhythms and rituals of the place are obscure and vaguely menacing: Here children and the odd burro run wild, the grimy local diner's fish-in-batter is missing a key ingredient ("This fish has no fish in it," Artiom says wonderingly), and wage-earning opportunities run to blood donation and cybersex performance. Or, "You could sell a kidney," jokes Alfie (Paddy Considine), the conscientious arcade manager who dons a tux to call bingo, gives informal English lessons to Artiom, and nurses a crush on Tanya.

In its most superficial outlines, *Last Resort* resembles the brand of "gritty" docudramas on headline topics that often glut the prime-time schedules of BBC and its most credible competitor, Channel 4. Artiom falls in with the local young miscreants, drinking and thieving. Tanya, an illustrator of children's books in Russia, does eventually agree to the entreaties of the local Internet-sleaze merchant: One day she finds herself writhing on a bed as a lollipop-licking schoolgirl in pigtails for the delectation of her online audience, and promptly begins to cry. A network programming executive could tick plenty of boxes on the sensational checklist: juvenile delinquency, single motherhood, illegal immigration, porn, tears. Pawlikowski's concerns, however, exist out of time and place: a loving, unusually reciprocal relationship between mother and child (Artiom is the voice of reason more often than not and does, perhaps, more than his share of parenting) and a tender, organically developed romance between two cautious outsiders, Tanya the stranded emigrant and Alfie the self-exiled ex-con.

Pawlikowski is the most economical of filmmakers: When the deadbeat "fianceé" finally rings Tanya on Stonehaven's sole working pay phone, Pawlikowski cuts directly from Tanya answering the call to the young mother weeping in her son's lap. (They also sing; he toys affectionately with her hair.) The decisive conversation, which would make for a histrionic set piece in other hands, is elided completely. Yet *Last Resort* isn't austere, despite its gloomy environs: Stripped to a bare minimum of plot mechanics and exposition, the seventy-three-minute film is all texture, grace notes, treasured artifacts. Alfie loves Tanya's painting of a colorful ark, crowned with flowers and boarded by happy animals as well as an intact nuclear family—an incongruous bouquet of harmonious nature amid Tanya's florescent-lit institutional environs. The movie proceeds less by plot developments than by tiny shifts and modulations of tone; affections deepen and stakes are raised inch by precious inch.

As its title suggests, *Last Resort* is the chronicle of an enforced holiday, beachfront property included. In Pawlikowski's next and latest film, *My Summer of Love*—shot amid the crags and rolling greens of the valley between Yorkshire and Lancashire—teenage girls from opposite ends of the socioeconomic spectrum experience the perks and pitfalls of class tourism. The movie distills Helen Cross's bracing, lurid 2001 novel of the same name down to its core relationship: In a near-empty Yorkshire of an unspecified (pre–cell phone) era, Tamsin (Emily Blunt), a wealthy troublemaker home from boarding school, meets Mona (Natalie Press), an orphaned working-class teen who lives with her brother, Phil (*Last Resort*'s Considine), above a pub that he's busy transforming into a "spiritual center." ("I miss my brother," she sobs; for Mona, Phil died when he was born again.) Riding into Mona's purview on a white horse, accessorized with kerchief and hoop earrings, Tamsin has all the bearings of a chivalrous pirate-prince, the gentle(wo)man rogue of a fairytale adventure, here to rescue the foundling damsel from a bored, alcohol-soaked torpor. On the grounds of Tamsin's ivy-sheathed Tudor estate, another Dreamland welcomes Mona, who luxuriates with her posh conspirator in a hothouse of wine, sex, aristocratic leisure, and what feels like love, with occasional delinquent intrusions into the increasingly irrelevant and ridiculous outside world.

A literary adaptation in the loosest sense, *My Summer of Love* edges toward genre traps but always backs slyly away from them; the fervent cross-class romance and gathering threat of violence unavoidably summon *Heavenly Creatures* (1994), while the droll wild-girls riotousness is descended from Vera Chytilova's *Daisies* (1966). With verdant, near-pointillist Super 16 imagery (again by Lenczewski with additional photography by David Scott), the movie visualizes the thrill of disconnect inside the girls' pulsing cocoon of transgressive infatuation—the dizzying sensations of stunned joy and shared secrecy, the effulgent strangeness of familiar surroundings—aided by the woozy electronic surge of Alison Goldfrapp and Will Gregory's score, which trips along on moon-surface gravity and Goldfrapp's drawling, sleepy-siren vocals.

The edge-of-seventeen duo romp and loaf in what seems to be a vivid, webbed-light dream: "I tried to keep the whole film in a strange in-between land," says Pawlikowski, whose camera typically avoids any acknowledgment of storefronts, billboards, or other omnipresent emblems of commercialized contemporary existence. Mona soon wakes from this sun-dappled reverie to find herself inside a mere passing fancy. Her faith in this yin-yang connection proves to be as fervent and misplaced as her brother's newfound religiosity or the quixotic romanticism of *Twockers*' Trevor and *Last Resort*'s Tanya. Indeed, Pawlikowski's great passion thus far has been his empathic adoration for lovelorn tilters at windmills, and impetuous, spirited Mona is his most endearing, richly multidimensional character yet: sweet and skeptical in equal measure, blistered and bruised by bad luck yet still hopeful and open, possessed of a sharp, mischievous wit yet perilously naive. Aptly for a director who so admires *Badlands*, the remarkable Natalie Press possesses some of the unhatched, spectral purity of the young Sissy Spacek. And for a filmmaker so enamored with outsiders, it's worth noting that, both times Pawlikowski has focused on an English teen as his protagonist, he has cast freckled redheads—this in a country where such coloring is openly regarded as a mild affliction and where the term "ginger" is an insult.

As the jaded audience probably realizes long before the whip-smart but ingenuous and vulnerable Mona can, Tamsin is a method actress, mistress of the italicized gesture, a virtuoso of slapdash pretension. She moves and speechifies on the likes of Nietzsche and Edith Piaf (she lived "such a wonderfully tragic life," Tamsin purrs while "La Foule" plays) as if a camera were forever trained upon her. To Tamsin, Mona is an exotic, somewhat pitiable plaything, worthy of a condescending visitor's transient interest—the novelty will last as long as summer break: no dad, dead mum, crazy brother (when Mona mentions that Phil has done time in prison, Tamsin positively stirs with arousal). No money, little schooling, the stigma of a heavy regional accent. What a wonderfully tragic life! And bestowing all the noblesse oblige of the privileged fantasist on her luckless friend, Tamsin reciprocates with her own inventive misfortunes—dead sister, monstrous father—which grow more flagrantly baroque day by day. It's in her inadvertently cruel spinnings of fact and fiction that the relationship retrospectively gains a subtly inflected political dimension: the blasé, even unthinking exploitation of the poor by the rich. Shielded by the protective quilting of wealth and the regal bearing of entitlement that goes with it, Tamsin can stew in her romance-novel dreams all she likes; Mona, as she herself finally realizes, cannot.

"I have to stop dreaming," Tanya declares to Alfie late in *Last Resort*. "I've been dreaming all my life." One of Pawlikowski's trademarks is the strong character at the mercy of her illusions, which cohere and collide with those of her loved ones. Whether stuck in a foreign country, or adrift on a country estate around the corner from a suddenly foreign home, the heroines of *Last Resort* and *My Summer of Love* are aliens in a bizarre milieu, sleeping beauties who at last rouse themselves and stride purposefully away from a stagnant now into an uncertain future, one they can assess with lucid eyes. Forcibly divested of their illusions, they gain strength and resolve, but—aptly for a filmmaker whose favorite setting is in-between—Pawlikowski leaves candidly ambiguous whether they've lost more than they've found.

Notes

1. Unless otherwise noted, all quotations from Pawel Pawlikowski are taken from interviews by the author on March 17 and May 1, 2005.

2. Quoted in "Director's filmography" of Artificial Eye DVD release of *Last Resort*.

8

Jonathan Romney

Bela Tarr

We tend to take for granted the luxury of watching a filmmaker's career from the start, as it develops over the years. But the way most filmmakers come to widespread attention follows the pattern of something like catastrophe theory. Their names remain unknown outside their own countries, gradually become intriguing rumors, then suddenly—as they reach what one fashionable theory calls the "tipping point"—achieve cult status or full-blown fame. And then we have the challenge of reconstructing their work backwards—of trying to fathom how these directors got to where they were when the world caught up.

An especially perplexing case is Hungary's Bela Tarr, who reached his own tipping point with the Cannes premiere of his *Werckmeister Harmonies*. This haunting film, in which Tarr for the first time introduces a tinge of Lynch-like surrealism, is the obvious film to establish his reputation on the international circuit (although its commercial future is still to be decided). His previous film *Satantango* (1994) had acquired a legendary reputation, largely because it was so little seen and so daunting—a somber, enigmatic seven-and-a-quarter hours orchestrated in long, slow sequence shots.

Regarding *Satantango*, most of us had to rely on hearsay and the enthusiasm of such critics as Jonathan Rosenbaum and Susan Sontag; the latter identified Tarr's work as one of a select few "heroic violations" of current cinematic norms. Tarr's rather shadowy status is appropriate, given that a key theme of his latest work is the spread of rumor—murmurs of apocalyptic marvels and of ambivalent savior-cum-charlatan figures on the horizon. Seen after *Satantango* and *Werckmeister Harmonies*, the back catalogue comes as something of a shock. The early Tarr seems very much a straight social realist, with his portraits of blue-collar and marginal strugglers. *Family Nest* (1979) is about a young woman obliged to share a cramped apartment with her in-laws. *The Outsider* (1980) is a portrait of a young violinist and factory worker and his disenfranchised friends. In *Prefab People* (1982), the most austere of this trilogy, a married couple circles endlessly around in frustration and recrimination. These films are very much *cinema povera*, tending toward tightly enclosed close-ups, with backgrounds largely implied rather than shown. This style has led to comparisons with Cassavetes, although Tarr says he and his long-term partner-cum-editor Agnes Hranitsky only discovered Cassavetes after *Prefab People*. Although Tarr is not enthusiastic about Ken Loach, the comparison is hard to resist—especially in the excruciatingly comic scene in *Family Nest* where the heroine confronts an ineffectual housing officer.

The proletarian trilogy is a far cry from the complex, elaborately staged fabulations of the recent films, with their vast tableaux, elastic manipulations of time and space, and apocalyptic resonance—all of which make them comparable to Tarkovsky, Angelopoulos, and, an avowed influence, Hungary's own Miklos Jancso. Yet there is a distinct continuity between the two Tarrs. A consistent thread is a fascination for the hard presence of faces and places, the distinctive unglamorous roughness of (largely) nonprofessional actors and their environments. Even if, in the later films, Tarr creates composite locations or modifies real space to his own design (constructing a fake apartment from which to view the colliery landscape of *Damnation*), the later mythic terrains have the same matter-of-fact concreteness as the barrooms of *The Outsider*. Tarr sets up his camera and lets us know that the action is happening *here and now*: that there is no escape from the time and place where the fiction occurs.

This is particularly true in two intermediate experiments. *Macbeth* (1982), for Hungarian television, comprises only two shots—one a brief prologue, the other lasting approximately an hour as the action glides seamlessly from close-up to close-up around the corridors of Dunsinane, until exploding into a full-blown climactic battle. *Autumn Almanac* (1985) is set in a single apartment, the venue for a series of territorial confrontations among five characters; with its unearthly lighting scheme of blue and orange and stylized, claustrophobia-inducing sets, the film resembles a Bergman chamber piece filmed by Raul Ruiz (especially in such trick shots as a fight filmed from under a glass floor). The style of *Macbeth* is a logical development of the earlier films, which are not nearly as straightforwardly naturalistic as they seem. Their feeling of lives closing in is accompanied by a powerful circularity: In *Prefab People* the same scene is more or less repeated exactly, as the husband packs his bags and walks out. Both times, the following scene shows him back again, without explanation; it is uncertain whether we have seen two takes of the same scene, or a critical moment that must endlessly repeat itself. Such elision is also a constant: in the early films, lives happen faster than their protagonists can keep up with them, as if in a drastically compressed, sparsely edited version of real time.

From *Damnation* (1988) onward, Tarr's films seem to be set less on earth than in an inhospitable suburb of hell: *Damnation*'s central image is of a chain of coal trucks suspended on cables above a town, creaking inexorably round in a baleful circuit. Of Tarr's later black-and-white films, *Damnation* is the least satisfying, its oppressive mood dangerously close to self-parodic art-cinema miserabilism. It was, however, the first film in which Tarr and Hranitsky explored open landscapes, and it was their first collaboration with screenwriter and novelist Laszlo Krasznahorkai, whose own vision forms a tight fit with theirs from here on. *Satantango* and *Werckmeister Harmonies*, co-written by Tarr and Krasznahorkai, are both adaptations of novels by the latter. *Satantango* is by all accounts a faithful adaptation, at least where structure is concerned: the film is divided into twelve parts, like the novel, each closing with a narrative voice-over from the book. The first, wordless section, a seven-and-a-half-minute single shot, sets the tone: a herd of cattle drifts out of a barn onto a muddy patch of open ground, and wander off to the left, a few of them mating on the way: the camera follows, first in a pan, then tracking past the houses of an apparently deserted village, before the cattle disappear between the houses. The whole is accompanied by a ghostly, premonitory sound of deep tolling bells. This is more than just mood-setting: this sequence sets the film apart in a virtually subaquatic parallel universe of its own; torrential rain falls almost continually through the film, making Gabor Medvigy's stark black and white photography all the more imposing an achievement.

Satantango is very much a film about nature and the elements, in a European Romantic tradition, albeit in a deglamorizing, disaffected style that could be described as satanic ruralism. Its characters—nearly all fools, drunkards, scoundrels, or wrecks—are dwarfed by the natural world, which is either punitive and unforgiving, or entirely inscrutable. One tracking shot closes in slowly on an owl perched on a ledge, coolly and unnervingly returning the camera's gaze. In two extraordinary sequences, the trickster figure Irimias (Jeremiah: prophet of doom) strides with his henchmen down a city street, through a storm of detritus. But Irimias (played as a mercurial, charismatic figure by the film's composer Mihaly Vig) is at once a Lucifer and a Jesus, and he seems equal to the wind, as if it were his natural harbinger. The weather invokes a metaphysical sense of coming apocalypse, signaled by the bells that continue to toll throughout.

The fragmentary narrative concerns a village whose abject inhabitants are on the verge of dividing up their treacherous spoils when they hear that the much-feared Irimias and sidekick Petrina have returned from the dead. It is unclear why Irimias might be seeking revenge, but by the time he arrives (having signed on as a police informer), a young girl has poisoned herself, and the villagers inexplicably trust Irinias to act as the voice of moral conscience. He instructs them to uproot and move to a distant mansion where they will form a new community; once they arrive, he orders them to scatter, sending them off into ignominious exile.

As in the early films, important links are missing. The narrative is structured into overlapping mosaic fragments; or, as Tarr has explained, it follows the six-steps-forward six-steps-back pattern of a tango. Individual sequences tend to break free of the overall shape, like symphonic movements, acquiring an autonomous drive and duration of their own. One sequence in particular dramatizes the dialectic of order and chaos: in a pub hoedown even more anarchic than the one in *Damnation*, the drunken villagers collide in an orgiastic jolly-up accompanied by a maddeningly repetitive accordion riff. Elsewhere, language itself seems drunk on its feet: one man's narrative becomes a near-abstract Beckettian litany, an percussive background battery of verbiage.

The film's most daring play with duration and nonevent lasts for an hour. A boozy doctor staggers out into the open to refill his flask; wheezing along like Hank Quinlan in *Touch of Evil*, he stops to shelter with two prostitutes in a barn, then nearly reaches the pub during the drunkards' dance; fading in and out of visibility in the rain and darkness, he is at the very last moment led off course by a young girl and collapses in the forest. In another sequence, which intersects with the doctor outside the pub, the same girl tortures a cat at some length (the scene was faked under veterinary supervision, with agonizing howls dubbed on afterward) before taking poison. Several sequences overlap in this way, key events repeated from different camera angles; this structure fragments rather than binds together the narrative, reinforcing the theme of collapse and dispersal. The extraordinary length, both of the film and of individual sequences, makes us feel that the deeper we get into *Satantango*, the further we get into chaos, the further we stray from any linear narrative track.

The film ends with the doctor's surprise reappearance. He sets out into the countryside, where the bells are still tolling, and finds their deathly boom parodied by a madman hitting a bit of metal and ranting that the Turks are coming. The doctor returns home, boards himself up into pitch darkness, then in voice-over apparently begins to retell the story of *Satantango* from scratch. As the film ends, we feel we are waking from a bad dream that is about to start again. But who exactly is dreaming the dream, telling the story? *Satantango*'s self-reflexive drama has several author/director figures. The doctor himself keeps files on the villagers and makes drawings of his backyard, as if storyboarding his corner of the world. Irimias, the author of everyone's downfall, is in turn working for the police: the whole intrigue apparently unwinds so that two bored cops in a city office can at last file reports on the villagers in fabulously derogatory terms, a wonderfully farcical deflation of the film's metaphysical resonance.

Satantango is a monstrous prodigy—a cathedral of a film, albeit forbiddingly skeletal in its architecture. Arguably, though, *Werckmeister Harmonies* is the more self-contained, satisfying work, partly because of Tarr's daring in turning Krasznahorkai's novel *The Melancholy of Resistance* (so far, his only one available in English translation) into an entirely separate entity. The book's obsessive outpouring of language, with its long, involved sentences and philosophical digressions, is reshaped in a film that for the most part abandons language in favor of silence and the impactful image. Whole passages of the novel disappear, while Tarr's climactic hospital sequence takes its cue from a single sentence. The film reduces the novel to crucial moments and heightens those moments to the extreme, as though Tarr were using the book as the basis of an opera. In one sense, the film is as much of a monster as its predecessor: it took four years to shoot, on and off, and seven directors of photography (including Medvigy, Jörg Widmer, and American independent filmmaker Rob Tregenza), all of which is belied by an entirely consistent tone. A circus—in reality, one huge corrugated metal truck containing stuffed whale—comes to a small town, accompanied by a crowd of marauding followers. Valuska, a gentle postman and Dostoevskian lucid madman, witnesses these marvels; he pays for his innocence by ending up a mute wreck (a silenced dissident?) in an empty asylum ward. Tarr says he finally decided to make the film when he met the gaunt Lars Rudolph, whose haggard stare as Valuska certainly embodies the "look" of the film: he could be a Munch painting come to life.

Valuska is obsessed with cosmology, and the first scene shows him choreographing the local drunks into a working model of the universe. His uncle Mr. Eszter (Peter Fitz), a world-weary aesthete, is also trying more obscurely to recreate order, by reconstructing musical harmony as it was before the tempered system of tuning devised by Bach's contemporary Werckmeister. Yet order and chaos are closely aligned: just as Eszter's ideal harmony might, we suspect, turn out to resemble pure dissonance, so another source of chaos is the reactionary movement for cleanliness spearheaded by Eszter's estranged wife—a stout Hanna Schygulla, barely recognizable until she turns on a seductively domineering gaze.

The much-feared cataclysm finally erupts, apparently at the behest of the mysterious Prince—another carnival attraction seen in a terrifying Murnau-esque shadow show as a deformed shape on a wall, uttering ominous imprecations in a mechanical Hitlerian bark. The climax is one of the most nightmarish irruptions of violence in recent cinema, all the more so for being muted and ritualized. A mob of men marches in hypnotic rhythm, the camera hovering in front of them, rising, falling, drifting from side to side before this inexorable river of hostility. A single shot then accompanies the crowd through a run-down hospital, where they smash up the fittings and attack its inmates: throughout, we hear not a single threat or a scream of pain. A naked, skeletal old man appears in a pool of light—this stark manifestation and the inmates' striped pyjamas irrevocably suggestive of the Holocaust—and the crowd silently withdraws, the camera tracking slowly round a corner to reveal Valuska aghast in hiding.

Again, this tale of catastrophe has several authors: Valuska and Eszter, with their different "mad" versions of harmony; Mrs Eszter, who may have orchestrated the whole affair as a way of seizing political power; and the Prince, who is either the executive spirit of discord or an entirely ineffectual embodiment of universal madness. Tarr's pessimism about humanity takes a memorably burlesque turn in the scene where two small boys act out a parody of military authority, bashing on drums and screeching bellicose rhetoric into an electric fan. *Werckmeister Harmonies* could be taken as a general commentary on self-destructive folly, but it is hard not to read it partly as a political parable, not to see both it and *Satantango* as alluding to the breakdown of an artificial social order after the collapse of Eastern European communism. *The Melancholy of Resistance*, published in 1989, seems horribly prescient about the rise of murderous nationalisms in the nineties, and Tarr's adaptation appears to play on this with hindsight. Tarr has denied any political echoes—yet he seems to signal them by holding his camera steadily at some length on the only image in the dilapidated, archaic world of *Werckmeister Harmonies* that belongs unequivocally to the late twentieth century: a hovering spy helicopter. This may be a manifestation of the authoritarian state opportunistically moving in after the slaughter. But as Tarr returns its blank gaze, we can equally see it as a token of the patient, stark lucidity that characterizes his work, from his early essays in the everyday right up to the extraordinary bleak phantasmagoria of his latest films.

9

MICHAEL ATKINSON

Blunt Force Trauma

Andrzej Zulawski

"HE DEIGNS TO TAKE NOTICE of the circumstances of his life," Sartre wrote of Genet, "only insofar as they seem to repeat the original drama of lost paradise."

Repeating the original drama of lost paradise—isn't it why we adore the mutineer, the apostate, the idiocrat? The defiant crackpot has long been humankind's ultimate hero, for whom defying divinity and divine orthodoxy remains the imperative act of self, in direct contradiction to every aeon-established prescription for psychic happiness. Selflessness is bliss, but it is in the human blood to find transcendent vindication in the all-or-nothing Fuck You, regardless of the penalties. Consider how we go moon over filmmakers who tangle assholes with the world's costliest and most cumbersome art medium: Gance's and Von Stroheim's self-immolating gargantuanism, Fuller's renegade hyperbole, Rivette's cumbersome marathon-making, Pasolini's gay paganism, Cassavetes's outlaw intimacy, Herzog's gonzo post-colonialism, Carax's pulsing artificialia.

That Tarkovsky, Paradjanov, and Sokurov followed their abstruse visions despite their government's virtually insurmountable obstructions only lends their films a gleam of superhuman nobility. One could go on.

Of course, having become an *auteur damneé* is its own glory, whether the resistance resides in the films or merely in the backstory or both.

Everyone will invoke their favorite martyr, but before them all I will pit Andrzej Zulawski. Few other filmmakers have maintained, come hell or high water, as defiantly consistent a voice, and no one's cinematic voice is as divisive, as ludicrously anarchic, as viciously overwrought. Saying Zulawski is an acquired taste is handling him with tongs; a filmgoer either has the flesh-in-the-teeth lust for emotional, visual, and narrative pandemonium—the Zulawski gene, as it were—or they do not. Naturally, Zulawski partisans are few but fierce; if an argument can be made for him, it would necessarily be in the form of a bludgeoning harangue. As a generally regarded world cinema presence, however, he is a scourge, a film festival incubus, an atavistic cult godling, an infrequently distributable pariah.

Americans might only know him by *Possession* (1981), the only AZ film to gain any kind of U.S. distribution (an exploitation grindhouse run in 1983 arranged by amateur entrepreneurs), and enough of a hyperventilating madhouse keen to warn off unprepared viewers for the rest of their natural lives. Roundly dismissed as a cranked-up, tongue-in-cheek horror exercise, *Possession* becomes a different species of meateater once you realize, by way of Zulawski's other films, that the man is as serious as cancer. At the same time, on virtually every film, Zulawski has known epic production troubles like a dog knows fleas—frequently landing only a portion of his script's scenes in the can and then jerry-rigging a movie from that. The hinge upon which his career turns—*On the Silver Globe*—is in its present, semi-finished form (it's a "broken thing," Zulawski maintains) one of cinema's most appalling, breathtaking follies, and the most frightening art film you will never see.

It's easy to be inflamed when characterizing Zulawski because he is himself a creature of extreme experience. For him, there is no edge, only the abyss. Take a fairly prototypical example: *L'Amour Braque* (1985), a Tourette's-syndrome French-gangster version of Dostoyevsky's *The Idiot*, in which an opening bank robbery sequence is performed (by actors and camera) as if by the Ritz Brothers on microdots, the soundtrack a caterwaul of hoots and yowls, the claustrophobic framing of the actors threatening at any moment to explode into hysterical *Hair*-like dance numbers. In which manic elan passes well over the brink into psychotic delirium. In which the dialogue is a stylized, rhythmic pidgin even French audiences had difficulty deciphering. In which John Woo-style shoot-outs bloom out of lovers' agony and blaze over a pink Cadillac's hood in front of the Folies Bergere. In which the "idiot" hero's heartbreak over the caprices of masochistic moll Sophie Marceau resembles the angst of an electrocuted marionette. In which homicidal rapists do handstands before setting their victims on fire. In which every moment is acted as if at the absolute peak of skull-splitting emotional crisis—spontaneous vomiting and seizures are commonplace.

Most of Zulawski's films happen in a day-ward version of the present day, a world of artists, models, aristocrats, and murderers where Love is an irradiated crater of torturous misunderstanding, bloody betrayal, and frustrated devotion. His visual style is comprised largely of off-kilter, floor-level traveling shots and fish-eyed clusters of contorting humanness, but there's no foretelling how Zulawski will shoot a particular scene—the camera might spasm and rocket-ascend on a crane at any moment, or chase after a character as he or she mauls his or herself out of romantic anguish. Even so, it's his manhandling of actors that is both Zulawski's most distinguishing trait and his most disquieting, pursuing as he does the frenetically irrational like a melodramatic R. D. Laing, convinced that primal-scream apoplexy is the sanest response to a mad world.

Not much has been written about Zulawski, and virtually none of it in English, but when he is described at all he's described simply as a hyperbolist. True, as far as it goes, but Zulawski doesn't quite rise sui generis from the Euro-soil. His sensibility is in-grown surrealist—not in terms of imagery (which is most often grounded if absurd) but in terms of emotional eruption, disorienting texture, mad-love worship, tonal anarchism, dedication to pure and absolute liberty. It's the native attitude the pioneering surrealists saw and all-too-calculatedly co-opted in the twenties, but which poured forth naturally from Sade, Mallarmé, Lautréamont, Vaché, Artaud. Though by all reports as sane as a schoolmarm, Zulawski traffics on one level in the spirit and ideas of lunatics. On another, the influence of Jerzy Grotowski—whose transformative, acrobatic, "poor" theater performances struggled to undermine the secure distance of the spectator—and of Haitian voodoo (both acknowledged by Zulawski) suggest a more rational, albeit otherworldly, strategy.

The career began in the French and Polish film schools, where he apprenticed under Wajda. After publishing as a novelist and a film critic, and directing two modest TV films, Zulawski debuted in 1971 with *The Third Part of the Night*, a wrenching, over-the-waterfall-in-a-barrel nightmare about Nazi occupation that is virtually divested of historical markers, instead focusing in the director's particular manner on mad panic and Theater of Cruelty catharsis. In the first scene, the tortured hero (Leszek Teleszynski) has his family butchered by Gestapo, and from there the film is an unceasing bolt through a clammy dys-Europa. In fact, the movie's context is so abstracted and soaked with queasy paranoia, so crowded with doppelgangers, raving lunacy, sudden corpses, secret signals, and intimations of plague, that the mad-scramble upshot is baldly Kafkaesque. Finally, the Resistance-bound hero becomes a startlingly horrible variety of collaborator, joining a lab-coated assembly line of self-vampirizing workers who systemically inject their own blood into the bowels of monstrous lice.

If you're going to make a mark on Euro-cinema, then or now, this is one way to do it, but Zulawski was censored for his troubles, and the film's release was abbreviated. Still, it fared better than his next film, the historical phantasia *Diabel* (1972), which the Polish censors sat on for sixteen years. As breathless and rabid as his first film, *Diabel* is set during the 1783 Prussian conflict, but self-evidently critiques Poland's antiprotest machinations circa 1968; the scenario follows a young antiroyalist (Teleszynski again) as he is manipulated by a mysterious demiurge/government spook into betraying his ideals and slaughtering virtually everyone around him. Typically, synopsis does the movie no favors; Zulawski's mise-en-scène evokes the viewpoint of drunken delusionist hunted by wolves through the backwoods of County Grimm, and the tableaux of human suffering and debauchery witnessed makes the contemporaneous lurid-history-maven Ken Russell look like an unimaginative priest.

Even when it was released in Poland in 1988, *Diabel* was thoroughgoingly *maudit* (reportedly, even the Catholic Church attempted to depublicize it), but his next film, *L'Important c'est d'Aimer* (1975), was a relative hit, and therefore Europe's first widespread taste of Zulawskian madness. A somewhat orthodox tale of infidelity and temptation in outline (based on Christopher Frank's novel *La Nuit Américaine*, the film's title apparently changed in deference to Truffaut), the movie is classic nuttiness, the sexual tension between rogue photog Fabio Testi, down-on-her-luck actress Romy Schneider, and absurd husband Jacques Dutronc, surrounded by gangsters, porn, Z-movie gore, Rimbaud quotes, Shakespearean affectations, and Klaus Kinski as a Truman Capote-ish theater queen. The camera careens, the music napalms, the actors explode at each other like lava spouts (except Testi, who glowers). Miraculously, the film was publicly accepted to the degree that Schneider won a Cesar, yet it occurs to you that the real miracle is the quantity of Zulawski's output, since it seems each and every movie is a desperate matter of life or death.

How do you pass blithely from one movie to the next, when each howls like an innocent in the fires of Hell? International both in its production and in its box office success, *D'Aimer* created a romantic textual template for many of Zulawski's later films, but he spent the cachet he'd earned instead on an even more personal project: *On the Silver Globe*, an adaptation of his granduncle Jerzy Zulawski's famous Moon Trilogy (second only to the novels of Stanislaw Lem in the annals of Eastern

European sci-fi, and also reputedly the initial inspiration for Fritz Lang and Thea von Harbou's *The Woman in the Moon*). Like Jakubisko's *The Deserter and the Nomads*, Sokurov's *Days of Eclipse*, and Tarkovsky's *Solaris*, Zulawski's erstwhile epic rethinks futuristic "speculative fiction" as a gritty, metaphoric rummage through civilization's ancillary zones. Imagining the moon as a postapocalyptic/neoprimeval earthscape, Zulawski shot in the Gobi desert, on the Crimean banks of the Black Sea, and on Poland's Baltic coast, and what exists intact of the film's original conception has the raw, monolithic force of a pagan vision. The story involves a disastrous moon mission spawning a primitive society that, a few generations down the road, hails an investigating cosmonaut as their messiah and warrior-king in the battle against a race of winged mutants. Zulawski's stylistic approach is still dominated by wide-angle warping, rocketing hand-held traveling shots, and behavioral extremism, but here something else has hit like lightning: breathtakingly horrible, brutal, stark images worthy of both Dante and Doré. Hordes of black-robed savages enacting mysterious rituals on white-sanded beaches; the sea water in flames behind a slow-motion shore battle between moon-men and mutants; scenes played out in decaying caverns or ruins the size of a soccer stadium; the cinema's most extraordinary crucifixion; a mob of heretics impaled—as in, Vlad-the-Impaler-impaled, through the rectum—on 25-foot, intestine-roped stakes on the same beach, captured by Zulawski in a crane shot that launches high enough to hear one of the poor bastards choke out a few last words of protest.

Naturally, Polish authorities were aghast, and with more than three-quarters of the film photographed, in 1978 Ministry of Culture functionary Janusz Wilhelmi halted production and ordered everything destroyed. Zulawski struggled for a few years to restart the film, even returning to the Gobi to retrieve materials abandoned there. Eventually, the light went out, and Zulawski evacuated Poland for good. When he returned after democraticization in 1986, either Film Polski or the movie's devoted cast and crew or a combination therein convinced Zulawski to finish the film, merely for a single Cannes screening and for archival use. Editing, post-dubbing and shooting new footage (much of it views of contemporary Warsaw, with a cameo by Krystyna Janda, carpeted by ruminative explanatory narration), Zulawski fashioned a kind of self-memorializing creole-movie, hardly unlike several similar self-interrogatory anti-achievements by Godard and hearkening back to the ultimate failure to be a movie, Jones's *Duck Amuck*. (Zulawski correspondent Daniel Bird has told me that AZ would be "appalled" if *On the Silver Globe* were ever shown commercially, and that getting him to talk about it is "like drawing blood from a stone.") In whatever form, *On the Silver Globe* remains one of the most unforgettable visual assaults in movie history.

Thereafter, Zulawski became French, but *Possession*, his first film after his heartbreaking expatriation and perhaps his most wrathful, was shot in English and included a Carlos Rimbaldi monster that—conveniently, for some—ghettoized the movie as fantasy exploitation. What it is is a Petite Guignol plunge into marital fracture: Isabelle Adjani and Sam Neill are an unhappy West Berlin couple tortured by the fact of Adjani's infidelity—not with the human lover who's as baffled as Neill is, but with a cephalopod-like creature Adjani somehow produces and nurtures into maturation as a replacement mate in her bedroom. (A bloody mid-film birth scene with Adjani in a subway station is either a flashback to the creature's germination or the miscarriage of its spawn; Zulawski never comes clean.) Two years after Cronenberg's *The Brood*, Zulawski mutates this taboo-busting scenario from an expression of biological rage to the acute manifestation of crushed romantic dreams: eventually, the tentacled thing grows into a simulacrum of Neill, into a man perfectly formed around the needs of his woman and child. (Politically, the time bomb starts ticking once we actually see Adjani making love to the thing.) Attaining the screaming pitch of an emergency Caesarean section, *Possession* doesn't soft-pedal its horror for the sake of its metaphor, which is easily obscured by the discomfiting bedlam. In fact, the grisly glimpses of Rimbaldi's hippogriff aren't nearly as upsetting as the ravenous pas de deux of the protagonists, who come close to simply sinking their canines into each other's throats. Thus, it was prosecuted as a bannable "video nastie" in England despite having won Adjani a Cesar and a best actress trophy at Cannes.

In the decades since, Zulawski has persevered in being Zulawski despite the opprobrium of the international film culture, his scenarios favoring feverish Romanticism over the earlier films' fantastical desperation. Suddenly, he had virtually every beautiful French actress eager to enroll in his superego-decimating School of Flesh, all of them naked in flayed spirit as well as body. Valerie Kaprisky is stripped, objectified, humiliated and abused in *La Femme Publique* (1984) by a mad film director (!) adapting Dostoyevsky (!), whose plan involves the eventual assassination of a Catholic cleric (!!). For *L'Amour Braque*, Zulawski arrived at Sophie Marceau (in a Louise Brooks wig), fell in love with her, and starred her in three more films. Suitably, the Sacha Vierny-shot *Mes Nuits Sont Plus Belles Que Vos Jours* (1989) is a sweeter, more contented day-trip through Zulawski's safari park, with bemused brain-tumor patient Jacques Dutronc living out his final days courting nightclub clairvoyant Marceau and creating a frustrated bulwark against their respective pasts as traumatized children. Zulawski full-nelsons his cast into compositions as obtuse as Eisenstein's in *Ivan the Terrible* (likewise, his same-year adaptation of

Boris Godunov has spectacularly muscular visuals, and might be only bested by Syberberg's *Parsifal* as the most inventive opera-on-film ever made), but the emphasis has subtly shifted from Zulawski's viewpoint to those of his characters. However feral the filmmaking and acting, *Mes Nuits* has a warm glow (it's the closest he's come to making a comedy), and it's easy to translate the hero's near-lunatic devotion to Marceau as the director's heart singing.

Marceau fueled the same dynamic in *The Blue Note* (1991) and *La Fidélité* (2000), the former a reconsideration of the Chopin-Sand relationship, the latter a loony but generous contemporary passion play based on La Fayette's *The Princess of Cleves* (like de Oliveira's *The Letter*), in which Marceau becomes torn between two men and chooses loyalty over passion, an ironic theme for Zulawski to ponder that grew more so once Marceau left him in 2001. In 1999, Marceau returned to Poland to make *Szamanka*, a nightshriek of hopelessness about a disturbed waif (first-timer Iwona Petry, who, it is rumored, descended herself into institutionable depression after working with Zulawski) with the insolent-angel, open-mouthed beauty of an over-fucked porn amateur, who attends classes as an anthropology student whenever she's not being sexually used by virtually every man to cross her path. Linking up with sweaty, hot-tempered anthro prof Boguslaw Linda—who is otherwise engaged in excavating the semi-preserved body of a bronze-age shaman from under an oblivious patch of industrial asphalt—the titular heroine enters by way of a Last Tango but exits somewhere south of suffering, squirming, and fidgeting and cataleptically surrendering her way out of reality.

Set to military drumrolls, *Szamanka*'s scores of sex scenes are as joyless and barren as *La Fidelite*'s are swoony; Poland, it seems, will always be Poland. But far from being subjective to national sensibility, Zulawski is truly a hermeticist: perhaps no other filmmaker who uses live actors has gone so far in creating his own personal outland: psychosocially anarchic and mad for freedom—that is, freedom from decorum, restraint, ethos, social control, privacy, taste, ambivalence, shrewdness, normalcy. Of course, life is absurd there. Is it a wonder only the steeliest of filmgoers wish to visit?

10

Laura Sinagra

Sharunas Bartas

One of Lithuanian director Sharunas Bartas's best films, *The Corridor* (1994), a meditation on mid-nineties life in post-Soviet Vilnius, posits the city as a filthy human anthill where wordless inhabitants of a nondescript apartment house shuffle amid cold-looking rooms. Some sit motionless in half-lit chambers. Others imbibe alcohol with neither shame nor relish. Ambient sounds bleeds through walls—traffic noise mixes with huffs of blurred recrimination. Radio static obscures snatches of pop songs bleating romantic palliatives. Shots out the flat-block windows attend on silhouetted throngs moving in a resolute rush. Inside, the aged and middle-aged exist in close quarters with children too inexpressive for innocence. One couple stares motionlessly at one another as if the slightest twitch could invite a messy sexual melee. At what could be called the film's dramatic high point, a child sets fire to line-dried sheets and is subsequently shoved into a rank pool. Throughout, the director himself prowls the titular passages, less a voyeur than a ghost condemned to inhabit these spaces, cursed with motion, moving forward like an enervated shark.

Like the work of Alexander Sokurov or Bela Tarr, Bartas's films are both documents of post-Soviet malaise and broader reflections on Europe's forgotten urban corners and impoverished expanses. But even by the standards of Eastern European miserablism, his methods are extreme, taking silence and detachment far beyond periodic abstraction and positing a truly gutted self—one for which capitalism has no use. His has been called a "cinema of waiting," but there's not usually a sense in his films that his subjects hope for change. In fact, Bartas more often ponders the ontological effects of a linguistic deprivation and a loss of agency so complete that not one of the denizens of his mute communities seems to even remember the relationship between desire and satisfaction.

The near-wordlessness of Bartas's films seems also to comment on the plight of the Lithuanian language itself. The lacunae where his subjects' words should be fill with the linguistic history of the place—to which written language came relatively late, and official common language has never been assured. Relentless sackings, tsarist Russification, tugs of Polish and German war, short-lived independence, and Stalinist re-Russification have left a legacy of official documents that flip variously from script to script. Bartas's films bear the weight of broken promises in several dialects. Of course, this abandonment of speech also nudges Bartas's films—their soundtracks clanging and whooshing in a pastiche of string-laden laments and the *musique concrete* of daily life—toward a version of universal, though certainly Europhilic, expression.

Graduating from the Moscow Film School in 1986, Bartas became an activist for independent film before the breakup of the Soviet Union. Intent on making movies in his home country, he founded its first independent studio, Vilnius's Studio Kinema, in 1989. After making several shorts there, Bartas garnered international attention with two films shot in the western Russian no-man's-land of Kaliningrad. This documentary and narrative duet *In Memory of a Day Gone By* (1990) and *Three Days* (1991) both, in a sense, star a grim city, the former Prussian port Konigsberg.

For the purposes of representing the fatigue of a political past that's left humans ill-equipped to even feign agency, one could hardy have chosen a better backdrop than this orphan place, cut off from mainland Russia by neighboring states, all by then moving steadily NATO-ward. Since Bartas made his films, this blighted city, with its poverty and growing AIDS problem, has continued to be a hub of organized crime, an ideal transport point for trafficking sex workers and Afghan heroin.

Memory is a sketch of the city, surveilling the poor and lame who move through its portside mists, observing subjects in a way that *The Corridor* would later revisit. Detours to the snowy countryside showcase the gorgeous, indifferent landscapes that would also become Bartas's hallmarks. The more plot-driven *Three Days* follows a trio—two transient men who meet up with a woman, played by the actress who would become Bartas's filmic muse, Katerina Golubeva—as they wander through the streets searching for a place to have sex. Crawling in rooming house windows, their efforts are thwarted by the presence of people living in roach-motel conditions. The idea is, of course, that dwarfed against the scope of callous geo-economics, our three questing bundles of sinew and synapse can only revert to primal instinct. But in this rusted-out environment, they can't achieve even this basic goal, finding public and private spaces equally inhospitable.

Gaining momentum for his projects after this point, Bartas followed *Three Days* (1991) with *The Corridor* (1994), and *Few of Us* (1996). Respectively, they move his critique first to the claustrophobic heart of Vilnius, then outward to the Siberian hinterlands. Golubeva, her wide-set eyes conveying world-historic futility, anchors both films. Her luscious blankness and a kind of feral athleticism even in repose provide the director with his most riveting embodiment of his country's latent sensual life. Golubeva, of course, would go on to star as the supernaturally unhinged foundling in Bartas pal Leos Carax's *Pola X*. (In a move that almost evidenced a sense of humor, Bartas played that film's black-turtlenecked caricature of an industrial composer, leading a scrap-metal orchestra amid the gear-grind of a factory that doubled as cacophonous artist squat).

In his own films, however, the director never suggests humor as a coping device. While several of the films feature moments of drunken revelry, communal inebriation never has a sympathetic function. Whether his waxed subjects chortle and howl or silently drain the dregs, the attendant atmosphere of these episodes only increases the sense of doom and danger. When Bartas moves in on the faces of his carousing unfortunates, there is surface merriment but still no sense of interior life.

Though sometimes Bartas seems to have scouted only the most cartoonish faces, he certainly is able in these films to elicit a kind of empty stare that deepens the quality of the silence. Golubeva's face, shot in a mirror in *The Corridor*, never suggests emerging identity, but simply furthers Bartas's equation of humans with elemental materials—hair, eyes, glass, wood. People are like the furniture they require, as present and tacitly enabling of sloth, boozing, and joyless retreats into sleep. By simply "being," his subjects announce a presence devoid of urgency. Their countenances are landscapes, and human actions are only as knowable—placidly predictable or violently mutable—as observed natural phenomena. Time and again, Bartas connects beaten landscapes with the contours of bone and skin. The dumb durability of each. The life of a body mimics the life of a mountain, enduring and unaware of government or ideology, until it wears to nonexistence.

In the far-flung *Few of Us*, which picks up where Bartas's 1986 student short "Tolofaria" left off, he contrasts tiny, rank interiors with jaw-dropping open expanse. The film begins stunningly as Golubeva is helicoptered in to a snowy Siberian village. We never know why she's brought here to make her way among the local Tolofars, a formerly nomadic group forced to settle the remote region in the early 1900s. Bartas may be commenting on the displacement of hundreds of thousands of Lithuanians to Siberia under various regimes, but also, placing Golubeva the midst of this particular group obviously speaks to racial tensions in the multiethnic former Soviet Union. As the larger world focuses on conflicts in Chechnya and Georgia, the director seeks out a forgotten pocket of rural squalor.

The Siberian mountain landscape, of course, also makes for several striking shots. The most symbolic finds Golubeva edging down an unstable rock face, pebbles cascading from under her slipping boots. In the cabin-like interiors, cigarette smoke moves across faces like clouds obscuring the moon. In the natural world, a white reindeer stands in painterly contrast to a drab dwelling. Later we watch it loll, in a distant shot, across Bartas's fixed frame. Again there is boozy carousing. Again a sense of menace. This time, the violence is more kinetic. Golubeva's interloper is tacitly threatened and some kind of violence ensues outside our view, leaving a body in its wake. Watching her depart after the murderous scuffle, we're as unsure of her trajectory as we were about the circumstances of her arrival.

After these two strong two films, Bartas's next project, 1997's better-financed *The House*, was a misstep. With his reputation growing in Europe, he was able to draw on a hotshot performer pool that included actors like Valeria Bruni-Tedeschi, Alex Descas, and his creative booster Carax. Unfortunately, the film plays almost like a parody of *The Corridor*. Suddenly, the blankness that seemed to come so easily becomes the one thing that none of the actors can carry off. As they meander though a dilapidated mansion similar to the one in Gus Van Sant's *Last Days*, the players seem bent on overtly conveying pain at the burden of history. Obviously, this kind of expressive agony is just what Bartas avoided up to this point. Each wince and sigh depletes the power of the project.

In one scene, Bruni-Tedeschi plays with two hand puppets, punching and crumpling them convincingly, but, compared to a similar device in *Memory*, where a Kaliningrad vagrant works a sad marionette for apathetic passersby, this sequence seems overwrought. Prowling the halls, Portuguese actor Francisco Nascimento seems on the verge of laughter, dutifully pacing from room to room like he's searching for the catering spread, never capturing the meaningless trudge of his obvious antecedent, Bartas's own blank-corridor creeper. Unlike Golubeva and previous ad hoc actors and nonprofessionals, these heat-seeking mutes clearly find it difficult to remain silent. When Bartas succeeds, his subjects need to seem beyond the promise of speech, their fathomless silence telegraphing an inability to even remember how emitted sound attaches to consensus meaning.

By 2001 Bartas is back on track with *Freedom*. This time, his merciless landscapes are the roiling sea and the North African desert. Apropos of the black-market trafficking now such a troublesome by-product of EU border-dissolution, *Freedom*'s stateless trio engages in a mysterious smuggling transaction in choppy open waters, then on land on a remote, stark desert shore. Once again, the faces of the three, one woman and two men, are explored with cartographic thoroughness, and this time, the natural landscape itself has the look of a naked body. In one scene, the woman walks without emotion into the brutal surf, buffeted and staggering, as if trying not to kill herself but to merge with it. There's no difference between the sea, the sand, and the self. As in *Few of Us*, the unforgiving landscapes offer beauty that provides no protection or solace. Fiery pink and yellow sunsets and the mist that rolls over the dunes hardly inspire these forlorn three to any kind of reverie. And of course, their freedom is the same freedom afforded to all Bartas's subjects—the freedom to exist off the capitalist grid, outside the only available frameworks for articulating identity.

For *Seven Invisible Men*, the director's 2005 offering, he returns to Europe—namely Lithuania, Poland, and the Crimea. This time, the requisite displacement is represented by three travelers (two of whom seem to have a sexual history) motoring through the region, inexplicably on the lam. Opening sequences privilege the breathtaking, seemingly benign countryside traversed by this haggard trio, juxtaposing pure-dawn beauty with ominous glimpses of dilapidated farms and the ruins of collective production.

At first, in contrast to the subjects of *Freedom*, and Bartas's Golubeva vehicles, the members of this trio, with their incessant smoking and thousand-yard stares, carry a whiff of insouciant art-house glamour. There is even the sense, perhaps because of their motion, that a narrative plot may emerge. More verbal than most of Bartas's films, this one explores the despair of characters self-aware enough to at least ask repeatedly, albeit with a heavy larding of existential dejection, "What are we going to do?"

What they do is run out of escape velocity and throw their meager lot in with some stock Bartas types, scruffy unfortunates of various ages and implied intimacies holed up in a dwelling where the sting of scarcity is dulled at intervals with booze and slurry song. The film echoes the racial and sexual overtones in *Few of Us*, its ethnic mix creating a cultural tinderbox. In today's world, however, it seems less like the central personages have parachuted into an unfamiliar milieu and more like they have attempted escape and come full circle, crashing into a gaggle of fellow nomads with as little inspiration or means for change as they.

In this crumbling house, Bartas's usual threat of violence and danger mounts. The energy is sexualized as the man in the central couple lazily takes up with a new bored waif. The remaining traveler harasses some trapped women, and the rest of the restless men seem scuzzily pleased to leer at young girls whom the film implies will be corrupted soon enough. A soliloquy by one young man obviously driven to madness functions as the film's curdled heart. Subsequent bloody displays of power mean less than nothing in this traditionally contested bit of the Ukraine—a land over which none of the groups here hold claim. In a sense, none of the men and women in *Seven Invisible Men* are visible at all to the marketplace that has discarded them. But Bartas continues to see them, and see them, and see them.

PART 3

Documentarians and Mad Scientists

11

David Sterritt

Ken Jacobs

Film critics and movie buffs often toss around the word "experimental" as a synonym for "unorthodox," meaning the work in question is somehow out of the mainstream. This is why many filmmakers prefer "avant-garde," another vague term—meaning "advance guard" and suggesting that, say, Michael Bay somehow wants to "catch up" with Michael Snow and his adventurous ilk. Words like "underground" and "poetic" are even more nebulous, diffuse, and all-around unsatisfactory.

Sometimes "experimental" is a useful term after all, though, since some filmmakers really are experimental in their outlook—not in a fiddling-around sense (like mad alchemists throwing elements together to see what might happen) but in the sense of continually tinkering with the fundamental meanings, methods, and raw materials of cinema. Ken Jacobs is one of these not-so-mad scientists. What does a Jacobs film look like? It's difficult to generalize about his work, except to say he rarely deals in storytelling. He believes in cinema that opens up the world for its audience, instead of closing it off by wrapping plots and characters into neatly tied-up packages. Instead of "actors acting" he likes to fill his movies with friends and family members "caught between who they are and their fantasy aspirations," as he put it in one of our interviews. He's also very fond of manipulating "found footage" from preexisting films. Beyond this, his works are extremely varied in content and length, ranging from four minutes to more than six hours of always unpredictable material. At the time I'm writing this, admirers are awaiting a milestone in Jacobs's decades-long career: the release of what may be his magnum opus, *Star Spangled to Death*, on DVD in its full six-hour-plus version. Although he's very much a filmmaker, Jacobs has finally joined many other experimental screen artists (even the late Stan Brakhage, who resisted video's siren song until near the end of his life) in considering the use of a home-viewing format to preserve and disseminate a major film-based work. And no question about it, *Star Spangled to Death* is as major as they come. I first saw it many years ago in an unfinished 16mm form, when it consisted mainly of black-and-white footage Jacobs had shot in New York's then-low-rent Brooklyn Bridge neighborhood, where he lived. The stars were an assortment of Jacobs's friends (most notably Jack Smith, his frequent collaborator and a dazzling filmmaker—*Flaming Creatures*, *Scotch Tape*—in his own right) striking poses, making faces, and cutting up. The overall result was a series of dream-like visions transmuting the oppressed conditions of the poor and marginalized into carnivalesque celebrations of the cast-off life—and bitter critiques of the money-driven, other-directed society that had made them poor and marginalized in the first place.

In its final form—if it ever truly has a final form, since Jacobs is likely to keep tinkering with its elements forever—the completed *Star Spangled to Death* is all this and much, much more. Two of its three "chapters" are dominated by found footage, ranging from dated instructional and travelogue material (the sort favored by Bruce Conner, arguably the greatest found-footage filmmaker) to such embodiments of American sociocultural dysfunction as Richard Nixon's fabled "Checkers" speech and a 1950s television show explaining how tortures inflicted on laboratory monkeys are on the verge of unveiling the profoundest secrets of human emotion for the everlasting benefit of network viewers. This is intercut with the street-theater acting (acting up? acting out?) of Jacobs and his friends—including Smith as The Spirit Not Of Life But Of Living and failed painter Jerry Sims as Suffering, among others—in extraordinarily subtle ways. For just one example, the swaying of a man filmed by Jacobs's camera, who might be davening in the fashion of Jewish prayer, echoes the rocking of traumatized monkeys in the psychology-lab footage. Misery takes literally innumerable forms, one is reminded, and has been misconstrued in equally uncountable ways over the millennia. Eventually, as promised in a brief promo-trailer for the movie's second half, the people filmed by Jacobs largely take over the picture from the salvaged material that has dominated the previous hours. Direct criticism of contemporary evils also escalates, not omitting the Iraq atrocities of George W. Bush and his cronies, still going strong as the film reached its final (so far) shape.

While he is a screen artist for the ages, Jacobs is also deeply engaged with the manifold malevolence of his own historical time. To say *Star Spangled to Death* is Jacobs's magnum opus doesn't mean it's a summa of everything he's essayed and accomplished over the years. It doesn't get into 3-D effects, for instance, although few things have fascinated Jacobs more than the possibility of expanding vision—and hence perception, and hence thought—by coaxing three-dimensional visions from the two-dimensional stuff of cinematic film stock.

His most exotic and successful method for accomplishing this is the perfectly named Nervous System, which he invented (yes, the not-so-mad scientist hard at work) and has displayed in a wide array of venues. Simply described, the system uses two 16mm projectors to project a pair of identical (but slightly unsynchronized) film strips onto a single screen space, one frame at a time, while a sort of propeller spins between the projector lamps at high speeds, blocking them alternately from view. Jacobs himself operates the frame-by-frame progression of the strips, and controls the sound effects that often complement the imagery; thus "performance" is a better term than "screening" to describe a Nervous System event. His wife and longtime partner Flo often participates as well. Jacobs is most proud of the more "abstract" works he's created for the system, such as *Bi Temporal Vision: The Sea*, a 1994 piece that stretches about 15 seconds of film material (ocean waves) into more than an hour of pure visual delirium. I prefer applications of the Nervous System involving more figurative footage, such as the deeply moving 1990 work *Two Wrenching Departures*, a tribute to Jacobs's erstwhile collaborators Jack Smith and Bob Fleischner, who had both recently died. In any case, almost anything can become grist for the system, as titles like *Making Light of History: The Philippines Adventure* and *Ontic Antics Starring Laurel and Hardy* indicate.

Nor does the Nervous System exhaust Jacobs's lofty 3-D aspirations. His other devices include a method whereby you view a flat image with a piece of darkened celluloid covering one of your eyes, and a method that requires you to view side-by-side images (shot with a stereoscopic 16mm camera that made it briefly to the market years ago) with your eyes crossed. The first of these works very well, the second even better (if you have strong eye muscles, at least). And of course Jacobs has made plenty of movies, in the sense of regular film projected on a regular screen for regular viewing. Not that the movies have regular content. Among his major classics are *Blonde Cobra* and *Little Stabs at Happiness*, shot in 1959 and edited into final form in 1963, both starring Smith's shenanigans and the former calling for a radio to be played (tuned to talk, not music) at particular points during the action. *Tom, Tom, the Piper's Son*, completed in 1969, elongates and elaborates a brief silent-film chase picture—possibly shot in 1905 by G. W. "Billy" Bitzer, the legendary D. W. Griffith cameraman—into an exhaustive (and exhausting) feast of stop-and-go cinematics. *The Doctor's Dream*, made in 1978, reedits a "normal" commercial movie according to an arbitrary set of parameters, transmuting an ordinary entertainment into a strange, oddly disturbing hallucination. And so on, comprising a filmography too extensive to be further detailed here. Paying a visit to Jacobs in his lower Manhattan loft, one enters a crowded workspace overflowing with books, records, artifacts, equipment, and cinematic flotsam. It makes a warm and comfortable home for the director, Flo, and in earlier times their two children, as well as a combination studio, library, and lab. Almost anything can happen there, as I was reminded when I ran into him on the street (we live fairly near each other) and he started enthusing about his work on "3-D poems," whatever those might be. Later that day my fax machine coughed up a few pages of exactly these, dispatched by Ken posthaste. Look at the identical side-by-side stanzas with your eyes crossed to just the right degree, and sure enough, they pop out as three-dimensionally as can be. "I definitely am inquiring," Jacobs said when I asked him once about the energy behind his work. "I'm interested in a number of fronts. Some of them have to do with history, and an understanding of how [people] work. . . . I've invested in kids, and I want them to live. I've invested my feelings in the world, and I want it to continue."

His other interests include "time and movement," and the discoveries that can be made by examining "strange caricatures of the past" in old movies. He calls these "eternalisms," and he can ferret them out of all sorts of footage. Sometimes he rephotographs the material, as in *Tom, Tom, the Piper's Son*, and sometimes he simply presents it the way he found it, as in *Urban Peasants*, an unaltered 1975 collation of as-is home movies accompanied by a "How to Speak Yiddish" recording, and *Perfect Film*, a 1985 reel of TV outtakes (shot after Malcolm X's assassination) that Jacobs literally discovered in a trash bin. He's fascinated by the possibility of finding truth and beauty in outmoded film images—or if not full-scale truth and beauty, at least "some kind of genuine commotion going on, something happening." In other words, this is not a stony-faced quest for solemn verities. "I'm amused by this," Jacobs says. "Everything tickles me. I get a big kick out of it." Early influences on Jacobs included such great movies as *City Lights*, by Charles Chaplin, and *The Bicycle Thief*, by Vittorio De Sica, as well as Herman Melville and Miguel de Cervantes novels. When still a teenager he was also deeply impressed by an "art photograph" he saw in *Life* magazine, showing people whimsically draped in sheets but with ordinary trouser legs, shoes, and socks visible down below. Jacobs was fascinated by this "contradiction between fantasy and reality," and by what it suggested about "where the mind can go while the body remains."

His life was never the same after this vision of what it might be like "to be [living] in the seedy reality of the '40s and '50s, and yet to have a head full of dreams." Jacobs decided to express his ideas in an ambitious movie, but soon realized Hollywood wasn't about to knock on his door. So he started filming the original version of *Star Spangled to Death*, shot "for pennies, with leftover [film] scraps." Around the same time he studied painting with Hans Hofmann for two years. By a dozen years later, when he founded the film department at the State University of New York at Binghamton, he had some fifteen movies either completed or in progress. Since then he has made many more as well as videos, theater pieces, "shadow plays," and performance works.

Although he once hoped for a large mainstream audience, Jacobs decided as early as the 1950s that he had been "dreaming and idealizing 'the people' in a kind of '30s left-wing way," as he later put it, and that mass audiences would probably not take an interest in his offbeat sensibility. Resigning himself to the fact that such spectators will always prefer Hollywood-type films, he followed his own nonconforming, "Baud'larian" path—reaching a small number of viewers, but putting a special value on them since they share his disdain for mass-produced "art" that cares more about packaging than content. Jacobs feels mass-marketed movies do a lot of harm to people who mindlessly and continuously feed on them, since such films cancel out the ideals and dreams their audiences might otherwise have. "It could well be that romance is in people until it's beaten out of them . . . or bored out of them," he says. He feels that the roots of today's mass-audience culture are in the 1950s, a time when "you were supposed to adjust and conform to 'reality' . . . and you were 'sick' and 'out of it' unless you acknowledged and adapted to this." Jacobs warns that "the coercive pressure to 'adapt to reality' means to give up and fall in line. Maturity is defined as acquiescence." To counter this mentality, Jacobs asks his audience to participate in the creative process—by thinking actively about what's on-screen, instead of letting it simply wash over them. "This is keeping the mind alive," he says. "Otherwise we just have habits; we're mechanistic." Using cinema to its fullest potential, according to Jacobs, means concentrating on the act of discovery rather than churning out polished productions.

Asked to define the aesthetic "gold" he wants to "mine" in his work, he answers, "Pleasure. Amusement. Pain. Realization . . . To see where [my mind] will take me, and where this technology will take me . . . And to exercise this power in a way that doesn't mean enslavement or subjugation to others."

12

George Toles

A Few Moments of Arousal in a Film by Martin Arnold

The French theorist and filmmaker Jean Epstein famously argued in the 1920s that the essence of cinema was to be found in "the form of the sensual moment that he called *photogenie*—fleeting fragments of experience that provide pleasure in ways that the viewer cannot describe verbally or rationalize cognitively."[1] Inside those penetrating, swift-brushing, enticing points of time, those sweetly painful hooks for the eye of memory, something akin to "pure immersion in the image" becomes possible.[2] Maya Deren later offered an argument for a similar, moment-based film aesthetics, extolling the camera's power to place not only faces and objects but the slipstream of time itself "under the microscope." We might call the camera's lifting up of ragged, flyaway instants for magically prolonged scrutiny, *time close-ups*.

Austrian experimental filmmaker Martin Arnold makes movies that might be said to consist entirely of time close-ups. The images he selects for fetishistic stretching and intensification are culled from tiny, seemingly inconsequential narrative fragments of black-and-white Hollywood films made under the combined restraints of the Production Code and hermetic, studio backlot shooting. Part of the viewer's assigned task with Arnold's densely packed shorts is to experience these familiar confinements of old

Hollywood as a kind of palpable armature. Within the hazy (or time-fogged) gray settings that duplicate the major human gathering places in typical homes and apartments (kitchen, living room, hallway, bedroom), the characters who attempt to complete their everyday routines are somehow stymied, interrupted, and caught—as if suddenly naked and unknown to themselves—in the act. They submit, without understanding why, to private ordeals of frenzied sensation while going through customarily simple procedures in their rooms. Meanwhile, the rooms themselves, the clothes the characters wear, the objects that loom too large in their accustomed places, seem to protest against the outbreak of impulse, and work to press the characters back into their former, recognizable molds. The spaces, in other words, are at odds with a suddenly unhinged subjective time flow, which wrenches the characters onto a new track of wayward, extravagant self-expression. Like the man without a shadow, the faded monochrome inhabitants of Arnold's shorts seem bent on reunion with a lost dimension of their being that will somehow give weight and presence to their actions.

Time opens a portal that carries them away, for a repetitive, senseless, yet hyper-lucid interval, from their vacant imitations of life. Suppose it lay within this time out of time's power to bind characters more securely to the previously vague and unremarkable particulars of their generic movie settings. Suppose the details of setting, in other words, seem to grow up around them like the heavy, fateful furnishings of a Carl Dreyer chamber. Suppose these sharpened details acquire the capacity to transfix the eye, even to the point of painfulness, because of their implacable, newfound *thereness*. A small, lit lamp standing on a nondescript table in the corner, for example, though it occupies limited space in the frame, can feel monumental as it turns so starkly still and frozen behind Judy Garland jitterily entrapped by the word of a song. As Judy tries to finish singing the word "alone," with face and gestures flailing to find the elusive, perfect sound that will allow her to be released from "aloneness," the table lamp behind her seems to call her back to a stability and self-containment that she has lost touch with. Judy's seizure lends a calm, almost godlike sovereignty to whatever in her surroundings resists seizure. In the new time dispensation of the Arnold world, moments not only open up to swallow viewer and character alike, but also "pursue us," in a phrase of Schopenhauer's, "like a taskmaster with a whip."[3] It is as though we are forced backward, with the characters, through the hoop of moments we had thought we had successfully passed through, in order to get them right, to make some crucial but elusive correction. Never has it been such a challenge to get free of one simple action in its appointed moment, and onto the next. Perhaps we feel the full force of Schopenhauer's claim that "whenever we may live we always stand, with our consciousness, at the central point of time . . . each of us [bearing] within him the unmoving mid-point of the whole of endless time."[4] Time, which can be regarded as "merely the form of phenomena," has become cavernous in Arnold as it would be onstage if actors were not only to forget their lines but their very roles and the play itself, along with their natural sense of how to move and speak.

Martin Arnold's way with film time is to imbue it with psychology—specifically, the psychology of an obsessive-compulsive who is obliged to perform a whole host of small actions repetitively, back and forth, as though each one were a crucial phase in an endless ritual of appeasement. I recently saw a production of a play by Ross McMillan entitled *Legion*, in which the central female character (an obsessive-compulsive) cannot move from her living room to her bedroom without performing a variety of preparatory actions, four times each, culminating with four identical approaches to, and retreats from, the bedroom doorway. Having reached this point in her sequence, she is allowed to turn around and hop over the threshold backward, and if she lands in the right spot must then rapidly slam the door four times, making certain that it is fully closed after every equally decisive attempt. If she does not fail here, she is granted access to her room and can face the bed, where further trials await her. The playwright has explained the obsessive-compulsive's goal, or need, in terms of a desire to somehow step outside of history—one's own history as well as the more general history of everyone else's struggles. Having given history the slip, one enters a kind of private cathedral, where one can partake of shadow-actions in a sphere so separate from "recorded life" that what one does is like writing letters on the roof of the mouth with the tongue: no legible, impure, incriminating traces are left. However elaborate the lead-ups to an act become, and however many missteps one makes in the process, only the completed actions count as real-life activity. The preparations not only make real acts possible, they purify them in advance, though no one else will have any notion of how or why this is so. The numbered, ritualized approaches to an act are like a secret prayer, drafted in invisible ink. Obsessive-compulsive maneuvers are a time-out from the requirements dictated by social forms and socialized others. So much of real, historical time is spent making wearisome concessions to authorities other than the higher, unanswerable, stopwatch-wielding deity within. One's accumulated repetitions have the efficacy of divine grace. Someday their true meaning and perfected form will be revealed, and our spirit—laboring so long in a lonely cave out of the sight of men—will be set free, transfigured. A further function of these private repetitions is to offer momentary reprieves from the less manageable life pressures on either side of them.

Martin Arnold's films seem to penetrate the inner sanctum of the obsessive-compulsive's previously well-guarded lair. He is entranced by the potential relation of obsessive-compulsive stop-time to Epstein's photogenie: beautifully transient film images paradoxically deep enough to drown in. The effect of motion in Arnold's films is hectically immobilized, comparable to the way in which the obsessive-compulsive's hand-washing or teeth-counting are both a visual stutter and a magical lift off from the ordinary, anxious uncertainty of experience. The private drama of scrupulous repetition is performed, under a spell, for some kind of personal God, a God perhaps for whom no one else is real or of any consequence. Arnold seizes upon this privacy as something that can be maintained (on film, at any rate) in another's presence, even as one is enacting strenuously peculiar behavior. For the Arnold obsessive-compulsive, it is a matter of losing touch with one's sense of another person's capacity to observe what one is doing and think ill of it. One can be stroking someone in a mechanically insistent way or sending her, many times over, an unambiguous predatory look, while feeling that one is as protectively cloaked as in a daydream. The other figure is a prop for one to manipulate, who will mirror one's repetitions with synchronized, counted actions of her own. As one of Arnold's titles declares, there is no escaping the root condition of "alone." Whether our name is Andy Hardy or Joseph K. we try to take some of our limitless "waste," at the hands of life, and in our solitude convert it back into the very stuff of life. What might have been wasted or lost need not be. Instead of repetition wearing things out, the act of repeating becomes a sacred proof of consequence. By delaying, almost endlessly, our advance to the next point, we finally know what it might mean to get somewhere.

Moments luxuriously expand as Arnold's dreamers seem to circle around them, like gasping swimmers, poised for some ultimate surrender. The hovering instant acquires the fluid spaciousness of a lake. And as one obsessive-compulsive rite gives way to another and then another, a whole series of adjoining time-lakes open up. Let's call them Finger Lakes, after that unfailingly poetic region of upper New York state. While the viewer of an Arnold film may initially be struck by jagged, comically frantic, or tedious duplications of pointless on-screen activity, there is a fairly rapid change of perspective whereby we become attuned to an eerily intense, expressive ceremony, whose phases have an air of necessity. Within the terms of this ceremony, the logic of the repeating gesture and minute gradations of expression powerfully manifests itself. The form of the action is wiped smooth by our new relation to film time, as though its wrenching discontinuity progressively revealed a stillness at the heart of things. For

Arnold, the takeover of conventional old movie images by obsessive-compulsive rites is meant to rescue a plenteous field of the unconscious living just beneath the hurried, automatic transitions, and the almost interchangeable entrances and exits designed for the characters of studio narratives. In the Andy Hardy stories, for example, where thought and impulse are entirely lost to learned response, things move too fast and slickly for any pure moment to break free. What Arnold's interventions unearth from them, therefore, are previously unfelt, invisible moments in a perpetually disruptive cinematic flow. Nothing in the films' original sequence of events either expected or needed to leave a strong, distinct impression. The clock-time of the Andy Hardy movies, played at proper speed, is the time of a faceless day, somehow lived through without being experienced, and impossible to recall after the fact in its bloodless particulars. Moments that declare their separateness, and make a bid for memory heat and sticking power, can only do so by being shunted onto another track of time—one devoted to the "petrified fragility" of obsessive-compulsive repetition. In this realm of beautiful "liquid geometry," even a tiny eye movement or momentary shadow on one's cheek can strike the memory with the force of a beloved old building collapsing in slow motion.[5] The oscillating, repeating emphasis of a particular flicker of emotion on a face or action of a hand makes it seem to hover between a condition of still-pending arrival and disappearance, reminding me of the way that a falling building is still there in the mind's eye for a short period after its descent. The memory somehow holds it up (still intact) while one observes its silent, irreversible toppling. (I am reminded here of the astonishing archival footage of the great Toronto fire of 1904, and of the demolition of gutted buildings that took place in its aftermath.)

Let us conclude by glancing at a few Jean Epstein moments drawn from the very beginning of Arnold's 1998 short, *Alone: Life Wastes Andy Hardy*. We are immediately plunged into the murk, and resultant shock, of "out in the open" mother–son sexual feelings. Before we decide that we know what the joke is, or what sort of knowledge should be brought to bear in our response to the images (the correct attitude, as it were), we would be well-advised to remind ourselves that we understand far less about such feelings than we imagine we do. What, after all, are the firm boundaries of love? Another thing of which we have limited knowledge is how images of such entanglement are connected to matters beyond sex and beyond the reach of what we can either find words for or adequately represent. The moments draw some of their troubling power from their ability to suggest what is mobile and expressible in the life of feeling and what lies paralyzed beneath it.

Alone begins with a medium close-up two-shot of young Mickey Rooney, who is strangely shorn of his trademark, overanimated dynamism, and a plain, moonfaced woman of indeterminate age whom we have reason to assume is his mother. The mother seems to be adrift in a somber reverie. She is not looking at her son, but outward, as though retrieving a crumpled, momentous memory image from an enfolding mist. We seem to have jumped into a scene that has been building for some time; the actors seem poised near the trip wire of a climactic revelation. We barely have time to register Mickey's expression before he boldly moves behind his mother and presses his lips against her cheek; his mouth and nose, as he sets to work, are hidden by her imposing, centrally placed head. His long hold on the kiss while he lingers, frozen in place, reminds us unmistakably of a vampire leaning in to drink deep from a female victim. As this association is formed we notice that his hands are clasping both of her upper arms. One hand circumspectly stays within the bounds of the short sleeve dress fabric, above her exposed arm; the other hand (on our left) dangerously contacts the skin below the sleeve, in what appears a conscious trespass. Then the other hand, emboldened by his partner's success, slyly follows suit. These hands become key players (nearly autonomous creatures of instinct) in the repetition compulsion seduction drama that ensues.

From the first moment of the film, we hear what appears to be a ghostly, distorted organ accompaniment, floating up to us from the ocean floor of the unconscious. I picture a shadowy Captain Nemo at his underwater keyboard in the Nautilus. Perhaps there is a faint echo of the music of early radio/television soap operas, but transmuted through a combination of wavering, punctures, heartbeat reverberations, backtracking, and the sense of lonely distance into an authentic dirge. The music is like a muffled cry for release or rescue, but finding neither, it can only turn in on itself futilely and retrace its well-worn steps in the mournful labyrinth. Andy's preliminary, almost thoughtless embrace of his mother is like a tender feeling that has gotten stuck, tar baby-style, en route to completion. Through a combination of accident and vague inclination, Mickey (or his namesake, "Andy") has coaxed his mother's long-entombed sexual urges back to the surface in a quiet kitchen after supper, and as a result of his transgression both son and mother seem enchained to each other in an unbreakable spell. They seem to have stumbled, by separate paths, into one of those "out of time" moments in a dream where it feels confusingly necessary to tarry. As the moment expands, its overdetermined details claim their entire concentration. They seem to be working their way through an action together that for the time being seems to be all there is. Yet, however intensely they respond to each other's presence and touch, they are somehow equally intensely alone.

It is striking how much of the "fiery fount" of Andy's inner life appears to flow out of his nervous, hungry fingers. By working over mother's dress sleeves, so avidly, responsive to its textures, folds, capacity for bunching and smoothing out, they communicate the startling power of this fabric to heighten arousal. Andy alternates between vertical hand travels (up and down the sleeves to the naked arms: is he keeping count?) and a gripping pressure, as though squeezing the arms closer to the body. The latter action has an aural accompaniment which turns mother's torso into a massive accordion. Individual fingers acquire trembling definition as we absorb their depth of fixation. They are like matches about to ignite through their frictional brushing of the fabric surface. As the hands proceed to lend the "clinging" garment sexual force the viewer's eye is distressingly drawn to a suddenly ample-looking "V" of visible flesh beneath the collar of mother's dress. Though there is a long row of buttons on this graceless floral print frock that have been carefully fastened (an Auntie Em special), one begins to detect a glimmering seductive intention to leave a portion of the body exposed at the top. Some of the buttons, one notes with suspicion, have been left undone. Why? The button line is closed well above the bust line, but Andy's squeezing action causes the large bosom to heave noticeably and make the parade of buttons quiver, as if conducting the woman's sexual current upward. Andy's outfit includes suspenders whose tightness, especially when he moves rhythmically against her (another action worth counting), forms a symmetry with the button row, against whose confinement the flesh seems audibly protesting.

The most miraculous feature of this shard of Arnold's narrative is the mother's demeanor. Once we have made maximum allowance for all the changes that a director can make in our perceptions of what is going on at a particular moment through time manipulation and sound and optical layering, there still remains the mysterious, and seemingly unaltered, truth of facial expression. What the mother's face reveals when we submit it to duly skeptical scrutiny is a person openly, unreservedly in the grip of desire. One may struggle to disbelieve this expression and try to transform it into something less extreme, more accommodating, say, to the spirit of parody, but the face holds the imprint of excitation indelibly for the entire duration of Andy's interaction with her. It is as though the emotional equivalent of an egg that has gone bad has been cracked and spilled out on heretofore reliable facial terrain. The countenance is reborn under this fresh sticky coat—become radiant with sulfurous hunger. She consistently declares whenever our look returns to her that she is ripe for the taking, and has firmly settled the inner struggle about surrendering herself completely to her son. As we proceed in the expanding moment, her "made up mind" seems to deepen its determination to savor every surprising sensation that comes to her. There is no turning back and no point in denying that this is the fulfillment she now requires and that she has *earned* through a life of homely toil and sacrifice. The mother calmly accepts her newfound voluptuary status and seems unable to recall why she should be alarmed, even on her son's behalf. In the free fall of this dream thought, she is willing all her attributes to be sleekly animal and inviting. Her carefully prim hairstyle transforms as Andy nuzzles against her, as he feels the tresses loosen against his cheek and inhales their fragrance. The hair, as we attend to it, could now almost be *designed* to ensnare him, to lead him to just this place of undoing. Similarly, her lipstick and makeup begin to strike us as plausible further stratagems—aimed precisely at her boy. "I wondered how long it would take you to notice me . . . all these elaborate preparations, invisible to others, with which I hoped, some day, to catch your eye. At last you understand, and because you do, I understand as well." Without her eyes shifting position, she slowly parts her lips as he presses on, and emits a noise that mingles a sharp intake of breath with a slowed-down chattering (or possibly clacking) of teeth. She wills her mouth and warmly shadowed chin to take on more animal colors and as the sound of her teeth become a ticking clock, she seems to be tearfully relieved to have reached the end of mothering. At last the time has come to remove, together with her garments, her maternal disguise.

Martin Arnold has spoken in an interview of his desire to have "the movements on the screen" in his films extend "to the body of the spectator." He would like us to feel involuntarily "attached to the figures by strings," and to have us vibrate (erotically, nervously) as these strings are plucked and stretched by the figures' hypnotically coercive, obsessively repeated movements.[6] As the laws that govern the steadfast appearance of the things we most depend on seem to be revoked, one by one, before our eyes, we sink through the image surface and graze, ever so slightly, the barely intelligible thing in itself. How do we construe it in this long moment of touching?

Notes

1. Leo Charney, "In a Moment: Film and the Philosophy of Modernity" in *Cinema and the Invention of Modern Life*, edited by Leo Charney and Vanessa R. Schwartz (Berkeley: University of California Press, 1995), 285.

2. Ibid.

3. Arthur Schopenhauer, *On the Suffering of the World*, trans. by R. J. Hollingdale (London: Penguin, 2004), 5.

4. Ibid., 41.

5. Both of the quoted phrases are taken from John Golding's review of Mark Rothko's *The Artist's Reality: Philosophies of Art* in *The New York Review of Books* Volume LII, Number 4 (March 10, 2005), 41.

6. Scott MacDonald, "Martin Arnold," in *A Critical Cinema: Interviews with Independent Filmmakers* (Berkeley: University of California Press, 1998), 347–62.

13

Godfrey Cheshire

Ross McElwee

For Southern artists, all images implicate the past, just as every voyage of self-discovery leads inexo'rably back to one's roots. Each journey outward and away whispers of eventual homecoming, with all its tangled emotions. Well into *Bright Leaves*, Ross McElwee inspects footage of his father he shot in the 1970s. The elder McElwee, a conservative doctor who lived in Charlotte, N.C., has been dead several years, and Ross finds decreasing comfort in his lingering filmic ghost. "As time goes by, my father is beginning to seem less and less real to me in these images," he broods. "Having this footage doesn't help very much, or at least not as much as I thought it would. What does help is the land itself, being back here again—North Carolina still seems, in a kind of understated way, like the most beautiful place on earth to me. And woven right into this landscape that I'm so fond of is tobacco." By the time McElwee eulogizes North Carolina's beauty, his father's flickering, fading image has given way to a gorgeous emerald-green landscape, one that jars with mention of the state's deadliest, if most lucrative, agricultural product.

In its rapid-fire linkage of fathers, cinema, mortality, and his Southern homeland, this brief passage is quintessential McElwee. The themes invoked reach beyond the filmmaker's own family history (including, in *Bright Leaves*, a would-be tobacco baron great-grandfather whom McElwee imagines was the inspiration for an old Gary Cooper movie) and indicate a dogged personal itinerary that has now become an encompassing cinematic odyssey. During the last quarter-century, McElwee has fashioned a still-evolving autobiographical cycle that comprises what is arguably the American cinema's most remarkable and sustained meditation on time, place, identity, and their filmic representations. No doubt his work invites responses as personal as the films themselves. Growing up in North Carolina in the same era as McElwee, I was fascinated by movies about the South but also acutely aware that they invariably reflected an outsider's point of view. No matter how lovingly a Southern book or play might be adapted, the filmmakers—and usually the film itself—came from elsewhere, and the alien provenance was eventually betrayed. The bad accents, missed nuances, or condescending tone were perhaps inevitable, given that there was no indigenous Southern cinema.

Granted, Southerners might consume vast quantities of regional fiction that portray them essentially as they like to see themselves. But McElwee, I realized on first encountering his work, was doing something else, because *he* was something else: a willing apostate, a Southerner who had not only fled north for school (M.I.T.) and remained but had also embraced his expatriate status. His great subject might be "my life and my family's life down South," yet the insider's viewpoint was that of an outsider, too—the key to an ongoing ambivalence that seesaws between romantic identification and ironic distance.

Certainly, the need to establish that distance was in part generational. The South was convulsed by the Civil Rights 1960s as it had been by the Civil War 1860s. The forty-minute *Backyard*—which is almost uncanny in how fully it announces the themes, subject matter, style, and even several of the main characters of his future work (the film was shot in the 1970s though not completed until 1984)—opens with photographs of proper, besuited Dr. McElwee standing next to shaggy, bearded Ross McElwee, whose voiceover recalls that when his father asked about his plans after college, he listed possibilities that, besides filmmaking, included working for black voter registration or the peace movement and entering a Buddhist monastery. You can feel the sizzle of the Republican surgeon's ire at this response.

Lolling around his plush home with 16mm camera in hand, Ross studies Charlotte life with a painter's appreciation for its relaxed rhythms, sensual beauty, and incidental absurdity. The camera conceals Ross and projects his coolly scrutinizing eye on his father's comfortable life. This passive-aggressive intrusiveness pays special attention to the interaction between the McElwees and three longtime black retainers. That their subtly compromised intimacies are remnants of the Old South is underscored by a ditty, sung by McElwee's grandmother, in which a wise black

Mammy advises a "pickaninny" abused by white children to "stay in your own backyard." Yet the film's underlying melancholy stems from a backstory recounted in bits: one McElwee brother died in a boating accident years before, and Ross's mother of cancer more recently. Ultimately, the questions of family that Ross seems to thrust at his dad demand a restitution that could come, if at all, only in heaven.

Charleen (1980), also shot in Charlotte in the 1970s, is an ideal counterpoint to *Backyard* in its treatment of a de facto matriarch of the New South. Charleen Swansea, whom McElwee first encountered in high school, is an irrepressible forty-two-year-old who teaches poetry to school kids and has two teenagers (by a previous marriage) as well as a twenty-five-year-old lover. She left home as a youngster looking for new fathers and was "adopted" by Ezra Pound, who evidently kindled her determination to be passionate and anticonventional at all costs. While she will reappear in McElwee's films as Greek chorus, mother confessor, reality principle, and Eternal Feminine, the hilariously profane Charleen obviously served Ross as an important role model in how to escape the Joycean nets of a suburban upbringing. In *Charleen*, her insistence on honest, warts-and-all description eventually doubles back on her: rather than ending as an appreciative tribute to an extraordinary teacher (which she is), the film verges into darker, more private territory, showing her with hands bandaged, confessing to the jealousy and fear of aging that led her to smash her straying lover's windows.

Sherman's March (1986), the film that put McElwee on the art-house map (it was one of the most successful American documentaries prior to the current era), takes his penchant for chronicling his own life and scrutinizing the South to epic length, and does so in a way that slyly reveals the elements of literary, theatrical, and cinematic contrivance that underlie his brand of documentary. If the Ross who appeared in *Backyard* was something of a mask, a persona offering a guarded bridge between author and audience, the same character here becomes an ingenious comic creation whose angst-y, confessional sincerity is at once transparently heartfelt and conveniently deceptive. The filmmaker starts to make a film about General Sherman's destructive foray, but after his love life self-destructs, he begins to chronicle encounters with women as he meanders through the Carolinas and Georgia. Even if McElwee is leading us on, there's no shortage of genuine nerve in how much his method leaves to chance and in how determinedly he tries to push his romantic discontents to the breaking point.

Revisiting his father, who still regards his filmmaking as a useless frivolity, Ross again uses his camera as both shield and sword. Charleen, trying to get him to engage with a Charleston girl, snaps, "This isn't art, it's life!" All the same, he knows what he's doing. The fluidity and eloquence of McElwee's technique here still impress, while the portraits of the seven women he spends time with—among them an aspiring actress, a linguist, a rock singer, an anti-nuke activist, and a husband-seeking Mormon—are as keenly appreciative of female beauty and complexity as any Truffaut film (McElwee's discretion about his involvement with all seven only enhances his own courtly image). Beyond its autobiographical drollery, the film's bemused view of such regional eccentricities as survivalists and Burt Reynolds–worship make it the most striking film about the American South since David O. Selznick made his own pilgrimage in Sherman's path.

Given the success of *Sherman's March*, it was natural that McElwee would continue in the same vein. So *Time Indefinite* starts in a light mood. At a family gathering, Ross announces his engagement—at last!—to filmmaker Marilyn Levine. The two are married in a good-humored ceremony attended by his father and Charleen, and the happy prospect of parenthood arrives. Though Ross views the cost of baby furniture with mock-horror, his excitement at Marilyn's pregnancy is palpable. Then, mortality strikes a triple blow. Ross's grandmother dies, his father (who had not been ill) suffers a fatal seizure, and Marilyn miscarries. How can filming continue? For months, it doesn't. Ross only picks up the camera again when he returns South. In Charlotte, he goes through his father's clothes and spends time with Melvin and Lucille, a black couple who've worked for the McElwees for decades (they also appear in *Backyard*). In South Carolina he listens to Charleen's horrific account of how Jim (her young lover in *Charleen*) committed suicide by setting their house afire with himself inside. The world seems to reflect Ross' darkness.

If *Sherman's March* was a lyrical picaresque, buoyed by the filmmaker's footloose spontaneity, *Time Indefinite* has a novel's dense, thoughtful gravity, unfolding in slow-dawning recognition of the bonds that family, responsibility, and death inevitably impose. The earlier film's witty broodings on nuclear apocalypse, though genuine, were so tonally useful that they could also seem opportunistic; in the later film, as the "Ross" mask melts into a real face, the shock of personal loss and the slow lessons of grief movingly honor life's difficult, day-to-day trials. In my view, there is no more profound or beautiful nonfiction film about family. And the South—which isn't a thematic preoccupation in two other McElwee films with autobiographical threads, *Something to Do with the Wall* (1990) and *Six O'Clock News* (1996)—is hardly incidental to its final shape and larger meanings.

Natives of the South who live elsewhere often continue to identify themselves as Southerners and use the term "going home" both in its ordinary sense and to connote returning South. McElwee's work gives a cinematic dimension to this double consciousness. In *Bright Leaves*, worrying that Adrian, his Boston-bred, now-adolescent son will not know his heritage, Ross takes his camera "home" again. He meets cousin John McElwee, a drawling Tar Heel cinephile whose home contains an astonishing collection of old movies (on 35mm and 16mm) and cinema memorabilia. Amid this trove, Ross encounters *Bright Leaf*, a 1950 Michael Curtiz film in which Gary Cooper plays a nineteenth-century Southerner struggling against a wily opponent in the tobacco trade. Speculating that the character was based on his great-grandfather John Harvey McElwee, Ross begins digging into the life story and surviving traces of his ancestor while probing the problematic legacy of North Carolina tobacco. During his search he comes to regard *Bright Leaf* as a "home movie" concealed within a Hollywood melodrama and even questions one of its stars, Patricia Neal, about how her off-screen romance with Gary Cooper gave the film another kind of documentary dimension.

Though McElwee kids his own "metaphysical" musings, his work reveals true Southern cosmology. The South appears as Eden, which gains its idyllic glow only in retrospect, defined by the shadow of some enticing serpent—be it slavery or war or even tobacco. How could a place so beautiful produce such a dark stain? That's the order of things here. The apple harbors a worm; tragedy's pull is inescapable; siblings and parents die before you can fix their images. As McElwee looks around, and back, he sees how tobacco has lent its stain to his family saga. After John Harvey lost his fortune, three subsequent McElwee generations produce doctors who treat innumerable cancer patients. Yet, even their skills can't hold mortality at bay, as the legions of afflicted smokers indicates. Among them is Charleen's sister, whose demise prompts one of the film's visits to a cemetery.

Ironically, even the demon itself seems in danger. Though tobacco museums flourish, the culture they commemorate is rapidly vanishing, as Ross discovers when he films a small-town "Tobacco Day" parade that, after decades of tradition, will henceforth be known as "Farmers Day." If he doesn't stop to reflect that celluloid is fading off into the cultural horizon as rapidly as cigarettes, it's perhaps because the natural Southern reaction is to whistle in the dark, crack a few jokes, or invoke legends of the glorious past—say, concocting a tale about Gary Cooper playing one's great-granddad. Such imaginative feints may not bring the departed back to life or prevent their pictures from fading, but they do keep our amorous dance with meaning at full sway, and with luck, they will sustain us until the next time we look homeward for our better angels.

14

Patricia Aufderheide

Judith Helfand

Secret Stories, Video Diaries, and Toxic Comedy

SOME PEOPLE ARE BORN EXILES from mainstream media, some choose it, and some have exile thrust upon them. Judith Helfand is in the last category, and she has never intended to stay there. Before the age of forty, Helfand directed or codirected three full-length, award-winning documentaries shown on national television. The first was *The Uprising of '34* (1995, co-directed with the legendary documentarian George Stoney), about a 1934 national textile strike that in the South became a massacre of textile workers, the history of which was then suppressed for decades. The backbone of the film is composed of intimate interviews, often overbrimming with long-pent-up emotion, conducted with the relatives and descendants of murdered workers; the words themselves testify to decades of enforced silence. The Academy of Motion Picture Arts and Sciences voted *The Uprising of '34* one of 1995's ten best documentaries.

In *A Healthy Baby Girl* (1997), Helfand chronicled in video-diary form her family's coming to terms with her uterine cancer as a result of her mother being prescribed DES, an antimiscarriage drug that the pharmaceutical company knew could be deadly. The film is artfully artless, seemingly a girlish video diary, but of a hideously premature experience of near-death. The chronicle of personal recovery evolves into a statement of outrage. The film was both an expose of the social devastation caused by chemical company negligence and also a mother-daughter relationship story. It won a Peabody Award for Excellence in Journalism and Public Education.

Blue Vinyl (2002, co-directed with Dan Gold) took Helfand on a search for the environmental implications of vinyl, which her parents have chosen for the new exterior of their home; she finds that polyvinyl-chloride creates cancer-causing dioxin at the beginning and end of its life cycle. By this time, Helfand's artless persona was well-honed. She took that persona on a walk around the world, with a piece of her parents' new vinyl siding under her arm. She became the personification of the little guy in a big corporate world, but one who simply refuses to be a victim. The film took the Sundance Film Festival cinematography award, was nominated by the International Documentary Association for "Best Documentary," won the 2002 Environmental Messenger of the Year from the Environmental Grantmakers Association, and garnered two Emmy Nominations for "Best Research" and "Best Documentary," among other awards. After successful festival debuts, the first two films showed on one of public TV's premiere documentary series, *P.O.V.*, and the third showed on HBO.

Judith Helfand is an independent filmmaker because there is noplace in American filmmaking that gives full-time filmmaking jobs to people who make social documentaries. She is an independent investigative researcher because mainstream media doesn't welcome dissidents who ask embarrassing questions about large corporations. She is also an original and irrepressible personality, an untamed presence in a world of documentary that is increasingly dominated by branded, technically competent, knee-jerk sensationalist product and far-too-obedient makers. But she doesn't cultivate a reputation as an exile or outlier; rather, she attempts to make films for all of us. In the process of doing so, she has charted new territory in documentary. She has done so by putting a sharply social spin on the personal-essay genre, by incorporating humor in her social messages, and by building partnerships with social activist organizations throughout the filmmaking process.

Helfand has aggressively reshaped the long-standing independent tradition of personal essay documentary, and turned it toward explicit social critique and social action. The personal essay film turns on the character of the filmmaker, which of course is always a creation. Helfand has created a persona that, far from the idiosyncratic, exploratory and tentative one that many other filmmakers adopt in pursuit of themselves (think of Ross McElwee with *Sherman's March* or Rea Tajiri with *History and Memory*), is quite assertive and well-defined.

In her films she plays the role of an ordinary Jewish-American, middle-class girl, someone who was ready to grow up to be an ordinary Jewish-American, middle-class woman. What has exiled her from that ambition is corporate fecklessness, which exposed her family to DES and blighted her reproductive future. She is now someone denied the rights of ordinariness, someone whose mission is to defend the right of people leading ordinary lives not to be similarly plunged into extremity and tragedy. The precise social specificity of her identity—in suburban Long Island, to be exact—becomes a calling card to viewers and a claim that, like them, she is someone who has the right to ordinary happiness.

She says that the link between her own misfortunes and those of others in corporate America dawned on her while working on *Uprising*. She was interviewing a miner afflicted with black lung. The miner asked her why she wasn't at home having babies, and she told him about her hysterectomy, caused by a drug company's irresponsibility. He seemed astonished, not that it had happened but that it had happened to a white, middle-class girl. It was then, she has said, that she understood that they had in common a vulnerability to corporate power.

In *A Healthy Baby Girl*, there is an elision between personal therapy and public activism. The camera becomes her ally in rebuilding her life and her relationship with her mother, which simultaneously is an exposé of corporate greed. The film's mission is explicit at the start, when Helfand and her lawyer, with whom she filed a lawsuit against the Eli Lilly pharmaceutical company that made the DES prescribed to her mother, discuss her motives for filming. She says that it is her way of coping, and of resisting her mother's feelings of shame and guilt. "My mother is one of nine million mothers, I am one of three million daughters. This is very public," she says before breaking into tears.

The video-diary format testifies constantly to the overlap between private and public, never more vividly than when her mother tries to hide from the camera. The mother and daughter are attending a DES convention, where it sinks in for both that a relapse of cancer is possible. The mother flees from the camera, and the screen goes dark. The wireless microphone picks up a hallway conversation, where the mother repeats, "I'm a private person," and says she can't go on being in the film. The daughter insists that it's to make their story public, so that they won't have to stand in a hallway and cry, that she is working. Eventually the mother agrees.

Blue Vinyl continues and elaborates the techniques and perspective of *A Healthy Baby Girl*. The diary format is back, and so is the sometimes petulant, a little spoiled, stubbornly public central figure of Helfand, the voice of ordinary citizens. Her parents also return, similarly playing the role of bemused middle-class "private people," taken aback by their daughter but even more taken aback by the upturning of their lifelong assumption that they could trust the large corporate institutions that embed them. She shows herself vulnerable and nervous while preparing to face the spokesman for The Vinyl Institute, and when she does, the David-Goliath meeting turns out well for David.

Helfand has also pioneered in developing a new genre of documentary: the self-described "toxic comedy." The term refers not to jokes or happy endings but to a tone of wry insouciance and cheerful resistance to corporate greed and indifference to human suffering. It also points specifically to the central problem her films address: corporate poisoning of individual lives. *A Healthy Baby Girl* employs offbeat humor throughout, connecting the domestic with the public. For example, a discussion of whether the filmmaker's ova might also be contaminated with DES happens in the family's kitchen, as the mother cooks—of course—scrambled eggs. In *Blue Vinyl*, Helfand goes everywhere with a piece of her parents' vinyl siding under her arm, metonymically taking her house with her and making it everybody's house. (The organizing Web site associated with the film is called myhouseisyourhouse.org.)

Documentarians have, since the origins of film, made a special claim on viewer attention because they speak the truth, and documentary form is blessed or burdened with an expectation that it participate in what theorist Bill Nichols calls the "discourses of sobriety." Helfand participates in this tradition, although she never has made the fatal mistake of assuming that anyone would care. As she has developed her persona and learned from her experiences, she has also developed a capacity for storytelling that celebrates the joy in autonomy—whether it's in being able to ask the questions, or seek out others in a common quest, or to find alternatives to seemingly enchaining social options.

Other documentarians also employ little-guy humor for serious purposes. Michael Moore (*Roger and Me*, *The Big One*, *Bowling for Columbine*, and *Fahrenheit 911*) creates an honest-working-man persona, someone who guilelessly exposes the guile, hypocrisy, false claims, and pretension of the powerful. In *Super Size Me*, Morgan Spurlock is the genial all-American who can challenge McDonald's implicit equation with all-Americanness just because he is such a burger-and-fries kind of guy.

Helfand's feminine little-guy is both more vulnerable (she uses her own body as an example of corporate invasion of individual autonomy) and more collaborative. She evokes sympathy, extends it, and seeks out collaborators, on-screen and off. Her questions are those of a lay person, not even of an accuser. She uses her seeming harmlessness to dramatic advantage, for instance to contrast the personality-filled individual and the soulless corporate world (represented among others by a drug company representative who mouths embarrassing platitudes in *A Healthy Baby Girl* and the bulletproof spokesman from the Vinyl Institute in *Blue Vinyl*). She also dramatizes the commonalities between her own quest and that of the organized and outraged (for instance, the DES daughters in *A Healthy Baby Girl* and mobilized citizens of Lake Charles, Mississippi, afflicted with multifarious health problems from dioxin in *Blue Vinyl*).

Finally, Helfand has articulated the process of making social documentary as a social process with activist partners. There has always been a tension in social documentary between the filmmaker and the social activist. Most social documentarians have been more filmmaker than social activist, and many depend on others to use their films effectively. What Helfand has so distinctively done is to erode the distinction between filmmaking and "outreach." She has done this by seeking out social actors in the story she is telling, and developing strategic alliances as she goes along. Thus, with *Uprising*, Helfand and Stoney showed pieces of the film repeatedly to older interviewees, to younger organizers, to anti-union people, and to organizers on health and safety issues. Workshopping the film, as she describes it, transformed the film and convinced her of the importance of a collective process in shaping any work that was intended to effect social change. In *A Healthy Baby Girl*, she built alliances with DES daughter organizations, with environmental justice organizations, and with Jewish groups in preview screenings of the film. In *Blue Vinyl*, she developed a working relationship with the Lake Charles community activists early on, a relationship that then led to a grant for the film from The Ford Foundation.

This strategy is so important to Helfand's work that she, in company with organizer Robert West, launched Working Films (workingfilms.org). The organization describes itself as "an activist-driven bridge between high quality documentary filmmaking and serious grassroots organizing." The organization argues that "social justice docs can be as resonant and effective as they are engaging and entertaining."

Judith Helfand's work marries personality, story, and passion for social justice. "At the core there always has to be a relationship at stake," she has said, "and a heart at risk of being broken. That is what happens in most of my films—that we were able find that heart that was at risk of being broken, and we were committed to fixing it."

Helfand continues to work on environmental health issues. Her next project focuses on global warming and climate change.

PART 4

Lost between Genre and Myth-Making

15

Guy Maddin

The Beardo

José Mojica Marins

What image comes to mind when a stranger on the street approaches and utters the words "Coffin Joe"? For it's some that bootblack, bristle-brush beard; for others those jellyfish eyes. Of course, a healthy number focus on the horny, curling fingernails, and a precious few contrarians (precious to me when, as so often, *I* am that stranger on the street) will blather on dazedly about Coffin Joe's stove-top hat, which he might have personally snatched off Lincoln's dying, gay head in the Ford Theatre those many years ago. Ah, but no beard, eyes, fingernails, or even hat for me: I say the man's lower lip tells us all we need to know, resting easy as it does on those coarse black chin whiskers, fat and satisfied like a satiated cutworm or like the vulva of a woman who's been quite willingly stuffed into a hyper-realistic cow costume and rolled into a busy bullpen. That shiny, rosy kissy-lip *is* Coffin Joe to me, and all the more so when it peels lazily back to release waves of booming laughter.

For all the years I spent musing dreamily about that dangling skindootle, I never knew about the existence of another man with a similarly fleshy mandible: a Brazilian horror-movie director named José Mojica

Marins. How much warmer my bed might have been had I only known there were more than one of those tumescent, buttock-like mouth curtains out in the world! Now I'm told they're one and the same, Mojica and Coffin Joe, and I feel glad for my ignorance. Going back to one after dreaming of two might have struck me dead.

Mojica and his bottom lip were born in Sao Paolo in 1935, and there they've been ever since, making movies and raising hell! He hit one right out of the park with his very first effort: a short about flying coffins from outer space blasting the local priests with death rays. His earliest effort to make a feature left a series of dead or double-amputee actresses in its wake—as soon as he cast his distaff lead, she would drown in a pool, or contract tuberculosis, or involve herself in a mutilating car accident; and so Mojica would begin his search anew. (Any director recognizes this as only the typical casting experience carried out to a slightly exaggerated extreme.) Of course we know that, after a few career false starts with a Western and a drama of reckless youth (pointless genres for a talent like Mojica's), he had a spooky, history-making dream which resulted in the creation of Coffin Joe, the star of his first horror movie *At Midnight I'll Take Your Soul.* Mojica played the character himself, naturally.

Though it was made in 1964, the first Coffin Joe adventure looks at least thirty years older than that. Joe—more Portugesely known as Zé do Caixão—is a strutting undertaker with a resonant laugh and a coarse, anticlerical manner, who terrorizes the provincial bozos in his town by eating meat on a Friday while mocking their holy-day processions (which don't look much fun anyway). On the side, Joe lusts after his best friend's wife; all the more so after his initial advances to her are met with a vicious chomp on that gorgeous crimson wattle. Properly motivated now, he commits a series of unholy outrages in his pursuit of the girl, and eventually ends up in a graveyard, terrorized by the ghosts of his victims until his eyes bug out (via unconvincing prostheses) and he appears to be dead. His shimmering underlip quivers no more. The soundtrack emits much screaming!

Thankfully Coffin Joe was not really dead, or I might never have heard of him. The box-office success of his horror debut assured a sequel, so Mojica gathered up his faithful crew, converted a synagogue into a movie studio and made *Tonight I'll Incarnate In Your Corpse* (1967). Ho ho, is that a threat or a promise? This one featured even more random screaming on the soundtrack, a color sequence set in a Hell that resembles the ice planet Hoth as set decorated by Damien Hirst, and lots of great beardo action. And it was a marvelous hit! What an enchanting place mid-sixties Brazil must have been.

By then, Coffin Joe was the Freddy Krueger of his day. And yet it was hard for the great bellowing maniac to attract the money for his newest Joe adventure (a real problem, sometimes, in continuing characters, as I have found in my fruitless efforts to fund a series of feature-length episodes about *Archangel*'s Lt. Boles). But Mojica persisted, and came up with a truly bewitching—and not a little upsetting—concoction: *Awakening of the Beast* (1970). Again the soundtrack is composed of near-constant screaming (a daring gambit, ill suited to cross-promotion), and almost every shot seems to have been made with a different type of film stock. Brutal spankings are meted out to the female cast members! Flaccid bottoms are painted with faces! A mad hippie shepherd violates women with his crook! All this; and with that wet liver-slab of a lip convulsing in jollity, the world tilts a little further on its axis. *Ha-ha-ha-ha!*

No one has ever made another movie like it, and no one ever will. But here I must part company with the accepted wisdom of the Coffin Joe appreciation community. As the most frenzied film appearance of the be-whiskered super-anti-hero (he appeared once more in a sort of clip show best-of called *Hallucinations of a Deranged Mind* (1978) and the 1974 proto–*Wes Craven's New Nightmare* meta-movie *Black Exorcism*), *Awakening of the Beast* is held in the highest esteem—Mojica's masterpiece, they say. The finest film he ever made. But no, and a thousand times, no!

For we must acknowledge *Finis Hominis* (1971), the movie Mojica made after *Awakening of the Beast*—the movie he made, you might say, after his beast had been fully awakened. By this point Mojica was tired of being identified with his most famous (not to mention, practically his only) character, Coffin Joe, and who can blame him? How often could you endure walking the streets of Sao Paolo and being asked on the spot to perform that iconic staccato laugh or to pull down your lower lip for the entertainment of the children? Only so long; and so it was with Mojica. His reaction was to create and essay a character in every way Joe's opposite: a beautiful man of peace and radiant light whose mission on earth was to help people, not harm them. Finis Hominis was such a man, never mind how much he looked like Coffin Joe.

He is first seen rising from the sea wearing his birthday suit, his great beard and prominent lower lip at first kept from the camera's view in a maddening tease. Naked, he strolls through Sao Paolo: across multiple lanes of traffic, through crowds of children, past lovers embracing, into the homes of wheelchair-bound old ladies. (One gets the feeling that the film was made for no other reason than to give Mojica a chance to do these things: a motivating principle I admire unreservedly.) The movie shifts to what might be the first scene in a formula thriller: a woman's car is stopped by a fallen tree, and a burly child-snatcher—the very image of Popeye's great nemesis Bluto—grabs her daughter and runs off, as she's restrained (with a rape likely to follow) by a pair of swarthy, fantastically attired miscreants. All it takes is an appearance by the bare-assed Finis and the criminals are burning leather back into the jungle from whence they sprang.

Through this opening sequence we see once again that Mojica will use any dirty bit of film stock he's given. Color, black and white, rejected by Edison as too old for use, doesn't matter. Every Mojica film looks like a pastiche filmed over months or years, when he might have worked on highly disciplined two-week schedules for all I know. Only Mojica, or his loyal hunchbacked assistant director Vilbur, know for sure.

Finis arrives at the home of a mysterious woman, who gives him an outfit to wear. It's a class act all the way, like Finis himself: a great bespangled coat of red, giant mood beads, golden sandals, a voyageur's *ceinture fléchée*, and a bulbous crimson turban to top it all off. Thus furbished, Finis strides into the world to do *even more good*. A blind beggar gets alms; an irritating paparazzo gets a boot to the chest and his camera flung into a duck pond. Finis glowers at everyone he passes, and a light, bouncy instrumental rendition of "Raindrops Keep Falling On My Head" plays on the soundtrack—the song's finest use in a film ever, by the way.

(A small digression: Little remarked upon are Mojica's talents as a needle-drop DJ or sound-collage artist. You just never know what his musical tracks are going to offer up next! Deprived of the hellscreams that decorated his Coffin Joe soundtracks, Mojica here employs an endless and completely random series of musical cues to add joyous and bewildering moods. From sprightly rock numbers or toneless ghost noises, the musical landscape shifts dizzyingly through a toy-piano rendition of the theme from *Goldfinger* to the Moldavian national anthem, to a cheerful sung tribute to Rio played over shots of a despairing man walking that city's streets, and to many other enchanting found sounds after that.)

Finis and his glorious raiment arrive at a church, where, over the feeble protestations of the priest, he gulps down all the sacramental wine. Smacking his big pork-chop lips (oh the mighty dangler!), he emerges from the church into the waiting arms of police, who stuff burly Finis into the back of their VW bug on charges of vagrancy and extreme panache. But the very next scene shows us monochrome footage of a radio newsreader, who informs us of Finis's immediate, apparently effortless escape.

He's next seen in a restaurant, eating his fill. As he makes his way to the door, a troublesome waiter approaches. "You must pay the bill," says the waiter. Finish responds, "Your bill is of the corporeal world. I will not pay it." This episode becomes the talk of the town, or at least the talk of two garrulous secretaries we see gossiping in a beautiful, shimmering black-and-white sequence gorgeously photographed by Mojica's long-suffering cameraman Giorgio Attili.

The scene shifts to a hospital, and here I think Mojica and his crew must have become a little confused. It's meant to be a dramatic sequence showing an injured girl suffering in the midst of a heartless or otherwise occupied hospital staff. The pathos is greatly undercut by the brown hue of the "blood" used on the girl—it's chocolate syrup, which we all know is what Hitch poured down the plug-hole in *Psycho*, but it doesn't serve the purpose so well in color. My theory is they forgot what film stock they were using that day: an understandable mistake that only lends to the charm of the movie. Anyway, Finis arrives and sees to it that the entire negligent staff—dozens of doctors and nurses—all crowd into the operating theater at once to take care of the girl. Like his spectacular escape from the police and clever dodging of a restaurant bill, this latest *grand folie* hits the front pages of every newspaper in Brazil.

At this point, we expect the powers that be to turn against Finis, to start banging together some crosses, warming up the boiling lead and so forth. This is a Jesus parable, isn't it? But Mojica is no kind of filmmaker if not an unpredictable one, and none of that happens. Instead, Finis, a Duracell Bunny of goodwill, keeps on helping. First he bails out an adulteress who's been chased from her love-bed by the cuckolded husband and his entire family. Before they can beat her to death, Finis intervenes and exposes their hypocrisy to each other and the world: a whole family of recreant leches, it turns out, right down to Granny! You almost want the movie to be about them now, but no, it's onward, ever onward, to the next moral lesson.

Which is a doozy, the dooziest of the entire movie. It begins with a middle-aged combover guy (slobbering over a nubile young girl): a millionaire, we learn, and his perfidious young wife. She's in league with the millionaire's family, who all live with him, and everyone wants him dead; he, meanwhile, is the sweetest, most naïve and trusting millionaire ever.

He's off on a trip; within seconds she's humping the nephew. Here we learn an important plot point: she can only cry while taking it, as we used to say in the schoolyard, up the hoop. And yet she loves it. This becomes important when the family apparently manages to kill the kindly millionaire by faking the young wife's death (a scene scored with a mind-blowing sonic whip-pan between tootling calliope music and the toneless moans of the damned).

I've often wondered what might be the best funeral scene ever filmed. *Imitation of Life* always seemed a shoo-in. But, apologies to Doug Sirk, it's just got to be the millionaire's funeral in *Finis Hominis*. Set to the woozy strains of *Auld Lang Syne*, we see that the widow's dry eyes are causing a scandal among the mourners. The conspirators are in a panic: how can they make her cry so as to stave off suspicion? Well, why not just bugger her right there in front of everyone, *right over the corpse of her husband!* Her slimy tears rain down across his forehead! None of the mourners seem to notice the act of sodomy occurring before them! The casket is about to close, when finally—finally!—Finis arrives and declares the man not dead at all but only a helpless cataleptic. He rises from the coffin as the mourners panic and flee. Best funeral scene ever!

The cult of Finis grows exponentially after that, but by then the eighty-minute running time of this delightful movie is almost up so it's time for him to make one last cliff-top announcement before disappearing from the world he's helped so much. He reveals the meaning of life (I won't spoil it for you); and in the middle of this über-dramatic sequence, Mojica the filmmaker (as opposed to Mojica the maniacal narcissist) can't resist a last jab at the mass-media machine, cutting to a technician in his RV-sized mobile unit who dispassionately declares, "This broadcast will beat all of our ratings records."

And so, having turned the world on its ear, Finis returns to the Sanatorium for Nervous Disorders, where he's a patient. "I told you he always comes back," a doctor says. An excellent punch line to a fine feature-length joke!

José Mojica Marins! A filmmaker for the rest of us. Forever he will stand erect before me in my dreams, his fat lower lip unrolled like a window blind, ready, willing, and oh so able to deliver his singular brand of enchantment.

16

Maitland McDonagh

Dellamorte Dellamore and Michele Soavi

Dellamorte Dellamore. It glides off the tongue like limoncello, sweet and tart and potent all at once, a marvelous title for a blackly ironic fairy tale suffused in equal parts with morbid eroticism and gut-crunching violence. So what possessed October Films, during its brief reign as king of the arty horror movie hill (by virtue of having released Guillermo del Toro's 1993 *Cronos*, Abel Ferrara's *The Addiction*, and Michael Almereyda's *Nadja* in rapid succession), to rechristen it *Cemetery Man*? Hiding Michele Soavi's remarkable achievement behind a title simultaneously lurid and banal was a stroke of invention on a par with releasing George Franju's sublimely shuddery *Eyes Without a Face* (1959) as *The Horror Chamber of Dr. Faustus*.

Meet Francesco Dellamorte (Rupert Everett), cemetery man. He's a soulful loner, almost Byronic in his brooding beauty—shown to great advantage in several lingering shower scenes. He's the caretaker of small town Buffalora's cemetery, where corpses have suddenly begun rising from their graves. "Returners," he calls them, as he sends them back with a well-placed bullet to the brain. Dellamorte's sidekick—equal part monstrous mascot, right-hand man, and butt of various childishly cruel jokes—is the cemetery's nearly-mute grounds keeper, Gnaghi. A bald brute with a child's mind, a gargoyle's grin, and the soul of a misunderstood dreamer, he's played by monstrously fat French pop star François Hadji-Lazaro, who's also featured in the gallery of grotesques assembled by Marc Caro and Jean-Pierre Jeunet for *City of Lost Children* (1995).

Lean and austerely dressed in black and white, Dellamorte has death written all over him. The Dellamore part arrives in the form of Italian supermodel Anna Falchi, credited only as "She." Arrives three times, in fact: Falchi is in turn a luscious young widow, the Mayor's starchy personal assistant, and a disingenuous prostitute, all faces of the archetypal unattainable woman, and all of whom Dellamorte loves and loses. At the same time, Gnaghi falls in love with the mayor's daughter, Valentina (Fabiana Formica); she spurns him in life, but her grisly death in a motorcycle accident—she's decapitated—sets the stage for a great romance. Working from a screenplay by Gianni Romoli (*La Scorta*), Soavi swirls together fright-night conventions, pop psychology, pulp nihilism, and romantic symbolism in a rich truffle of a horror movie.

The film's richly and self-consciously poetic title sounds like some sort of joke. But it is, in fact, in perfect sync with the film's languid, tarnished lushness. *Dellamorte Dellamore* doesn't have the bright, hard-edged look that many movies adapted from comics affect. Its look owes as much to late eighteenth/early nineteenth-century romantic painting as to horror-movie conventions or, for that matter, the starkly black-and-white *Dylan Dog* comics to which it's related. One reason Italian audiences flocked to *Dellamorte Dellamore* is its association with the hugely popular *Dylan Dog* series, created by recluse Tiziano Sclavi—who maintains a provocative air of mystery by refusing to be interviewed. Dylan Dog isn't a dog: he's a darkly handsome "investigator of nightmares" who lives at 7 Craven Road, London. He first appeared in 1986, investigating creepy cases that sometimes involved the supernatural and sometimes came down to sheer human nastiness. His name pays homage to Dylan Thomas, rather than Bob Dylan, and his world-weary antiheroism is equal parts art-school affectation and soul sickness. Italians love him: They love his coolness, his self-mockery, his pulpy intellectual pretensions, even his goofy butler, Groucho Marx. Pioneering semiotitian Umberto Eco once told the *New York Times* that *Dylan Dog* is his favorite nighttime reading, and didn't seem the least bit embarrassed at sharing his bedtime preference with the average Italian bike messenger. *Dylan Dog* is a rare thing in Italy, an authentically home-grown pop phenomenon that has nothing at all to do with America.

Dellamorte Dellamore isn't a *Dylan Dog* story per se; it's based on one of Sclavi's novels. But *Dylan Dog* by any other name is still *Dylan Dog*. Purists can haggle, but *Dellamorte Dellamore* is "Secret Agent" to *Dylan*

Dog's "The Prisoner," and casting the notoriously self-important Rupert Everett in the lead seals the deal: When Sclavi was first asked how Dylan Dog should be drawn, he replied, "like Rupert Everett." But Soavi's range of reference extends far beyond *Dylan Dog*. *Dellamorte Dellamore* is morbidly romantic and cruelly funny, its disparate influences written into every frame: *Night of the Living Dead*, René Magritte, Jean Rollin, *Re-Animator*, Todd Browning's *The Unknown*, Italian Westerns, Mario Bava's *Blood and Black Lace*, Matthew Gregory Lewis's *The Monk*, American sitcoms, *The Adventures of Baron Munchausen*, the offbeat horror-biker picture *Psychomania* . . . it's crammed with allusions, general and specific.

The credits roll over the image of an elaborate snow globe containing two small figures standing on the edge of a cliff, then we're introduced to Dellamorte. He's hunched gloomily in his chair, trying to have a quiet phone conversation while the grim and grisly ranks of the undead claw annoyingly on his door. The film ends on a revelatory note, with Gnaghi and Dellamorte trying to escape Buffalora, only to find that the road drops off into an inexplicable abyss—anyone who finds the closing scene confusing just hasn't been taking notice. *Dellamorte Dellamore* is utterly self-contained, a closed sphere in which time and chronology mean nothing, the dead and the living mingle freely, the glorious and the grotesque are inextricably intertwine, in which one woman can be three and three one, in which no personality is immutable—not even Dellamorte's. That said, *Dellamorte Dellamore*'s plot is picaresque (to put the best face on it), more a series of sketches than a sustained narrative. Dellamorte dispatches living corpses, spars with local functionaries who don't want to hear about his problems and falls in love with "She" in three different guises. He fails at romance and is chastised by Death himself for killing the dead, so he begins to murder the living as well, starting with the local toughs who taunt him in the town square. Some of the episodes are rich indeed: Dellamorte and the widow She making love on her late husband's grave. The visit from Death, who materializes out of a bonfire's swirling smuts. Dellamorte's murder of the prostitute She. The besotted Gnaghi's brief bliss with Valentina's smirking, wayward head—pure sitcom slapstick with a necrophilic twist. The attack of the rampaging troupe of zombie Boy Scouts, all prissy little uniforms and snapping teeth. Dellamorte's nightmarish visit to a local doctor, by whom he wants to be castrated. If they don't quite cohere, they're nevertheless hypnotic. Linear storytelling has never been the strong suit of Italian horror, and *Dellamorte Dellamore* wears its narrative laxity better than most because it's bound together by the intertwined themes of the carnal and the charnel.

Dellamorte Dellamore shifts tone rapidly between grim humor, ostentatious violence, and perverse sensuality, but above all maintains a delicate ambiguity about its internal world. What, exactly, is happening at Buffalora cemetery? Are corpses truly coming back, or is it all Dellamorte's delusion, born of too many nights spent brooding in his cottage in the city of the dead? Does he really fall in love with three identical women, each of whom exacerbates his neurotic sexual insecurities? Or are we watching an elaborate psychosexual nightmare? The first She intensifies his shameful impotence by telling him her late husband—a man so old Dellamorte assumed he was her father—was sexually insatiable. The second confesses a morbid fear of men's organs, so he tries to have his cut off. But when he recovers from the injection he receives instead (the doctor couldn't bring himself to amputate such a fine member), She tells him she's going to marry her boss. He raped her, she explains, but then they did it again nicely and she realized the error of her abstinent ways. The third She successfully takes Dellamorte to bed, but fails to mention that it's a cash transaction, provoking him to literally incendiary rage.

The film's cemetery scenes, with shuffling corpses dragging themselves out of the ground, could fit nicely into any particularly well-photographed cannibal zombie movie. But they're interspersed with Kafka-esque visits to various institutional quagmires. Take the office of Dellamorte's bureaucrat friend Franco (Anton Alexander), who helps him file the appropriate form for living dead problems: It's a Collyer brothers maze of paper and folders. Or the hospital where Franco lies following a suicide attempt, apparently a sparking refuge from the chaos of the world outside. Dellamorte walks in, slaughters doctors, nurses, and nuns, then walks away unnoticed, leaving the white tile floors glazed with blood. The Columbo-like police inspector, assigned to investigate the surprisingly large number of murders in apparently peaceful Buffalora, seems to be from another film—a comic gumshoe who never quite gets what's going on. And why doesn't he suspect Dellamorte, when substantial evidence places the gloomy outcast at the location of every crime? Immediately after the hospital massacre, the inspector spies Dellamorte on the stairs and tells him to clear out, because there's a madman on the loose, killing people.

Fans of Italian horror director Dario Argento and Euro-exploitation in general know Soavi's name; otherwise, he's an unknown quantity outside Italy. Born in Milan in 1957, Soavi began his career in movies as an actor, doomed by his blond, blue-eyed good looks to play Americans in knockoffs of popular U.S. films. Soavi found his first mentor in veteran exploitation director Aristede Massaccesi, whose breadth of sleazy genre credits is rivaled only by the number of pseudonyms under which he has worked. The best known—notorious is probably the better way of putting it—is Joe D'Amato. Over the course of several films, including Mad

Max knockoffs *2020 Texas Gladiators* (1982) and *Endgame—Bronx Lotta Finale* (1983), *Conan the Barbarian* knockoff *Ator the Invincible* (1983) and *Caligula* knockoff *Caligula: The Untold Story* (1981), Soavi tinkered with screenplays, worked as Massaccesi's personal assistant, and played bit parts. Soavi met Italian horror legend Argento when he auditioned for a role in *Inferno* (1980); the part went to Gabriele Lavia, but Soavi persuaded Argento to let him work on his next picture, *Tenebrae* (1982), and later played the thankless role of a police inspector in *Phenomena* (*Creepers*) (1985). His first stab at directing was a 1985 music video for Bill Wyman's spooky composition "Valley," from the soundtrack of *Phenomena*. It was Massaccesi who produced Soavi's first feature, *Bloody Bird* (1986, also called *Deliria*, *Stagefright*, and *Aquarius*), an assured slasher picture in which silly thespians rehearsing in an old, dark theater are terrorized by a psychopath in an oversized owl-head mask, but Argento's influence is all over the baroque visuals and voluptuous violence. Quentin Tarantino enthusiastically declared it "The best Italian horror film of the 1980s."

The Church (*La Chiesa*) (1990) was developed for Lamberto Bava, one of Argento's less-talented protégés despite his world-class bloodlines (his father was horror legend Mario Bava); Soavi came in at the eleventh hour. He and *Dellamorte* screenwriter Romoli did their best to whip the script—in which a cross section of unfortunates trapped in a cursed Cathedral devolve into a bloody orgy of demonic debauchery—into shape, and the result is a polished genre exercise distinguished by startlingly fluid camera work and inventive shot transitions. *The Sect* (*La Setta*) (1991), released in the United States on video as *The Devil's Daughter*, involves a satanic cult and the innocent school teacher upon whom they have evil designs, but its dreamy images—including a snowglobe that looks forward to *Dellamorte*, a tree twinkling with macabre talismans, and slyly sinister fluffy bunnies—are uniquely haunting. They're all indebted to Argento's convoluted narratives and distinctive visual palette, but you can see Soavi's own sensibility working its way to the surface. Soavi met his third mentor, mainstream surrealist Terry Gilliam, at a film festival in Brussels, and Gilliam hired him as second unit director on *The Adventures of Baron Munchausen* (1988)—whose spiral into logistical problems, infighting, executive interference, and costly scams turned it into a disaster of legendary proportions—which was no doubt instructive. Soavi credits Gilliam—who, like Argento, manifestly values style over storytelling—as a great influence. Gilliam says he wishes Soavi would get out of horror, that it's limiting him.

Dellamorte Dellamore was a substantial hit in Italy and was embraced at festivals like including London's Shock Around the Clock at the National Film Theater, where it made its English language debut in 1994.

But *Dellamorte Dellamore* failed to set the box office on fire—it's hard not to lay some blame on that title, which misled exploitation audiences and turned off the art-house crowd—and Soavi dropped out of sight, taking a break from filmmaking for family reasons. When he came back five years later, the Italian horror filone had dried up and he turned to television, churning out highly rated but formulaic crime pictures interspersed with more interesting projects, including a 2002 biography of St. Francis of Assisi and a 2003 film about real-life serial killer Donato Bilancia, who murdered seventeen people in and around Genoa in 1998.

Soavi's return to feature films seems imminent: At the time of this writing, he was in preproduction on *Arrivederci Amore, Ciao*, based on the bestselling thriller by Massimo Carlotto, famous in Italy for having spent seventeen Kafkaesque years fighting the law, three as a fugitive and more in jail, after being railroaded on a murder charge in 1976. Carlotto turned to crime writing after receiving a pardon in 1993. Further, old collaborator Gianni Romoli—who became an influential producer after getting his feet wet with *Dellamorte* (his credits include Turkish-born director Ferzan Ozpetek's acclaimed *Steam: The Turkish Bath* [1996], *His Secret Life* [2001], and *Facing Windows* [2003])—has offered Soavi the pick of two of his recent screenplays. One of Romoli's scripts is a vampire story called *Meridian Demons*, and the other a mega-budget remake of the hugely popular, 1941 Italian fantasy epic *The Iron Crown*, which Romoli calls "The Italian *Lord of the Rings*." So there's reason to hope that one of the brightest lights of the contemporary Italian cinefantastique will burn brightly for years to come.

17

Mark Peranson

Guy Maddin

Few artists are as underappreciated in their home country as Canadian filmmaker Guy Maddin, and few underappreciated artists have been as overexposed abroad. 2005 saw a brief respite in the Maddinmania that peaked in 2003, when three major, very different Maddin films—plus a book of his diaries and writings, *From the Atelier Tovar*—were in wide circulation: the stupendous silent movie-ballet *Dracula: Pages from a Virgin's Diary*; the experimental *Cowards Bend the Knee*, which mixes autobiography, hockey, *Electra*, and *The Hands of Orlac*; and the Isabella Rossellini-starring, "proper" feature film, *The Saddest Music in the World*. To grab a metaphor from one of Maddin's favorite pastimes, this output is the cinematic equivalent to the Wayne Gretzky-led Edmonton Oilers hockey dynasty of the late 1980s; it puts noted Japanese firebrand Miike Takeshi to shame. Currently, Maddin had two more films debut in 2005: a Super 8 featurette, *Brand Upon the Brain!*, set in a Vigo-like orphanage; and a short film about the wholly un-Maddinesque Roberto Rossellini, written and starring Maddin's newest friend, Rossellini's daughter.

As anyone who has had the pleasure of seeing a Maddin film surely knows, while the director has a keen knowledge of film history, his tastes fall far away from the documentary veracities of Italian neorealism. Born in the 1950s, Guy Maddin is stuck in the 1920s. Since 1985, Canada's poster boy for idiosyncracy has made seven highly personal features and a grab bag of shorts that, despite their surrealist trappings and affinity for silent cinema, are impossible to pigeonhole. Remaking melodramatic part-talkies that never existed, Maddin works in his own genre. Never too far removed from mythos, a movie reference, or his vaunted childhood anxieties, Maddin's riotous, emotionally masochistic curiosities entertain and confuse, delight and dislocate. Perhaps now's the time for Maddin: Nostalgia and romancing the past are currently as de rigeur as the glorification of kitsch, and the self-flagellating Maddin provides all these in spades.

Raised above his Aunt Lil's beauty salon—which became the studio for his feature debut, *Tales from the Gimli Hospital*—and Winnipeg's hockey arena, Maddin's Icelandic childhood on the Canadian Prairies was one of slothdom, craning his ears to the ambient crackling of late-night radio signals to catch Minnesota Twins ball games. (So he claims: Anything Maddin says should be taken with a shakerful of salt.) Along with glorious memories of scrubbing the backs of unibrowed Soviet hockey players, there was private tragedy: While Maddin was young, his hockey-manager father died and his older brother committed suicide. The eighties saw the creative flourishing of the Winnipeg Film Group, North America's most inspirational cold-weather co-op, led by prairie postmodern trailblazer John Paizs (Maddin appeared, in drag, as a nurse in Paizs's short *The International Style*). Maddin's primitivism stems from the limited means of these early days—using handheld cameras, monochrome film, and effects like Vaseline on the lens, he proves the most valuable tool is a pliable imagination.

While slacking off during these salad days with friends like eventual producer Greg Klymkiw and John Harvie (lead of Maddin's first short, 1985's *The Dead Father*), Maddin home-schooled in rabid cinephilia, watching 16mm noirs, melodramas, and silents borrowed from local libraries and projected in the apartment of University of Manitoba professor Stephen Snyder (his neighbor); remnants of these 1,001 nights speckle his own movies. Galloping through the Riefenstahl meets *Caligari*-influenced *Careful* (1992), for example, one finds allusions to Von Sternberg, Hitchcock, Keaton, Ophuls, Méliès, and Clair. One should also note Maddin and frequent screenwriter George Toles's literary tastes: Knut Hamsun, Robert Walser, and Bruno Schulz, among others, have all lent their frank and twisted thoughts for Maddin's cultivated concoctions. (An early curio found in *From the Atelier Tovar* is an autobiographical script titled *A Child Without Qualities*, *pace* Robert Musil.)

But the way Maddin juggles his sources is based on forgetfulness—both the viewers' and his own. After bringing up one reference, he quickly moves along, never allowing another filmmaker to cohabit his recaptured cinematic space for too long, never allowing viewers to dwell on the twisted narrative. Haunted by lovelorn amnesiacs, the films' surfaces bubble with the overwrought, illogical grippes of passion. "The only real themes that matter to me are how humans love each other or hate each other or are envious of each other," Maddin has said, and a recurring scene finds two lovers isolated in a honeymoon suite, experiencing an idyllic moment soon soured by point three of the triangle. Sexuality breeds psychosis in these most noir of worlds: Maddin's movies sweep viewers prettily towards death and disappointment.

Maddin relishes highly manneristic acting styles resembling those of silent heroes like Conrad Veidt, with the director surrogates (in the early films, played by a delirious, vamping Kyle McCullough, now a staff writer for *South Park*) trapped in hilarious, hallucinating states of self-pitying cowardice. (Maddin and McCullough still claim they devised a numerical system for acting, with Maddin shouting out a digit, and McCullough responding with a particular emotion.) Yet despite their anachronisms and deliberate continuity errors, these tongue-in-cheek films never descend into full-blown camp or wistful nostalgia. How could anyone want to return to the absurdly corked-up Tolzbad of *Careful*—a painfully precise depiction of childhood repression? Maddin complicates nostalgia by placing a grain of sand in each oyster: Something's foul in these culturally toxic films, though damned if you don't want to wolf those oysters down.

Maddin's debut, *Tales from the Gimli Hospital* (1988) came out of nowhere, and kind of remains there. In the film, a deadly pestilence rages through the idyllic Manitoba town of Gimli, sometime in the late nineteenth-century. Maddin's amusingly nonsensical first feature is a deadpan tone poem focusing on the jealous relationship between the delirious Einar and his rotund, jocular hospital-mate, Gunnar. As they undergo unconventional medical treatments, the two discover something in common: sexual relations with Gunnar's late wife. A disjointed series of self-hating Icelandic heritage moments filtered through a fishy surrealist sensibility and the entire vocabulary of silent cinema, *Gimli* is possessed by a pre-Code morality encompassing homoeroticism, necrophilia, and, why not, a black-faced minstrel. Using only one key light, it's the work of a primeval fetishist: The camera focuses in on unusual body parts, like kneecaps, the space between eyebrows, and, in an odd Icelandic Glima wrestling scene—a nod to Ulmer's *The Black Cat*—the buttocks. Made over eighteen months with a script jotted on Post-It notes—that earned Maddin's only Genie nomination until he won for *The Heart of the World*—*Gimli* was notoriously rejected by Toronto International Film Festival programmers, who mistook the layered, crackling ambient soundtrack for amateurish.

Even more alienating yet involving, the timeless *Archangel* (1991) went on to win Best Experimental Film from the National Society of Film Critics. Love lost, found, then lost again forever illuminates the shadows of Maddin's wildly opaque yet touching melo-noir-drama inhabited by a phalanx of amnesiacs—plagued by obsession, mustard gas apoplexia, or both. The circular narrative revolves around McCullough's John Boles (named after the wooden actor and WWI U.S. spy), a displaced soldier at the end of the Great War steeped in loss: for his country (Canada), his girl (Iris), and his leg (the right one). Arriving in Archangel, the Russian outpost where the war still raged on, Boles falls madly in love with Iris's double, Veronkha, who has forgotten she's married to a brain-injured war vet—who himself only remembers their wedding night. A post-traumatic fever dream, *Archangel* fixates more over von Sternbergian moments of ritual than narrative clarity. It's exceedingly faithful to the filmic and patriotic sentiments of the postwar, while being indebted to Mervyn LeRoy's *Random Harvest* and, of course, *Vertigo*, a film haunting Maddin's oeuvre like a holy whore. Still, the director makes innumerable original contributions, including an intestine strangling scene and film history's most memorable calm-before-the-storm involving fluffy bunny rabbits.

He followed it up with a work many consider just as strong. *Careful* combines the disrespected *träumerei* genre with the reviled pro-incest theme of Herman Melville's *Pierre*. In the Alpine villa of Tolzbad—Maddin's Oedipal Oz, where the mountains are named for Minnesota Twins players—one false move can spur off a fatal avalanche. This constant altitude of repression finds two families immersed in sibling rivalry and sexual shenanigans. Brothers Johann and Grigorss are butlers in training who dream about ravaging their widowed mother—and damned if they don't try. Their temptress, though, is Klara, Tolzbad's own Electra: Along with her sister, she too lusts after their paterfamilias. Brushed with a tincture of John Ruskin, Maddin's first color film resembles the sweaty two-strip pastel Technicolor of *The King of Jazz*, yet feels insanely modern. Along with implementing a dizzying array of Méliès-like in-camera effects—not one shot in this mountain movie is an exterior—*Careful* finds Maddin extra-cautious to deliver a coherent, Wagnerian narrative, where tragedy lurks behind the gestating hysteria like a child peeking out of the safety of the womb.

Despite these successes, Maddin's "art films," criticized for their incoherent elitism, had been bombing at home: returning home after *Careful*'s sold-out debut at the New York Film Festival, Maddin was informed of the film's dire first-week Toronto returns. Soon after, Maddin was in submerged in a career funk. The government funding agency Telefilm Canada had decided not to support *The Dikemaster's Daughter*, which was to star none other than Leni Riefenstahl, deeming it a "lateral move." This failure would haunt the troubled production of the hermetic *Twilight of the Ice Nymphs* (1997): interviewed on set, Maddin vowed he'd never make another film. (In *Ice Nymphs*, Frank Gorshin's Cain Ball proclaims: "A man with no independence has little to call his own!") Plagued by difficulties, including a lead who had to be redubbed, Maddin says the end result "came out of the birth canal stillborn," and I, for one, cannot disagree.

This awareness of the lassitude possible when in pursuing arch stylization to its limits led to the realization that things should be sped up. Wedding his visions to micro-montage and musical accompaniment, Maddin's fertile second coming sees the filmmaker tossing off playful, aesthetically overloaded works laughing at traditional storytelling. This stage began in 2000 with the Soviet-constructivist, sci-fi headrush *The Heart of the World*; the first of Maddin's project of remaking lost films, it was inspired by Abel Gance's *Le fin du monde*. Jet-propelled from an Uzi of inspiration, Maddin's masterpiece—one of the greatest short films ever made, period—is an entire melodrama in six minutes, frenetically edited to elide any need for plot development. Ironically, this primitive has got his groove back through the use of contemporary technology—Maddin's recent work, with its pacing and invisible reframing, is unimaginable without digital editing.

Teeming with Gothic Victorianisms, Maddin's work for hire *Dracula: Pages from a Virgin's Diary* might be the most faithful screen version of Stoker's 1897 novel, ramping up the era's racial/immigration anxiety as well as its famously prohibitive sexuality. More than merely a dance film made by a director with absolutely no interest in dance, *Dracula* is an authentic Expressionist silent feature shot in oft-tinted monochrome. With ballet reflected in mirrors, shrouded by plumes of fog, or sped up, *Dracula* feels like Michael Jackson's "Thriller" epic crossed with Dreyer's *Vampyr*. It would be easy to refer to its aesthetic as music-video based, but much like videos have lifted cinematographic and editing techniques from the avant-garde, Maddin discovered a new kind of cinema by reclaiming these innovations.

Further proof comes with Maddin's "autobiography," made as an installation for Toronto's Power Plant, viewed crouching through peepholes. (It has since been reworked as a stand-alone hour-long featurette, which might be the perfect format and length for Maddin.) The tremendous *Cowards Bend the Knee* is a Feuillade serial blenderized, jam-packed with enough kinetically photographed action to seem like a never-ending cliffhanger. If fiction is sometimes barely disguised autobiography, *Cowards* is its mirror image, twisted and poisoned wish-fulfillment: The mythomaniacal Maddin casts "himself" as a hockey sniper made lily-livered by mother and daughter femme fatales, and resurrects his father as the team's radio broadcaster and his own romantic antagonist.

Set in a shadow-suffused hockey arena and a Mabuse-like beauty salon-slash-abortion clinic lined with two-way mirrors—a throwback to Aunt Lil's old place—the plot drips with the Grecian formula, as sordid family secrets spawn unintentional murder most foul. Veering into penny-dreadful territory with the introduction of a vengeful ghost and uncontrollable extremities as windows into the unconscious, *Cowards* recalls *The Hands of Orlac*; Maddin fixates on his characters' groping and fisting expressionist paws, bathing them in ethereal light and chopping them into dazzling, iris-heavy micro-montages. Room to pant is provided by slo-mo replays, alternately poignant and explosive: lurid, frenzied moments of impulsive violence and carnivorous sexuality lend this bewitchingly onanistic work the sublime naughtiness of an antique hand-cranked skin flick. It all takes place, after all, within a drop of sperm.

Compared to this, Maddin's most recent "proper feature" at the time of writing, *Saddest Music*, almost disappoints. Almost. Set in 1933 Winnipeg, a town that has accumulated "a glistening wealth of unhappiness," the audience-friendly *Saddest Music* has the ham-fisted Maddin touch. A Canadian-born Broadway "producer of musical spectaculars" (Mark McKinney) returns to Winnipeg, penniless, and comes to represent the United States in a contest hatched by Lady Port-Huntley (Isabella Rossellini, gussied up to resemble her mom) to promote the brewery's peaty wares south of the border with the impending cessation of Prohibition. The film again finds brothers battling, this time over a nymphomaniac amnesiac (Maria de Medeiros's Narcissa); father and son as romantic rivals (for Isabella's legless Port-Huntley); and two forms of cowardice: McKinney's crass extrovert Chester Kent (named for Cagney's *Footlight Parade* lead), and his veiled, timid, and self-hating brother, Roderick (Ross McMillan, last heard as the dubbed voice in *Ice Nymphs*), reborn as sensitive Serbian cellist Gavrilo the Great.

A full-fledged musical shot on Super 8 and 16mm, *Saddest Music* is politics fused with autobiography. Although alluding to Busby Berkeley's Broadway Melodies and the paraplegic revenge melodramas of Lon Chaney (such as *The Penalty*), the standard that links the film on an emotional level is Jerome Kern's "The Song Is You." The grist for the mill is Maddin's career, with the true conflict between art and commerce. In spite of the director's vehement denials—as nothing's worse for the box office today than politics—*Saddest Music* encourages a reading as a powerful statement on American cultural imperialism, made in the country that has suffered from it the most. Desiring to put on a show that's "vulgar and obvious, full of gimmicks . . . sadness, but with sass and pizzazz," Chester sounds like he could be the Bush administration's media consultant. As the contest climaxes, Chester buys off the other nationals, directing fish-spearing Eskimos, Swiss pan flautists, and Indian sitar players in a mongrelized version of a song sure to cockle the heart of many aspiring Hollywoodians—"California, Here I Come." As always furiously independent, Maddin challenges us to agree that the saddest music in the world might be the sound that change makes when it jingle-jangles in the breast pocket of someone who makes his living by selling out.

18

Ed Halter

James Fotopoulos

In *The Nest* (2003), James Fotopoulos' most recent 16mm feature, things happen. A twentysomething Midwestern man and woman, young white professionals in an apartment of glass-topped tables and black leather furniture, go through a routine of getting dressed in the morning, leaving for work, returning, ordering out for food. Then the two discuss finding odd organic objects in their walls, with clumps of hair on them. A half-hour into the picture, the woman survives an off-screen car accident, and becomes bedridden. A second woman arrives, wearing a cheap glittery shirt. The man becomes violently ill. Another man, dressed like a secret agent from a children's spy-film, visits their apartment, and demands to know if they obtained any samples of shattered rocks from the car crash site.

Such are the traces of what could be pieced together as a story in *The Nest*; there are many other ambiguous moments in the film that may or may not take part in this narrative. Abstract images visit onscreen, set to throbbing electronic drones: drawings and sculptural tableaux, often combined in photographic superimpositions. One image looks like three cat-eyed aliens gloaming behind an electric cloud. Another appears to be two hammer-headed figurines of clay, seated facing one another, like little enigmas one might discover in a four-thousand-year-old sarcophagus, fragments of a symbolism long forgotten. The apartment is lit in a sickly low-wattage greenish-yellow, thick with shadow and buzzing with hypertrophied room-tone (sound is never merely naturalistic in Fotopoulos's works, which are as much audio compositions as visual). The film's rhythms shift gears without warning, swerving from staccato headache pulses to Warholian longueurs, then occasionally freezing entirely on one frame, as if the reel had paused in the gate. The standard interpretation of these stylistic qualities and dark-dreamy interludes as manifestations of the characters' interior states becomes stymied by the Beckett-flat dialogue, intoned in monotonous robot-speak by humans who appear and disappear as if through fractures in reality. Their words and actions occur with the hidden logic of a dream, on the teetering edge of dead solemnity and total preposterousness. It is like a discrete world of pure objects, as if understood preconsciously, without names.

Though he has often been classified as simply a far-out low-budget American independent filmmaker, works like *The Nest* make clear that twenty-eight-year-old Chicagoan James Fotopoulos needs consideration in another class entirely; as his career has progressed, it's clear that he has all along been pursuing a vision of moving-image artmaking that has little in common with movies as such. Though best known for a few 16mm features released on DVD and shuttled around the tiny avant-underground circuit, Fotopoulos has by now made the majority of his work in technologies other than film, and often remarks that his chosen medium is simply "audiovisual." Tellingly, his exhibitions have recently shifted to artworld locales: the 2004 Whitney Biennial, a smattering of galleries, a commissioned installation for Belgium's 2005 video art biennial Contour. Within the past five years, he has produced more than a hundred single-channel videos (of lengths ranging from under a minute to more than a couple of hours), at least twelve albums' worth of sound compositions, a book of more than 400 drawings, a series of music videos for the noise band Grandpa's Ghost, and countless paintings. His current undertaking, an exploratory presidential biography entitled *Richard Nixon*, promises to exist as a ten-plus-hour transmedia corpus in variably exhibitable sections.

The breadth of his artistic output is remarkable not only for its consistent quality—even the roughest of his works betray an unmistakable certitude of vision—but for the impecunious conditions under which his career has developed. Raised in a Greek-American working-class family in Norridge, Illinois, son of a policeman and a hair stylist, Fotopoulos is largely self-taught; he began making movies on Super-8 and video as a child, and dropped out of college after completing his first 16mm films. Until *Richard Nixon*, which received a grant from the Creative Capital Foundation, none of his projects received any considerable outside funding. Though Fotopoulos remains recognizable as an American independent filmmaker only when positioned at the category's ultima thule, he produces many of his longer works in the classic mode of director, complete with minuscule crew, casting-called actors, and festival premieres.

Like more traditional filmmakers, Fotopoulos very much invests in creating immersive worlds, but his worlds are ontologically uncertain, vibrating like optical illusions between enveloping alien universes, indexical records of their own low-budget making, and pure formal abstraction. These are dangerously tenuous states of being, hanging together by mere spider-threads; created from pieces of our existence, but existing parallel to it. When narratives do occur, they never take primacy over formal concerns; stories, characters, and acting styles prove as plastic as anything else.

Critics and others aligned with the traditions of American experimental filmmaking frequently embrace his work; others have responded with oddly vituperative dismissals, as if his very continued artistic existence offended them. Attempts to pin down his style in terms of known authors—frequent comparisons to Cronenberg and Lynch, for example—have thus never quite accounted for the singular nature of Fotopoulos's vision. His films may include something akin to Cronenberg's body-horror or Lynch's blank irrationality, but expressed through a cinematic materialism more in keeping with handcrafting avant-gardists like Stan Brakhage, Malcolm Le Grice, or Kurt Kren (and like Kren, he has a propensity for melding the crude and the refined, both in content and form). Amy Taubin offered that Fotopoulos's movies exist only as "laws unto themselves." Indeed, unlike so many of his peers—both artists and filmmakers—Fotopoulos creates without explicit reference to other media, historical or contemporary; his style is bereft of today's pervasively hyperlinked winking-pop impulse. Intent on perpetuating a self-contained esthetics, Fotopoulos is better described as neo-modernist than post-modernist.

His first three features are among his most accessible films, and introduce the stylistic elements and structural devices found throughout his work. *Zero* (1997), begun when Fotopoulos was still in his teens, involves a single actor, who portrays a man living in a squatter-style setting, muttering profanities and slurs to himself, and the female mannequin torso that provides his only company. His rants are broken by oneiric sequences of bodies, seed-like growths, and hand-painted firestorms; even the "real world" passages unfold on tinted 16mm monochrome stock that shifts from sepia to orange to purple. *Migrating Forms* (1999) takes place in the unremarkable urban apartment of a young man who is having an affair with a blonde. Most of the film consists of their awkward, semiritualistic interactions before sex, interspersed with silent anamorphic images of women. As their trysts continue, an impossibly large cyst appears on the woman's back; the man's cat drops dead; a small plague of bugs arrive. Whereas *Zero* appears to exteriorize the main character's sexual and thanatological drives, *Migrating Forms* takes these concerns and disperses them into the diffuse atmosphere of the film. Beginning and ending with pure black-and-white flicker sequences, *Migrating Forms* suggests a cyclical structure; at only eighty minutes, it feels like a perfectly crafted object.

From the single character of *Zero*, and the male-female dyad of *Migrating Forms*, Fotopoulos shifted into a whole underworld ecosystem for *Back Against the Wall* (2000), set in the seedy world of Chicago-area crypto-stripper "lingerie modeling" clubs. By far the closest the director has come to a standard narrative feature, it feels like an Edgar Ulmer flick updated to the late 1990s, partaking in a psycho-dramatic exploitation esthetic not merely for reasons of budget, but in order to capture the alienating experience of stumbling onto a particularly degenerate yet intricately structured pocket of society. The modeling clubs are never shown, though girls' mafia-like handlers brandish numerous guns (according to Fotopoulos, working .38s and an operational AK-47, provided by the same weapons man who supplied *Bonnie and Clyde*). One of the lead actors is deformed in such a way that his head melds directly onto his shoulders, as neckless as a yeti's.

Concurrent with the production of *Back Against the Wall*, Fotopoulos began *Christabel* (2001), his initial foray into longform video, and his first feature-length non-narrative work. Based on the Coleridge poem, *Christabel* is composed of four parts: two half-hour sequences shot in digital video, and two short codas in 16mm. The video sequences fracture and reassemble different parts of the poem: womens' voices intone the text, mixed into an overlapping drone; female actors re-enact moments from the narrative, edited in ghostly superimpositions; an echoing church bell clangs ("Whither they went I cannot tell— / I thought I heard, some minutes past, / Sounds as of a castle bell."), roughly matching the meter as well as what Coleridge calls the "beating heart" of Christabel. The 16mm sequences depict the poem's woodland setting (a frequent topos of Fotopoulos's short films).

After *Christabel*, Fotopoulos enters a new phase, beginning a breakneck streak of close to a hundred video productions that continued for five years, and completing two 16mm features in this period as well—*The Nest* and *Families* (2002), an intense black-and-white narrative of discrete episodes of disconnected love and sudden violence set among lower-middle-class twentysomethings. Done in 8mm and digital, the videos in many ways go much further into abstraction and the fracturing of experience into disconnected sensoria than his films ever have. Reminiscent of early video art or structural filmmaking—modes with a sculptural sense of time—

these unfold glacially, like moving through the architecture of an ultra-slow musical piece.

Some play like elaborate gallery loops but demand more attention than the at-a-glance style of contemporary art; these are the stripped-down descendants of the circular structure of *Migrating Forms*, opening and closing with images of 8mm video static, retaped off of monitors, which parallel the flickering bookends of his earlier film. In *Hymn* (2002), naked male and female bodies, superimposed and ghostly, fade in and out over an hour and a half of an almost even tone, as if *Christabel* had been smoothed out into a long thin substance. *The Lighthouse* (2004), at only ten minutes, explores a string of mostly nonrepresentational circular forms, created by distortions of light, set to a mix of soft, sandy shuffles. Fotopoulos produced clusters of shorter loops like this, exploring particular techniques. *The Cobweb*, *The Watchtower*, and *Celestial Visions* (all 2003), for example, were each made using a labor-intensive system of retaping off monitors, solarization, and changes in shutter speed on a 8mm video camera; the resulting images are thick with fat, blurry pixels, streaked out horizontally.

The longer videos, like *Jerusalem* (2003), *Esophagus* (2004), or *The Pearl* (2004), compile many kinds of technical experiments, collected into discrete slabs of time, which build, almost musically, over what can be a brutally extended length. These low-tech *gesamptkunstwerken* incorporate oil paintings, hand sketches, digital drawings, sculptures, actors, recorded dialogue (spoken by both humans and software agents), crude 3-D CGI, and original 16mm and video footage, processed and distorted thorough numerous means. The scripts are conversations between two individuals, sometimes a man and a woman, other times two electronic voices of indeterminate or neutral gender. Their discourse sounds vaguely paranormal, with echoes of cult lingo. "There was a white rectangle that appeared to be receding endlessly backward and the sides were completely black and they were in the middle, but they formed one person," intones a female voice in *Jerusalem*. "I'm penetrating the layers. I'm afraid," she says. "Don't be afraid, we are here with you," a man replies.

As always, the eerie, arch qualities are mixed in with absurd, poker-faced humor—an oft-overlooked aspect of his work. One of the most memorable characters of *The Pearl* is a mustachioed dildo, whose appearance Fotopoulos gives as equal weight to as any of his other effects. His most narrative video, *The Ant Hill* (2004), follows the degradations of a cult with such biblical formality that it can be viewed as grim comedy, and his latest, *Spine Face* (2005), includes actors in crude simian masks.

Why is Fotopoulos making this massive body of skillfully designed media, most of which has been exhibited nowhere? Many other contemporary experimental filmmakers work within a community of like-minded artists, who share certain idioms and concerns; others, schooled in the history of art practices, strive to place themselves fruitfully by expanding upon certain lineages and traditions; gallery video artists like Matthew Barney could be accused by pessimists of crafting careers expressly in response to the art world's insular market forces. Fotopoulos may not be completely innocent of any of these strategies, but his art feels like it springs from a more primary and absolute compulsion to create. By emerging from film into video art, he may bring a much-needed weight to a genre grown all too light, applying the rigor of experimental filmmaking to more current tools.

Considering his craft prowess, esthetic ambition, and obsessive productivity, it is by no means outrageous or presumptive to cite Fotopoulos as a kind of post-video answer to Stan Brakhage: a lone male explorer, delving far into the expressive possibilities of form through the interface of audio-visual technology. But whereas Brakhage's machine-age legacy stresses the carefully controlled purity of an expressly filmic vision, Fotopoulos embraces the chaotic impurities of continuously evolving electronic media. Just as Brakhage's camera-vision evolved in the age of cinephilia, Fotopoulos's digital drones and hypnotic pixels parallel our own daily immersion in computery realms.

19

Graham Fuller

Christopher Munch

For Those We Have Loved

Working patiently and quietly on the fringes of American independent film, Christopher Munch writes and directs movies that meditate quietly on the perennial struggle people face in communicating with those they love, on mortality, on the role of memory in the mosaic of consciousness, and the evanescence that drives his restless protagonists to grasp futilely, and often nobly, at impossible dreams, seeking permanence as they try to make sense of their lives. If Munch's vision seems at times melancholy, his films' beauty, their relaxed storytelling and their sharing of wisdom is unfashionably spiritual (in the secular sense of the word). And for all his characters' anxieties and creeping sense of failure, Munch's cinema is not in itself neurotic but serenely transcendent.

As well as two apprentice films, *Goldenoise* (1985), which wasn't completed, and *In Laura's Garden* (1987), Munch has made four features to date, none of which have enjoyed widespread distribution. *The Hours and Times* (1991) and *Harry and Max* (2004) are essentially chamber pieces about two intimately involved men in the pop music business struggling to reconcile their opposing needs, though that sounds reductive when referring to the first film's John Lennon and Brian Epstein. *Color of a*

Brisk and Leaping Day (1996) and *The Sleepy Time Gal* (2001) are more elaborate films, which, in collating pivotal moments in the vocational and romantic histories of two very different adventurers, become prismatic repositories of postwar Americana.

The Hours and Times speculates on what may have passed between John (Ian Hart) and Brian (David Angus), the Beatles's manager, when they went for a twelve-day holiday together in Barcelona, as they did in reality in April 1963, while Cynthia Lennon was still in the hospital with her and John's newborn son. Munch took the title from Shakespeare's 57th sonnet: "Being your slave, what should I do but tend/Upon the hours and times of your desire." Unrequitedly in love with John, Brian haplessly attempts to start an affair with him during their holiday, and constantly meets with his friend's scorn and rejection.

John, equally repulsed and fascinated by the idea of having sex with a man, at one point invites Brian into his bathroom, where he is soaking, to "scrub me back," but after they kiss and Brian steps naked into the tub, John immediately steps out of it and walks away. Munch later hints that they may have been intimate, though Brian's surprise at finding John asleep beside him in his room when he wakes one morning sustains not only the ambiguous nature of their relationship but the myth that Munch is weaving around the two friends, which any disclosure of sexual activity would deflate, as it would the metaphysical tone set by the title.

Munch is more concerned with the quotidian aspects of John and Brian's holiday, and with the playing out of the power games between them, than in answering the question: Did they or didn't they? After the black-and-white film opens with a murky opening montage of Barcelona—the docks (reminiscent of the waterfront in the Beatles's Liverpool), various Gaudi buildings, the Ramblas—John and Brian are shown flying to Spain. Sympathetically observed by Brian, John wakes from a nap and tells him: "I had a dream I was a circus clown, but the circus was underwater, somewhere in Japan I think, everything was blue, I think me [sic] costume was red." This not only indicates John's perverse iconoclasm but the unconscious nature of his relationship with Brian. As Donald Lyons has written in *Independent Visions* (Ballantine), "Brian compares John's dream to Matisse's 'La Danse,' whose patterns of interlocking dancers, with a solitary unlinked dancer, he describes to a quickly comprehending John. The dynamics of the relationship are before us, with a Japanese minimalism: adoring teacher; bright, teasing pupil." Brian's adoration is qualified by a tender paternal devotion, which John brusquely accepts. The real Lennon was raised without a father, of course. In *The Sleepy Time Gal* and *Harry and Max*, parents are a structuring absence (if not entirely absent in the latter). In *Color of a Brisk and Leaping Day*, the protagonist's father is cold and disapproving of his son. Munch himself lived with his activist-writer mother, growing up in La Jolla, though his astronomer father was present in his life and, the director says, taught him "problem-solving" skills.

In Barcelona, which John grudgingly warms to under Brian's cultured influence, they dine in John's room at the Avenida Palace Hotel—a two-shot that captures John standing above and behind Brian, that freezes their emotional and sexual dynamic for all time—and discuss Brian's sexual exploits with rough trade. John damns Brian with faint praise when he says, "I find you an engaging and remarkable man, Brian. I've never met a man like you, but I don't really want to have it off with you." Shortly after, when John later takes a call from Cynthia, he praises the originality of Gaudi's architecture and the way "it stands outside of time." Brian, middle-class and educated, is an original in John's rough, working-class rock 'n' roll milieu, and a man "out of time," partly because of his unfashionable kindness and urbanity, partly because, as the film has no need to remind us, the real Brian died less than four years later. Brian's later heartfelt suggestion in the film that he and John meet at a bench in Barcelona in ten years time, or at least recall their vacation, might seems like heavy-handed irony, yet it also implies that the movie's Brian, at least, was a dreamer, yes, but also a man who intended to live long enough to get nostalgic about his early thirties.

Brian takes John to see Ingmar Bergman's *The Silence* (whose themes resonate with Munch's film) and to a gay club, where they have a desultory conversation with a posh stockbroker; Brian flirts with a bellboy and talks to his mother on the phone. His and John's sadomasochistic idyll is interrupted when Marianne (Stephanie Pack), the liberated flight assistant John met on the plane, visits him, sidesteps his unsubtle (and deliberately uninviting) verbal advances, and twists with him to Little Richard's new single. This perfect heterosexual moment actually sets John free from his repressed feelings about Brian and enables him to love him—platonically or otherwise, we don't know—in his own remote, abrasive way. After they wake beside each other and go out on the hotel roof, Brian affectionately recalls standing beside John on a Liverpool rooftop and saying to him, "These times we have together are very special to me, you know that?"

These times, this hour—for that is the running length of *The Hours and Times*—eternalizes Brian's pursuit of John, which brings him torment, but also the comfort of knowing that it was he who shared those moments with him and the intensity of a relationship that, if imperfect, was validating. Munch, who has said he identified with Brian in the film, draws us into it with his mythic approach, but tells us a universal, empathetic story of romantic obsession.

Although Munch's next film, *Color of a Brisk and Leaping Day*, also has a male character forced to accept that his love for another man is not reciprocated, the true analogue to *The Hours and Times* is Munch's fourth picture, *Harry and Max*, which traces the shifting emotions in an evolving sexual relationship between two brothers. Pop star Harry (Bryce Johnson), 23, a former boy band idol, and Max (Cole Williams), 16, a schoolboy and current teen pop pinup, are first seen together on a winter camping weekend in the San Gabriel Mountains, and it's soon revealed they had sex on a previous vacation in Bermuda. Max, who performs oral sex on Harry under a blanket in their tent, is at first the more needy of the two, but gradually their roles switch.

The brothers' incestuous love and a sunlit flashback of them exploring together some ten years before hints at their having been left to their own devices by their parents. The flashback would imply a parental perspective, as if it were a home movie, except young Max carries a little film camera, which makes it unlikely they were being filmed, or watched. This strengthens the idea that they were neglected. It is significant that Max—who videotapes moments from the camping trip, too—is the one who wields the camera; it subtly suggests that he is the brother who sees most clearly, and, indeed, it will be Max who will takes responsibility for setting boundaries in their relationship. His relationship with the world is also more peacefully mature than Harry's: Max gardens and meditates; Harry drinks heavily and uses pornography—and a teen magazine pinup of Max—to help him masturbate.

A casualty of his early fame, Harry is a spiteful alcoholic in a state of permanent crisis. Mistaking his childhood need for love for a current need for sex, he begins to fixate on Max. What kind of jangled Oedipal state has he regressed into? It's not clear if Max symbolizes for Harry their mother, their father, or Harry's "perfect" prelapsarian self, whom he seeks to reclaim. Munch doesn't strain for psychological resolutions but offers a clue in the use of the boy-band phenomenon as a transparent metaphor for arrested development. Boy bands appeal primarily to adolescent girls, not to sexually threatening adults (like parents); despite having graduated to rock music, Harry only can relate sexually to his girlish, postadolescent brother—though he shares some terse, unenthusiastic phone calls with his girlfriend in New York.

Both brothers seek secondhand intimacy with each other by "casually" having sex with each other's discarded exes. Harry visits Josiah (Tom Gilroy), a former high school teacher of Max's with whom he had a brief, intense affair. He offers himself to Josiah in a sexually receptive position so that he can experience what Max experienced with him. Max sleeps with Harry's ex-girlfriend, the still grieving Nicky (Rain Phoenix), whom he has hitherto loved platonically. These intercut sequences create a dangerous little dance—not quite *La Ronde*—that underscores each brother's confusion and desperation. Its emotional consequence is revealed most vividly in Nicky's face, which can't conceal the self-loathing she feels after going to bed with the gay brother of the man she still loves. When Harry later visits her in the bar where she works, she conceals from him that she slept with Max—only for Harry to graphically describe his and Max's liaisons. Crucially, Max overhears this boast, and when Harry later comes on to him, he rejects him. It is the moment that frees Max from his childhood dependence on his increasingly arrogant brother, who is reminded of his self-destructiveness in a bitter encounter with their mother (Michelle Phillips), a feckless, peevish woman whose self-important role as Max's manager and protector is an insincere attempt to make up for failing her sons when they were kids. We later learn that Max fired her, severing their relationship.

Two years later, Harry visits Max in New York, where, an elfin, babyfaced teenager no longer, he is living contentedly with his painter boyfriend. The movie reaches a climax of sorts when Harry attempts to seduce Max by pretending he wants a threesome. Harry is rebuffed and he walks out, admitting his disgrace. Turning narrator, and recasting the story as a memoir, Max tells us how Harry became a more remote figure in his life, but a more mature man. As the movie flashes back again to the brothers as boys playing on an abandoned railroad line, Max recalls how he enjoyed his childhood with Harry. We last see him following Harry uphill on the camping trip, and noticing how the tracks have been torn up. This is a sign of time's inexorability, a nod to the same idea in *Color a Brisk and Leaping Day* (in which the dismantling of a railroad has more tragic import), and an echo of the consoling idea, intimated in *The Hours and Times*, that memories of love—or the attempt to love and be loved—are longer lasting and as potent as the thing itself.

Harry and Max is the talkiest of Munch's movies, but its steady, uninhibited flow taps the urgency with which Munch says he wrote the script. Although a societal taboo sits at the film's heart, Munch doesn't get very excited about it, and he assumes that his audience won't either. He approaches the subject of a nervily intensified fraternal love with such matter-of-factness that the issue of the brothers' erotic intimacy becomes less important than whether they will be able to resist its lure in the future and go on to discover their sovereign selves as adults. At times, the deliberately naïve and expository dialogue, the sudden sexual trysts, the constant discussion of them, Rob Sweeney's pleasing photography of banal domestic interiors, and the characters' displays of petulance, boorishness, outrage, and disappointment are wonderfully redolent of an afternoon soap opera, which is the drollest possible setting for a story enfolding boy-on-boy incest. It's a form of downbeat, alternative melodrama that doesn't betray or patronize the film's complex theme of how you move on emotionally when you've grown up in a dysfunctional family.

Munch's haunted elegy *Color of a Brisk and Leaping Day* is gorgeously named for a line in Octavio Paz's surrealist poem "Piedro del Sol" and cryptically bookended by quotations from the Parable of the Pearl of Great Price (Matthew 13: 45–46) and *The Rubaiyat of Omar Khayyam*. It begins with an epiphany: as Charles Ives's "The Unanswered Question," inspired by Emerson's transcendentalist poem "The Sphinx," wells up on the soundtrack, plumes of spray hover in the air as water cascades down a Yosemite mountainside. Lambently photographed by Sweeney, who was working as Munch's cinematographer for the first time, the image is one of many in the film that channels the dramatic black-and-white landscape photography of Ansel Adams, who was not only a philosophical descendant of Emerson but a conservationist defender of the Yosemite park.

Is the epiphany disrupted or heightened by the next image, which shows a steam-driven train coursing between a pine-studded slope and a river? It's a not quite unanswerable question, since Munch's film celebrates the mechanical splendor of the Yosemite Valley Railroad a little less than it celebrates the valley it has partially desecrated. Still, those two opening shots establish a dialectic between nature's transcendental grandeur and man's struggle to master it through industry—locomotives having their own esthetic appeal. The entire film, meanwhile, is encapsulated in a retrospective voiceover statement heard as a sedan idles down a residential suburban street just before nightfall: "The year the war came to a close was the year I fell in love for the first time, whether it was with a person or a place or just an idea, I couldn't have said. Later, of course, I came to realize it was all of these."

The speaker is John Lee (Peter Alexander)—young, educated, middle-class—who attempts to resurrect the Yosemite Valley Railroad in 1945 and 1946. The character is fictional, though Munch was inspired by the true story of an eighteen-year-old who had tried to purchase the railroad by making a securities transaction that would have allowed him to float a bond issue. The director saw the romance and the potential for a coming-of-age story in this failed effort.

An impeccably tailored engineering graduate, John is filling in as a trolley mechanic and has formed a rail club with a fellow worker, with whom he shares ancient footage of the Yosemite Valley Railroad, or "YV," when it was fully operational. John lives at an airless house in Pasadena (the suburb where Munch himself was born on Jun 17, 1962) with his snappish Chinese-American father, his icy French mother, and his sardonic, sexually frustrated teenage sister Wendy (Diane Larkin); there are strong hints of incest here, too. John's love of railroads is rooted in his pride in his Chinese ancestry: he is seeking to preserve the legacy of his grandfather, an immigrant laborer on the railroads built in the pioneer era. Against flickering silent footage of "coolies" laying tracks, John narrates a brief history of their experience, including the fact that government figures later sought to repatriate Chinese Americans. On a family trip to Yosemite, John asks his father to stop the car by the YV's El Portal station, which angers the stern paterfamilias, who has no time for his son's obsession. At the station, John learns the YV is to be sold for scrap; walking in the woods beyond, he and Wendy find an Indian artifact. The discovery charges the film with a sense of lives lived harmoniously in the valley before the railroad came—Munch constantly layers such cultural remnants of the past, or the passing—into the story as he elegizes the YV and the friendships John forges, even while depicting its last hurrah.

John's anger at the maltreatment of the Chinese is exacerbated when, on V.E. Day in Los Angeles, he and his pianist girlfriend, whose relationship is petering out because of his apparent inability to love, are jostled on a trolley by a drunken white sailor, who calls them "dirty Japs." The slur deepens John's resolve to own a railroad, for shortly afterward he overcomes official disdain for his scheme and persuades a railroad tycoon (John Diehl) to give him enough money to run the YV for a year. After parting with his yearning sister and patrician mother (whose taciturnity and emotional reserve he seems to have inherited), John leaves for Merced, where the railroad has its headquarters, and takes a room in the Yosemite park's iconic Ahwahnee Hotel with its granite façade and beamed interiors. Later he moves to a boarding house whose genteel old lady owner—who recalls the first days of the YVRR in 1907—is as much a symbol of a faded way of life as the Indian object.

Settling into his new role, John, the taciturn engineer Skeeter (played by Michael Stipe of R.E.M.), and the warm, avuncular former owner of the Yosemite Valley Railroad, Robinson (Henry Gibson), valiantly try to make the YV a going concern again, but neither its freight business nor its day-trip excursions are wanted in the age of road travel. When John returns from an unfruitful trip to raise government funding in the capital and learns that Robinson has died, something greater than the railroad's oldest champion is lost, and we sense the YV itself will soon follow. In fact, it is eventually reclaimed by the tycoon, who can make more money by shipping the rails to his Colorado railroad and scrapping the stock.

John's falling in love with a beautiful young park ranger, the Miwok Indian Nancy (Jeri Arrendondo), meanwhile, complicates his relationship with the railroad, and Skeeter especially. Although on their first meeting

Nancy denounces the YV for the damage it has done to the park, once they have acknowledged their tender feelings, each tries to reconcile their values with the other's. Nancy comes aboard the YV's plushest rail car and later sets out to visit John at Merced by rail; John takes an afternoon to attend one of her Miwok basket-weaving classes. That both are thwarted in these gestures is ominous for the relationship. From their first meeting, Skeeter harbors an unspoken love for John. In his shyness and stoicism, he cuts a more dignified figure than either Brian or Harry, who are emotionally sloppy in comparison; in the jealous act of sabotage he commits to stop Nancy completing her rail journey, he demonstrates that he is only human. When he and John part for good, the latter drives off to the right on in an old model T mounted on rails, but our eyes remain fixed on Skeeter loping off center-frame with his back to the camera. Apart from his dog, he is a man as isolated as any in an Antonioni film.

Everything is changing, or ending. Wendy—now living in New York but engaged to be married—visits John in Yosemite, but the spark between them has gone. John can only muster self-pity when, after a long absence, he and Nancy talk on an observation car. He asks her to visit him in Los Angeles, but she can tell his love has ended, as his pianist girlfriend could tell before her. As if to confirm his emotional failure to himself, and to put an abusive ending to the affair, John has a prostitute fellate him in a Chinatown brothel. The question she puts to him—"Are you more white or more Chinese?"—irritates the sore spot of John's mixed-race identity, as Nancy did when, thinking she was complementing him, she said, "You're in pretty good shape for a white guy who sits in an office." The combination of rigidity—John's irrational racial pride—and idealism may be "the terrible flaw in my character" he tells us, at the end of the movie, that cost YV its existence "as a common carrier." But Munch means this ironically, for he wants us to share the feeling that John's endeavor was heroic. We learn that he eventually went to work for his dad rewiring warehouses in Los Angeles and still paid court to that city's glorious station. We last see him, as we last saw Harry and Max, walking an abandoned track and consoling himself with the thought that "whatever is built lives on in the desert or inside a guy." What lives on in the viewer of Munch's masterpiece is John and Skeeter smiling at each other as John drives a loco for the first time, Robinson hugging John and telling him "you're family now" at the YV's grand reopening, and John and Nancy's first kiss.

Munch followed *Color of a Brisk and Leaping Day* with another elegy, *The Sleepy Time Gal*. It's not his last film, but it makes for a fitting conclusion to these thoughts about this unique filmmaker in that it is a highly personal statement about mortality and, specifically, the impending death of a dynamic middle-aged woman, a onetime bohemian, partly modeled on Munch's own mother. In its agonizing over unreasonable expectations that have not been fulfilled, the film is his most painfully existential, and it little matters that its dying protagonist appears to have gulped hungrily at every experience that has come her way.

In the summer of 1982, writer Frances (Jacqueline Bisset in her career performance) is visiting New York from San Francisco with her photographer son Morgan (Nick Stahl), a responsible twenty-year-old whose blunt but affectionate relationship with his mother has the hallmarks of autobiography, when she complains of a stomach pain and a bloated sensation. A diagnosis of stomach cancer sends her on a rigorous, unsentimental quest into the past to reexamine a life that valued social works over family needs and intellectual vitality over material gain. She considers her romantic vicissitudes and her parental failures. She has another son who is penniless and estranged from her, and a daughter whom she gave up for adoption at birth. Frances's soul-searching coincides with the search of the grown daughter, Rebecca (Martha Plimpton), a personally unfulfilled Wall Street lawyer, to find her mother.

This is Munch's most visually impressionistic and structurally kaleidoscopic film. It's also his most cosmopolitan and least time-bound. Moving from place to place within America, intercutting between Frances's stream of consciousness and the perspectives of Rebecca and Morgan, the movie pieces together the fragments of six decades lived fully—if not contentedly—without aspiring to complete a biographical portrait. This collage enfolds home-movie footage of Frances as a child (actually Munch's mother) and as a beautiful young woman; postcard images (frequently used by Munch in his films); shots of old New York, the Golden Gate Bridge, an old railroad station, other landmarks; a lover, Bob, when he was young and virile; images of the attack on the Fort Washington during the Revolutionary War (one of Frances's interests) and the George Washington Bridge now. Munch is telling us not just Frances's history but a history of America as Frances perceived it, something far more valuable than the official history.

As Frances tries to make sense of it all, she travels to Pennsylvania to visit Bob (Seymour Cassel), who is still married to the wife, Betty (Peggy Gormley), he was with when he fathered Rebecca. On a balloon ride, she expresses to him her regrets—"What's life but a shitload of missed chances?"—only for him to fire back a bromide that's of a piece with his cheerful attempt to woo her again, indicating he has never been the seeker Frances has been. Her conversations with Betty are more empathetic. Meanwhile Rebecca visits Daytona Beach to oversee the takeover of a radio station, and ends up spending a day by the shore with its owner, a sixtyish hep cat, Jimmy Dupree (Frankie Faison). They kiss as fireworks explode behind them and presumably sleep together. A flashback carries us back to the radio station to 1956 when Dupree was her mother's lover, and when she was a local legend as the station's late-night DJ, the seductive sleepy-time gal of the title. Though it adds an Oedipal twist to Rebecca's story, one without tragic consequences, the serendipity seems too contrived. More potent is Rebecca's mystical attraction to Daytona, a town she claims she doesn't like, and to the hospital where she doesn't know she was born.

Threaded through this storm of images, scenes and half-scenes, is Frances's present reality. She fights off her cancer temporarily—takes a new lover we never meet—and then learns it is terminal. She fights on, contemplates suicide, ails. Morgan is drily supportive to the last and replaces Frances at her elderly mother's bedside; a nurse (Amy Madigan) bears witness to Frances's last days. The last image in her mind is that of trees and bushes glimpsed from a car window as it rushes past—that this was what she saw driving to Bob's home on that last visit seems more likely to be a trace of vestigial guilt rather than any feelings about him that she has not already worked through. If it is guilt, it's on behalf of the widowed Betty, who, in a book she writes about Frances, recalls the misery of sleeping next to a man who was in love with another woman. Meeting Betty at her book signing is the closest Rebecca gets to meeting the mother she never knew, or recognized in print.

And this, surely, is one of the key points of Christopher Munch's cinema—that, as the angel Clarence says in Capra's *It's a Wonderful Life*, "each man's life touches so many others." It's a cinema of secret histories—in which Brian, Nicky and Josiah, Skeeter and Nancy, and Betty are as deep-feeling, and deeply felt, as the protagonists they orbit around—and of all our histories, and of the ancient lands on which they unfold.

PART 5

Defiant Lions of the New Wave Generation

20

David Thompson

Pleasures of the Flesh

Walerian Borowczyk

The strange case of Walerian Borowczyk, Polish-born animator, artist, and filmmaker, remains open even after his death at the age of eighty-two on February 3, 2006. The obituaries in France praised him for his artistic vision; those in Britain and the United States recounted the usual caveat that blighted his reputation amongst earnest cinephiles—that he became a pornographer. The charge comes from Borowczyk's embracing of a relaxation in French film censorship in the 1970s and his unashamed commitment to celebrating the female body, and it's one that will remain unresolved in a culture that prefers restraint, discretion, and a constant vigilance over any assault on taboo subjects or dedication to the erotic. The director's comment: "Anything that's beautiful is definitely not pornography. The very term belongs to legislation, not to art. Erotic films show the fascination that physical love exerts on us. Art has the right to engage itself with the most secret realms of our thoughts—that's its privilege."

Gradually his work is sneaking out from behind the covers once again on DVD, with an emphasis on the early, live action features: *Goto, Island of Love* (1968), a magnificent adult fairy tale about an isolated dictatorship in which a proud ruler is brought down by jealousy stoked by an ambitious worker; *Immoral Tales* (1974), four scandalous short tales relating in different time periods the triumph of sexual obsession over Christian convention and morality; and unquestionably Borowczyk's most notorious and provocative film, *The Beast* (1975), in which an American heiress has a recurring dream of ravishment by a hairy, bear-like monster with a huge penis. The fantasy eventually overwhelms the real world of her arranged marriage into a decadent French aristocracy. While *Goto*, made in austere black-and-white (with some subliminal—and sublime—flashes of color), is relatively chaste, its successors are dominated by a camera transfixed by female flesh, especially when glimpsed through sheer cloth or caressed by running water.

However, these titles (in regular circulation because the rights reside with Argos Films, the one French production house that has always supported him) give only a partial view of Borowczyk's achievements. He was born in Poland in 1923, studied painting at the Academy of Fine Arts in Krakow, and entered the film business by designing posters. In collaboration with another (also recently deceased) graphic artist, Jan Lenica, he turned to animation, which, through exposure at festivals and the rise of art-house distribution, won prizes, excited audiences, and garnered critical admiration. In *Dom* (1958), a sophisticated application of stop-motion and sound effects enables objects to take on a life of their own. A scurrying wig devours everything on a kitchen table. A mannequin head breaks apart when amorously stroked by a woman. The latter was played by Ligia Branice, the director's wife and muse, whose own special fragility would shine in his first live-action works.

Borowczyk's strange and provocative experiments in animation came to a peak with his move to France in the late 1950s. A trademark element (highly influential upon Terry Gilliam, for example) was the use of old documents and prints as source material, with Borowczyk cutting and manipulating the material to transform their shapes and purpose. His short-form masterpiece *Les Jeux des Anges* (1964) is an oblique representation of the rituals of the concentration camp. Painted gouaches depict box-like enclosures with mysterious sectioned organ pipes where human body parts are brought together and broken apart. *Renaissance* (1963) begins with an explosion in which the scattered and fragmented contents of a room gradually reassemble themselves, until the last object, a grenade, pulls its own pin and another blast returns the scene to chaos. It's as if Borowczyk saw life and death, creation and destruction, as equal in their power to inspire. Nowhere was this more directly expressed than in his astounding feature-length animation *Le Concert de M. and Mme. Kabal* (1967). Little seen today, it's a unique example of a hand-drawn film aimed at an adult audience. It combines scratchy black ink lines on a white background with a thoroughly abrasive soundtrack. The character of Mr. Kabal is a diminutive dreamer, his wife a monstrous figure prone to violent outbursts, and together they form a grotesque, warring couple who make their home amidst scuttling four-legged creatures and hovering butterflies. The surprise is that it's Mrs. Kabal who eventually transcends her dreams by creating an impossibly vast munitions factory within their house—but out of the mayhem she causes, an uneasy peace is eventually restored.

It's essential to remember this disturbing vision when looking at Borowczyk's live-action films. In the short *Rosalie* (1966), Branice plays a teenage girl accused of murdering her baby, and is filmed by the camera as if she is on the witness stand. While she tells her story of misery and exploitation, significant objects appear in full frame, assuming a weight equal to her tears in emotional impact. Throughout Borowczyk's films, the paraphernalia that surrounds people is as fascinating and potent as the creatures themselves. In a 1976 interview with Carlos Clarens in *Film Comment*, he remarked, "Through objects you discover human nature. Have you ever seen an object created by nature that had any rapport with man? Rarely. Only that which has been crafted by someone." Borowczyk's viewpoint is almost always frontal—you'll be hard-pressed to discover the conventional shot–reverse shot formula anywhere in his output. What you do find is a pervasive sense of film-watching as voyeurism—people are constantly shown looking through telescopes or spying through keyholes. The act of looking at things becomes the art of looking at things.

So if objects become living matter for Borowczyk, does that mean people become objectified by his camera? Let's say that it's an essential leap of faith the spectator has to make to enjoy his cinema and surrender to its peculiar beauty. By his own admission, Borowczyk was far more interested in the visual essence of his films than in telling psychological stories. He was often branded a surrealist, partly no doubt for the praise that he received from figures such Max Ernst and André Breton, who applauded Borowczyk's *imagination fulgurante*. But Borowczyk's attitude was more aligned to the painter-filmmaker, following a tradition traceable from Josef von Sternberg to Peter Greenaway. Borowczyk was a great admirer of *The Draughtsman's Contract* and, like Greenaway, would show off his art-history references, especially in his stunning recreation of Medieval tapestry forms in *Blanche* (1971), or Renaissance Italy in the Marguerite episode of *Three Immoral Women* (1978). But to my mind he's closer to von Sternberg, not only for mutual obsession with decor and materials, but for approaching the film image as an artist's canvas fit for the exploration of the unconscious—not to mention man's overwhelming adoration (and fear) of woman.

This, *bien sur*, is the anxious territory where Borowczyk's admirers and detractors diverge. The director himself demonstrated a shift in attitude throughout the feature films, and characteristically his generosity increased the more provocative his female characters became. At first, he cast Branice as a put-upon victim in *Goto* and *Blanche*, and then a similar misery dogged the heroine of *Story of Sin* (1975), made by Borowczyk on a rare return to Poland. An unashamed melodrama drawn from a *novel maudit* by Stefan Zeromski, the film depicts a young girl's persistent pursuit of her lover all over Europe, enduring a self-induced abortion and prostitution en route. Borowczyk's camera, far looser than before, delights in the bric-a-brac of the late nineteenth century—brass beds, phonographs, corsets, pornographic engravings—as much as the extreme human emotions on display.

The success of this film and the two he made for producer Anatole Dauman (*Immoral Tales*, *The Beast*) led him to the Hakim Brothers and the bizarre star coupling of Joe Dallesandro and Sylvia Kristel (hot from *Emmanuelle*) in *La Marge* (1976). Basing his script on a *prix Goncourt*–winning novel by André Pieyre de Mandiargues, the director was obliged to transpose the story from Franco's Spain to the demi-monde of mid-1970s Paris. But by clothing his characters predominantly in black, moving them around dark streets and sparse hotel rooms, and finally plunging down into a forbidding Metro, Borowczyk created a hallucinatory underworld for little Joe's Orpheus. His scenes with Kristel as the prostitute with whom he becomes obsessed have a surprisingly delicate intimacy. However, when Dallesandro exits the frame, she has little choice than to go back to business at a bar that is a distinctively Boro-world, filled with secret doorways and dusty cabinets containing ripe fruit.

But the women who are depicted in *Immoral Tales*, *The Beast*, and the highly enjoyable nuns-at-play romp *Behind Convent Walls* (1978) prove more resilient in the face of oppression and exploitation, and frequently discover their pleasures without the need of a masculine presence. In *Three Immoral Women*, a triptych of revenge stories, the vindictive heroines are triumphantly assertive and blithely disengaged from the men who cross them. In 1980 Borowczyk replaced Liliana Cavani to direct a version of Wedekind's *Lulu*, with the central character played by the child-woman Ann Bennent (sister of David Bennent, the stunted boy in *The Tin Drum*). Adhering to the words of the original play, this little-seen film is faithful to Wedekind's concept of the alluring female as the ultimate embodiment of male obsession. Borowczyk followed this in 1981 with another adaptation of a classic, of Stevenson's *Dr. Jekyll and Mr. Hyde*, but delved into its subtext to give greater weight to Jekyll's wife, Fanny Osbourne, who becomes an eager participant in his experiment to release humanity body and soul from all moral restraint. This foray into the fantastique is Borowczyk's last great film, though it's an unashamedly messy one—a passionate, delirious farce that slashes through the false respectability of Victorian society. Dr. Jekyll (the fey Udo Kier) immerses himself in a transforming bath and emerges as another creature altogether: tall, muscular, and seen—in a few subliminal shots—sporting a vicious phallus. Fanny is played by Italian actress Marina Pierro, who starred in most of Borowczyk's late features and became a muse to supplant Branice. While the latter usually portrayed a precious flower in danger of being trampled, Pierro's proud Italianate features, confident pose, and well-rounded body signified a perfect femininity for the Polish director. In his last film, *Love Rites* (1988), she plays a prostitute who turns the tables on her vain client and tortures him with bird-like talons attached to her fingers.

But how far were these last films the work of a brave auteur or a slave to the flesh markets? Borowczyk wanted to call his Stevenson adaptation *Le Cas étrange de Dr. Jekyll et Miss Osbourne*. His producers insisted on *Dr. Jekyll et les Femmes*, which is apparently sexier but makes little sense. His film based on Ovid, *The Art of Love* (1983), suffers from the inclusion of blatant inserts from an Italian porn film—while Borowczyk's actors admire the genitalia of equestrian statues, someone else plays with the real thing. And what to say about *Emmanuelle 5* (1987), officially described as "un film de Walerian Borowczyk"? The director himself only claimed authorship of the short film seen within the film, entitled *Love Express*, and said the rest was directed by his assistant. For sure, some of the imagery does suggest Borowczyk's eye at work (close-ups of sex toys, the archaic artifacts of an old train carriage), but the film is an incoherent embarrassment, the star Monique Gabrielle's well-buffed body and vacant expression far removed from the delicacy and natural imperfections of his previous heroines.

Sadly then, these are the aspects of Borowczyk's career that are mostly recounted now, measuring out a decline from purist art-house fare to luridly advertised skin flicks, mainly seen in versions dubbed by indifferent actors, censored by puritans, and corrupted by greedy producers. Borowczyk's last years saw him withdraw from a cinema wary of his intransigence and his obsessions. He made a few episodes for the classy erotic television show *Série rose* and published two books, one a volume of enchanting short stories, the other an embittered reflection on the increasing Pope-worship of his homeland after the fall of communism.

A few years ago, through Florence Dauman, who inherited Argos Films on the death of her father, I finally met the reclusive director, and slowly gained his confidence. I had hoped to make a documentary profile on him, and at times he became excited by the idea. But ultimately all that emerged was a self-shot monologue to camera and the editing of some behind-the-scenes footage from *The Beast* (visible on the Cult Epics DVD special edition). At least this rare material, which he called "The Beast Bis," shows the man obsessively arranging everything before his camera and illustrating every last gesture to his actors. As a self-sufficient animator and artist, collaboration was never really part of his game. Perhaps the solitary pleasures that Borowczyk often depicted—to misquote Godard, all he needed to make a film was a girl and a cucumber—were in a more mundane way reflected in his own modus operandi. Whatever the case, he was a singular man with a singular vision.

21

Joshua Clover

Chris Marker

The Return to Work at the Wonder Factory

To say that he's been "working outside Hollywood" is to fail rather abjectly to capture the geography of a half-century's labor outside the French national or transnational cinemas, outside even the most veiled studio system, outside the conventions of narrative and feature, eventually outside cinema itself, and always outside his name: "Chris Marker" (or Chris.Marker, as he signed for years) is simply the most familiar of a half-dozen filmonyms used in place of the banal French appellation into which he was born, as he was born into the bourgeois enclave of Neuilly-sur-Seine; here, perhaps, the suburb (an invention still relatively recent in 1921) achieves greater symbolic interest than usual as the first outside.

Such a strategy of reflexive exclusion might also serve to map Marker's filmography (the word "career" ought, for reasons that should be obvious, be excluded). The beginning is itself excluded: a handful of early films taking Marker's ur-form of the ethnopolitical travelogue (from 1954 to 1958, his jobs included editing the *Petite Planete* series of travel guides). Though at least one of these, *Letter from Siberia* (1958), is justly renowned, Marker has casually suppressed the five; for him, the material in advance of 1962, coincidentally the year of my birth, is over-awkward. The work on film reaches to the 1990s, during which Marker gracefully adopted "new media."

What remains can be divided—bluntly, as an elephant divides things—into Early Style, Late Style, and the missing years. Marker's canonical (if such a thing is possible; perhaps better to say "viewed") films come from the first and last of these: the early period (1962–1967) begins doubly with the direct cinema doc *Le Joli mai*, surveying the ambivalent Parisian spring at the end of the Algerian war, and a brief fiction he composed during *Le Joli mai*'s off days, *La Jetee*. The lattermost of these periods (1977 onward) pivots around the oneiric traveler's notebook *Sans Soleil* (1981), having commenced with either the opening or the closing sequence of the film called in English *A Grin Without A Cat* (*Le Fond de l'air est rouge*), a valediction for the difficult middle years. These years are difficult, in no small part, for how resistant the span (1967–1977) is to scholarship or even summary: a period in which the director made no films likely to be screened publicy in the United States or anywhere else.

And so it is here we shall have to look, if exclusion is the subject—even if, paradoxically, there is little here to look at (nothing, in fact, unless one is a habitue of international archives). To suggest that this zone is deserted would be awful; to offer it as the heart of the matter seems a different distortion. Suffice to say it's the area of greatest exclusion, the era in which he excluded himself from himself, from his own minor-key auteur status. The great majority of his work was collective, collaborative, unsigned—unmarked, one might say. Many of the titles from this period are attached to the SLON collective, which involved a *Cahier's* worth of French auteurs (including Alain Resnais, Agnes Varda, Claude Lelouch—and Jean-Luc Godard, busy finding his own way out). The acronym for *Societe pour le Lancement des Oeuvres Nouvelles* (Society for Launching New Works) is equally the Russian word for "elephant"; Marker has quite frequently represented himself through the figure of a cat, occasionally an owl, but the elephant doesn't make for a bad familiar. It's difficult to think of his films without being aware that they're frequently about memory, and are always memory itself.

The films' presence withing the constellation of memory is constant, if the alignment is shifting. Memory, surely, forced the medium; it seems clear that Marker turned from early success as a novelist and poet precisely because he decided that celluloid could better capture the material complex of time and space, and the passage of consciousness through it—heavily narrated celluloid, of course. Marker remains the most erudite and eloquent monologuist behind a camera (with the possible exception of Jean-Luc Godard, a ghostly presence in any accounting of Marker's life, just as Marker's story haunts Godard's). And if such reasoning drew Marker to the medium in the 1950s, a bookending decision seems to bring his filmwork to close in the 1990s, in favor of such multi-media and new-media projects as the 1990 video installation *Zapping Zone (Proposals for an Imaginary Television)*, and the CD hyperarchive *Immemory* (1998). Marker's formal ability is singular; perhaps this is why he has never fit comfortably into the category of "documentarian," despite the balance of his production. Leaving behind the fields of film stock, he made good on the simple declaration: "Electronic texture is the only one that can deal with sentiment, memory, and imagination."

That phrase isn't Marker's, originally; or perhaps it is. It appears quite near the center of *Sans Soleil*, spoken by a woman's voice as she reads through the letters of a vagabond cinejournalist eventually given the name Sandor Krasna, who is in turn citing a friend of his, a video-game designer and Tokyo artist named Hayao Yamaneko. They are all Marker, we suspect, as one is every character in a dream; similarly, the far-flung scenes share the quality of having each and all appeared *to him*, of aggregately becoming his past. "They have substituted themselves for my memory," the narrator says in a much-quoted passage on the ineluctable precession of images. "They *are* my memory."

Such involution structures the film, wandering from Guinea-Bissau and Cape Verde to San Francisco, from Iceland to France to the electronically synthesized "Zone," and returning most steadily to Tokyo: "These simple joys he had never felt—of returning to a country, a house, a family home—but 12 million anonymous inhabitants could supply him with them." Given it's maddening, fearless leap into *mise-en-abome*, it seems only sensible that the film is best described via Krasna's description of another: "He said only one film had been capable of portraying impossible memory, insane memory: Alfred Hitchcock's *Vertigo*. In the spiral of the titles he saw time covering a field ever wider as it moved away, a cyclone whose present moment contains, motionless, the eye."

Sans Soleil, is Late Style, as Theodor Adorno used the term regarding Beethoven: gathering and interrelating the interests which (as will become clear) have been present all along—finally not as independent phenomena but as "fragmentary, incomplete, elusive" moments in a continuing consciousness. The self-awareness of Late Style, of consciousness considering itself as itself, is signaled by reflexive gestures: footage from *Vertigo* is interrupted by a matching shot from *La Jetee*, which also happens to be the name of a Tokyo bar owned by Chris Marker, in which an earlier scene is shot. The definitive device, however, is the thematizing of abstract obsessions "made visible in unconcealed, untransformed barrenness." As the film turns in on itself, on how "the magical function of the eye is at the center of all things," memory and image come loose from particular memories, specific images.

The distinction between Early and Late Style suggests not interruption but continuity; what changes is the relationship to abstraction. *Le Joli mai* is exemplary of Early Style, of the focused, singular study; it's exemplary in turn of the direct cinema genre that Marker helped pioneer along with Jean Rouch, a form that would provide the deep grammar of modern documentary filmmaking. But if Rouch's tactic lay in attempting to quiet the buzz of polemic, to desubjectify the camera, Marker took a more impure tack: *Le Joli mai* mixes verité interviews and charged newsreel footage. It cannot finally commit to the simple justice of leaving an ethnographic record of how we lived, but must set this against the reflexive mediations of cinematic apparatus. Subjects' testimony about their lives is neither more nor less real than the life of images, and the record will perforce be a collocation of syntheses, counterweights, substitutions, competitions. This drama is recurrent, with varied tensions: *Le Mystere Koumiko* (1965), a curious and drifting engagement with a Japanese woman conducted both on film in Japan and by mail from Paris, sets the objective interview against the subjective (whimsical, even) interests of the filmmaker. Marker is notably unforthcoming about appearing on camera, but in his films, he has no interest in concealing the presence of the lens from the presence of life, or vice versa. Their relationship, as in *Le Joli mai* and many films on which he's worked, is dialectical. The present escapes into memory; all that is lived melts into images.

On days off from shooting *Le Joli mai*, Marker pointed his camera at a series of stills he had taken, narrated to form a cine-roman that leaps into motion only momentarily, just long enough for the object of the hero's obsession to turn her head toward the camera. *La Jetee*, named for the viewing pier at Orly airport where the film's one obsessive recollection is set, whorls out from an apocalyptic future lived beneath Paris, wherein the villains endeavor to send thralls into the past and future in search of rescue. Our hero, able to weather the journeys exactly because his hypertrophied memory has inured him to temporal difficulty, is eventually able to return to and enter the moment of that single remembered scene, vaguely glimpsed, that has haunted him since childhood.

In traversing this spiral jetty extending out into the lake of time, the remembered image is converted into life (and death) rather than the reverse. Seen from the perspective of Marker's larger work, however, the film is a confrontation not merely with the metacinematic, but with a more brute fact. The fundamental problem of memory for the individual is that one can't remember one's own death. Thus, this is the limit of *cinema verite* as well; the direct camera can recall subjects' lives for them, but the limit remains. The transit of that horizon requires the artifice of fiction; thus, with *La Jetee*, Marker turns for the first (and by some accounts, only) time to fiction film.

This fictive conceit—that the nameless lead is able to have "memories of the future"—renders other gestures in *La Jetee* rather uncanny, should one review the film from this end of history. The desperate mission at the heart of the film is, after all, "to call past and future to the rescue of the present." The captors of Paris seem to mutter in German, but the city is old and bombarded, some streets strewn with paving stones. "All that makes me think of a past or future war," he says elsewhere. Does it summon up recollections of 1940, or the Franco-Prussian war; does one imagine 1870, or conjure more closely *le joli mai* of 1968? Is not, in fact, the entire film somehow haunted by the May days yet to come, when the walls were scrawled with a verbal delirium and the clock seemed briefly to change hands? "Time builds itself painlessly around them," the narrator declares about a doomed reverie. "For landmarks they have the very taste of this moment they live and the scribbling on the walls."

For Marker, 1968 started the year before; he would later contend that "1967, rather than 1968, marked the turning point for the international revolutionary left," in Lupton's words. Thus would begin the middle period, in which Marker would participate in the making of such films as *The Battle of the Ten Million* and *The Sixth Face of the Pentagon*; a series of *Cinetracts* and another with each title beginning *On vous parle . . . Speaking of Brasil: Torture*, one was called; *Speaking of Chile: What Allende said*, another. Much from this period is brief, polemical, international—aggregately, it comprises a supermontage of liberations and repressions designed to show the globalization of struggle and the continuity of resistance. Hence the title of *Far From Vietnam*, echoing the analytic slogan "Vietnam is in our factories."

The most volatile film of this period in which Marker was involved is likely *A Bientut, j'espere* (1968, *Hope To See You Soon*), an account of the 1967 strikes at the vast Rhodiaceta textile factory in Besanaon, built largely from interviews taken during the stoppage. The strikes, by usual measure, failed; the film nonetheless captures the coming-to-consciousness of the spirit that would nearly topple the French government the following year with a general strike twenty million strong. The filmmakers were criticized for privileging misery over the workers' hopes, and focusing overmuch on the male workers; though numerous women labored in the factory, they appeared in the movie generally as wives.

Marker urged the workers to make their own films, a path down which they had already started. It's tempting to assign to this moment a hybrid soviet-hippie idealism, to think of the resultant Medvedkin Groups as a discursive flower of 1968: power to the people et cetera. But it is as well the logical endgame of direct cinema—the director having effaced himself so thoroughly that he evanesces, leaving the subject of the camera to become the subject of history.

That is to say, as noted earlier, this is the period of greatest exclusion for Marker. Such a condition is in some part a generalized quality of revolutionary moments; one recalls that *ecstasy* means to be outside oneself. Still, reflexive exclusion is also particular to Marker throughout; it's one of his constitutive qualities. The more he excludes himself, the more he becomes himself; the more absent, the more present.

The leftist publisher Francois Maspero (in the *On vous parle* reel devoted to him) notes that a publisher is known for three things: books published, books turned down, and books later published because of precedents he has set. This is an elegant schema, but perhaps a bit self-serving. It would be an error, and an ethically ambiguous one, to suggest that Marker was somehow a secret auteur of this era's bloom of ad hoc, antiprofessional documentary cinema, or that this flourishing somehow required the ceding of marquees pursued by SLON. Surely the Medvedkin Groups would have formed without him, under some name; surely the two students who grabbed a camera one June day to record *La reprise du travail aux usines Wonder á Saint-Ouen* (*Return to Work at the Wonder Factory at Saint Ouen*) would have managed, without assignable precedents, to film one small death in the death throes of 1968's refusal. It is not a moment about Chris Marker, but about the shape of modern social relations, whirling around a series of images, an anonymous woman and her tortured howl of *No*, her refusal to accept the breaking of the strike at the battery factory, wailing against union officials that she won't "go back to that prison," to the interior that is always outside of life.

And yet these moments must all be thought together, a complex of labors and conjectures, desires and negations, patient pursuits and sudden contingencies. Surely Marker wasn't in Saint Ouen; surely he was. Each such moment requires people to be there in order to happen, and to be recorded. But they conceive equally of a kind of ghost collectivity in which every conspirator is somehow present, during which these moments feel they are happening to everybody, how everybody with an eye is part of the field in which these hauntings of history manage to congeal into images, imaginings, memories.

22

Chuck Stephens

Moebius Dragstrip

Monte Hellman Circles Back

Monte Hellman makes Westerns. He's made them again and again. He's made them in Utah and he's made them in Europe; he's made them with horses and he's made them with hot rods. He's made them with Sam Peckinpah and he's made them with Samuel Beckett. Famously in the space of six weeks in the summer of 1966, he went into the desert with a small crew and a little of Roger Corman's money, and made two.

They didn't set out to be psychedelic, those two Westerns—*The Shooting* and *Ride the Whirlwind*—but they wrenched the skullcap off the form anyway, rearranged the tumbleweeds, left only what mattered. They stripped down a genre that had already been desiccated and gussied up and burned to the ground a hundred times over—stripped it down and rebuilt it from scratch, remade it in a thoroughly modern, thoroughly serious way, remade it so that the trail became a loop. So that every lonely rider could come around every lonely bend and find himself already there.

Doubling up, doubling back, seeing double, two at a time: For Hellman and his regulars it was both a way of doing business and a way of making sense. Jack Nicholson performed in and coproduced both of those Westerns, and wrote one of them himself. That was the business of it. Warren Oates stars in *The Shooting*—twice, as things turn out: two sides of someone named "Coin." That was the sense of it: cutting a corner and finding yourself already there.

It was, in part, a tradition that Hellman seemed bound to uphold. In 1956, Roger Corman went to Hawaii and directed two films back to back, *She Gods of the Shark Reef* and *Naked Paradise*, later retitled *Thunder Over Hawaii*. (He made six other films that same year.) In 1960, Corman went to Puerto Rico, directed two films, *The Last Woman on Earth* and *The Creature from the Haunted Sea*, and produced a third, *Battle of Blood Island*—within the space of five weeks. That same year, Corman went to South Dakota, directed *Ski Troop Attack* (featuring local ski teams from Deadwood and Lead high schools: "They turned a white hell red with enemy blood!"), and produced a loose retooling of *Naked Paradise* entitled *Beast from Haunted Cave*. This last film Corman entrusted to first-time director Monte Hellman.

Hellman (born Himmelbaum in 1932) spent much of the early sixties as one of Hollywood's intellectual fringe-dwellers, floating in and out of Jeff Corey's acting classes (where he'd meet Nicholson) and parlaying a background in drama at Stanford into a $55-a-week job sweeping out the film vaults at ABC. Occasionally he'd do some pickup work for Corman, shooting additional scenes for *The Last Woman on Earth* and *The Terror*.

It was a hand-to-mouth kind of time, as Corman would eventually recall: "A lot of people look at these films today and ask me if I was being existential. No. I was primarily aware that I was in trouble. I was shooting with hardly any money and less time."

"How'd I get involved with Roger Corman?" Hellman later echoed back to an interviewer. "Well, Roger lost $500 he invested in a stage version I did of Samuel Beckett's *Waiting for Godot*, so I thought I'd better pay him back by doing some films for him. Eventually, we made some Westerns, which was a bit of a full circle for us, because I'd staged *Godot* as a Western, too. Pozzo was a Texas rancher and Lucky was an Indian. I think I see a lot of things in terms of circles and circling back. It just seems that's what so much of human endeavor is."

At the time, though, that existential circle may have seemed a little looser—a little less like a noose, a little more like a hula hoop. Opening on the bottom of a double bill with Corman's *The Wasp Woman*, *Beast from Haunted Cave*—in which a giant-sized, cheapo-Cubist arachnid begins abducting women in answer to some *ur*-biological need—was, as Hellman fondly tells interested parties, his version of *Key Largo* . . . "but with a monster added."

Hellman has tried everything, tried it twice. In 1991 an article appeared in *The Village Voice*, anticipating—perhaps in the slow, lolling wake of the director's strange, estranged *Iguana*—some sort of Hellman renaissance; it was titled "Starting over, and over." The director told the writer: "Even if you believe in determinism you're living an existential life. You're an existentialist whether you know it or not."

Hellman was one of the great serious filmmakers of his generation. He wrote scripts with Jack Nicholson years before anyone knew the actor's name, elicited three of Warren Oates's finest performances, and directed one of the few American movies about cars and their drivers that really matter: *Two-Lane Blacktop*.

But other things matter, too—things like mistakes and delays, miscalculations and irruptions of the *ur*rational. Hellman directed spaghetti gunslinger Fabio Testi making love to Jenny Agutter under a waterfall, and *Guyana: Cult of the Damned*'s Stuart Whitman faking chopsocky alongside *A Better Tomorrow*'s Ti Lung, and the killer Santa Claus film, *Silent Night, Deadly Night 3: Better Watch Out!*

He hasn't finished a film since 1988.

Circling the Wagons

The first shot of *The Shooting* is a shot of a horse—a reaction shot. It is 1966, and *Lancelot du Lac* is still eight years away, but a circle is already emerging. ("Watch carefully *Lancelot*," wrote Chris Marker, once upon a time, "and Roger Corman's *The Red Baron*. They tell the same story.")

A sign reader, Willet Gashade (Warren Oates), returns to his camp, followed by someone. He makes it easy for them, leaves them a trail.

At the camp waits Coley (Will Hutchins), a sage brush naif with a piece of bad news: Leland Drum, a fellow camp-dweller, has been shot dead, and someone named Coin, the group's fourth wheel, has ridden off into the desert. (Throughout the film, the fourth figure keeps adding in and subtracting out from parties of three.)

From Coley's understanding, Drum and Coin had, in Gashade's absence, ridden "into town" and perhaps been a party to an incident: someone "rode down a man and a little person," Coley says Leland said, "maybe it was a child." Upon their return to camp, Drum and Coin had an argument, and Coin left. A little later, seated by the fire in the dark of night, Leland is fired upon, his face blown off by an unseen assailant.

Gashade's mind becomes "all unsettled" at the telling of it; then he gazes into the wind and announces, "Something's coming." A shot rings out, a crow caws murder from the sky; Coley kabuki-skedaddles across the frame, dusting his face and his footsteps with white flour from a flapping sack—a stage effect only one of Godot's muddled minions, or Thomas Pynchon's shanty-singing plebes, could so blithely perform.

Along the rise surrounding the camp, a figure appears: "It's a Woman!"

Perhaps her name is Destiny (it was in *Flight to Fury*)—we'll never know. For us, she is a mud-speckled Millie Perkins, once the embodiment of Anne Frank, now so coiled and venal she might be Kim Darby's *True Grit* adolescent grown into a Dodge City dominatrix. And she has a proposal: a thousand dollars to be shown the way to Kingsley—across the desert, in the direction Coin has taken.

The three set off: Coley smitten with the woman, who remains contemptuous of everything, while Gashade glares and figures, all unsettled, certain that the end of the trail won't be a pleasant one. Every now and then a nonexistent line is drawn, shots are fired into the vast nothingness, and perspectives are exchanged:

"I don't see no point to it," Gashade exclaims.

"There isn't any," the Woman explains.

And that's it, pretty much—except for Jack Nicholson. Trussed inside a leather ensemble—vest, tethers, riding gloves—too tight for a tiny toreador, and introduced with a closeup of his beady, Karen Black eyes so cut-to-shock that it might have ben torn from a Jack Kirby comic book, comes Nicholson's lightning-draw gunfighter, one Billy Spears. "I'm gonna blow your face off," he says to Coley, by way of how do you do. Is he the Woman's lover? No one seems to know.

Eventually, everybody chases everybody, faces them down, loses face—or finds a new one. Masks are worn—white flour, trail soot, pulped meat—or torn away, revealing features altogether like the ones we've seen before. Billy Spears shares the mutilation Jimmy Stewart once suffered in *The Man from Laramie*, and Gashade finds Coin, finds himself, finds time slowing down, film slowing down, everything melting into everything until the point is made: There isn't any.

Carole Eastman wrote *The Shooting* under the name Adrien Joyce (as she'd do for *Five Easy Pieces*), and she claimed that its climax was altogether topical: *The Shooting* was the first Zapruder-ized, quantum Western—the convulsive violence at the end of the trail analyzed until it atomized, scrutinized until it scrambled, all meaning left bleeding while the dust blows forward and the dust blows back. Only Nicholson walks away, at last the dandy, horribly damaged, staggering into the sun—or the hot lamps of fame. It was still only 1966.

Flight

In 1964, Hellman and Nicholson went to the Philippines for a few weeks and, Corman-style, finished *Back Door to Hell* and *Flight to Fury*; Nicholson wrote the latter, co-stars in both.

Murder, resignation to imminent death, hysterical nihilism—all these and Beaver Falls, Idaho; that's what *Back Door to Hell* and *Flight to Fury* have to offer, and I'm only talking about Nicholson's incarnations. A vacant grunt on a no-exit mission in the former, filmed first, he's given to vacillations between E.C. Comics-esque, Shocking War! banter (referring to his partner as "Sgt. Blood" and "Sgt. Courage"), and gazing across a room filled with uncomfortable Filipino bar girls and admitting: "I don't even know if I feel like feeling anything."

In the latter, he's a psycho who walks through Hell—Macao casinos; a plane wreck; raping, murdering banditos—in a pair of gradually filthier white bucks and a shit-eating, death's-head grin. The young actor meant it as a parody of his earliest work, *The Cry-Baby Killer*. "Nobody's gonna just put a name to me and that's it," Nicholson would later assert, in *Ride in the Whirlwind*.

Flight to Fury begins on a rickshaw driver's back, the wiry man running and padding, padding and running like Sisyphus, or like the rickshaw driver in Alain Robbe-Grillet's *La Maison des Rendezvous*—a novel, set in a Hong Kong whorehouse, Hellman long planned, but never managed, exactly, to film.

"You know anything about death?" Nicholson asks a girl next to him on the plane, minutes before her demise. "Punctuation . . . that's all it is."

"You're concentrating on the punctuation and forgetting about the sentence," she says.

Hellman later described *Flight to Fury* as his *Beat the Devil*. *Back Door to Hell* opened bottom-billed to *Hush . . . Hush, Sweet Charlotte*; it was filmed with the cooperation of the Philippine Department of National Defense. Both films end, numbingly, by the water.

When they returned from the Philippines, Hellman recalls, "Nicholson and I were ready to do a film for Corman that Jack was writing, called *Epitaph*. Jack and Millie Perkins were going to star; Jack's character was a young actor, and the story was about trying to raise money for an abortion—a totally taboo subject at the time. The plan was to use footage of Nicholson from the various television shows and movies he'd made up to that point. Corman had agreed to finance it, but when we got back from the Philippines he'd changed his mind and decided that the subject of abortion was 'too European.'

" 'But what about a Western?' he said. 'What about two Westerns?' "

A Road is a Road is a Road

In 1971, Monte Hellman finished only one film: a Western called *Two-Lane Blacktop*. There's a horse in it somewhere. The sixties were over, and watching the film it's difficult to imagine Hellman, who was thirty-nine years old at the time, having ever worn a flower in his hair.

Two-Lane Blacktop stars Warren Oates and Laurie Bird, along with singer-songwriter James Taylor and Beach Boys drummer Dennis Wilson. There are aficionados of both that insist the lank, untucked body temperaments of Robert Bresson's *The Devil, Probably* find their origin in *Two-Lane Blacktop*. No flowers, just hair.

"You all wouldn't be hippies, would you?" Alan Vint wants to know.

"No sir," Oates tells him, "these are hometown boys—we're a big family but we know how to keep it together, you know what I mean?"

Two-Lane Blacktop found its origin as a script by Will Corry. "It was a rehashing of a lot of Disney-type Fred MacMurray movies," Hellman recalled, "four kids in a convertible racing this Chevy, and the mechanic falls in love with the girl who has a little VW Bug, and she's chasing them across the country, and he's dropping his rags out the window to let her know where they are."

The film's screenwriter, Rudy Wurlitzer, eventual Buddhist and author of a series of existentio-absurdist novels (*Nog, Flats, Quake*), claimed he never finished reading Corry's version; tossed it out, bought a stack of hot rod magazines for reference, and rebuilt the script from scratch.

From the West to the East, the film provides a number of races and off-road excursions. The cars star: "I think we discovered that there were twenty-six different camera angles, in and around The Car," Hellman calculates. The young people's parts are also precisely calculated, functional. That is, each is designated by, named for, its function: The Driver (Taylor), The Mechanic (Wilson), The Girl (Byrd). "I can do this," The Girl asserts, failing her driving lesson but remaining true to function, nuzzling The Driver, getting under his hood.

Warren Oates's name is a bit more than his function; his name is his car's, GTO. He shares names throughout the film: jet pilot, test driver, gambler, location scout for a down-home movie about fast cars. And he has a different-colored cashmere sweater for every persuasion. And an ascot. And a bar in the boot. He is not eternal; if he doesn't get grounded pretty soon he's gonna go into orbit. But he's just gonna hang loose. Oates was forty-three years old, and his flat-tire mouth rarely held a friendlier smile.

He gets into a cross-country race with the '55 Chevy, for pink slips. That's the plot.

Will it help to reassert right here that *Two-Lane Blacktop* is a beautiful film—Gregory Sandor's stark, Americana-rama photography countermanding quite handily the post-Robert Frank grotesqueries so fashionable at the time? Or to revel in its movie-movieness: The "motorboating" projector hum that runs under the opening credits, yellow lines ruddering over pavement like damaged sprocket holes or a soundtrack optically strayed? Or the way the projector then quiets down, waits patiently for the film's elemental apocalypse?

In the meantime, Hellman concentrates on punctuation and forgets about sentence; not interested in topics, the film embraces moods—assertively so. Someone turns on the radio—a news broadcast—in the younger generation's car, a primer-gray '55 Chevy, and The Driver insists they "turn that shit off; it gets in the way." He feels like feeling something, but he doesn't want anybody putting a name to it.

Taylor is punchably snide and taciturn throughout; Wilson shaggy and disaffected, seemingly in tune only with the "she" that is The Car: "I think I may need to take a look at her rear end."

"I don't see anybody paying attention to my rear end," The Girl pouts.

On the contrary, The Girl's ultimately car-free ways foul everyone's emotional plugs, her perpindicularity to the men's forward motion sending the film's narrative momentum into a formalist spinout from which it will not recover. The chick just crosses the road to get to the other side, but the film ends in fire.

Esquire magazine, looking for an easy ride, called *Two-Lane Blacktop* "the movie of the year"—before they'd seen it. They were right, but what does it matter what you say about a film? Lew Wasserman, head of Universal, hated it, canceled its advertising budget. It opened July 4th weekend with no ad in *The New York Times*, and performed like water on a sparkler.

The Myths of Sisyphus

"I had been in Europe," Monte Hellman once told an interviewer, on his way to talking about something else, "and I was preparing a film which didn't get made . . . as many of my films don't."

Films Monte Hellman was offered, or prepared to make, but didn't: *Fat City* ("My biggest regret"); *The Last Picture Show* ("I was already signed to do *Two-Lane Blacktop*"); *Junior Bonner*; *Pat Garrett and Billy the Kid* (Hellman and Wurlitzer wrote the first version of the script); and *MacBird* (Arthur Kopit's satire of the Lyndon Johnson presidency).

Films Hellman wasn't prepared to make, but did: *Silent Night, Deadly Night 3: Better Watch Out!* ("I had absolutely no interest in making that film"); *Avalanche Express* (Hellman took over after director Mark Robson died midshoot); *The Greatest* (Hellman took over after director Tom Gries died midshoot).

Films on which Hellman worked but left: *Baretta* (pilot for Robert Blake TV series: "Blake baited me from my first day on that set, so I quit, even though Elisha Cook Jr., who was a guest star, kept telling me to 'take the money and run' ") and *Call Him Mr. Shatter* (a Hammer/Shaw Bros. coproduction starring Stuart Whitman and Ti Lung).

Films Hellman has developed and refers to as "alive and well and living in South Pasadena": *Dark Passion*, or is it *Red Rain* (based on a convict's prison diary); *Secret Warriors* ("a Charles McCarey, cold war story"); *Toy Soldiers* (about a radiation leak); *In a Dream of Passion* (the Alain Robbe-Grillet–based project set in a Hong Kong whorehouse); *The Last Go-Round* (based on something by Ken Kesey).

Films on which Hellman served as unit director: *The Big Red One* (S. Fuller) and *RoboCop* (P. Verhoeven). Films on which Hellman served as editor: *The Wild Angels* (R. Corman), *Bus Riley's Back in Town* (H. Hart), *Head* (B. Rafelson), *The Killer Elite* (S. Peckinpah), and *Fighting Mad* (J. Demme).

Michael Weldon's *Psychotronic Video Guide* asserts that Hellman edited action sequences featuring Harry Dean Stanton *into* Leone's *Fistful of Dollars* for television release. Weldon also asserts that one "Floyd Mutrux" wrote *Two-Lane Blacktop*. Here's a rock I looked under just because Hellman's editing credit was on it, and what a yummy-looking treat I found: *Target: Harry*, aka *How to Make It*, directed by Roger Corman, starring Victor Buono, Vic Morrow, Suzanne Pleshette, Charlotte Rampling, and Cesar Romero. Assistant director: Alain (*Série Noire*) Corneau.

Hellman: "I've always been attracted to the myth of Sisyphus, and I think there's a little bit of Sisyphus in all my films, the idea of an action that is repeated over and over again. You know, the man who climbs the mountain to push the stone to the top, and the stone rolls down, and he has to start all over, again and again."

Things still come up, sprouts of rumors of projects: an update of *Whirlwind*, an adaptation of Elmore Leonard's Hellmanical *Freaky Deaky*.

Handling Birds

In 1974, Monte Hellman finished a film called *Cockfighter*; it's a sequel to *Two-Lane Blacktop*, but it's not a Western. It is the best film to have been made from a novel by Charles Willeford, who once wrote novels set amongst Filipino bar girls (though the other two, *Miami Blues* and *The Woman Chaser*, have their finer facets: the character-rich equations of

Fred Ward, Jennifer Jason Leigh, and Charles Napier in the former, and the sublime balletics of Patrick Warburton in the latter).

Cockfighter opens inside a GTO, that is, inside Warren Oates's name-taking interior: "I learned to fly a plane; lost interest in it. Water-skiing, lost interest in it . . ." Oates is still smiling, but something else has crept in. Now he's a Melhorne handler named Frank Mansfield, a man who's been known to talk too much and is currently holding his tongue. "Anything that can fight to the death and not utter a sound . . . well . . . ," someone says, and you know who he's talking about. Right at the beginning, Frank loses his girlfriend, Laurie Bird, in a bet, to Harry Dean Stanton, the cowhand who'd put the moves on GTO three years before.

Hold the title of the film in your hand a minute. It's weighted like a sap. It feels more like a topic, less like a mood. In the course of things, one man shoves his finger up a rooster's ass, several men are robbed of their pants, and one proposes a drink to "the mystic realm of the great cock." And just like that, the film is loose, shambling, digressive, altogether affable, helped not a little by Nestor Almendros's photography (an expressive departure from Sandor's clean lines, a return to the L.A. funk of *Flight to Fury*), and Michael Frank's Van Dyke Parks-y score.

It is, amidst scenes of difficult-to-take bantam violence, Hellman's gentlest, most embraceable, most feminine film; it ends coolly, even joyously, in the trees. But it's also quite vigilant in its thematic dishevelment. At the climax, Oates tears the head off his cock and gives it to his estranged girlfriend, Mary Elizabeth (Rebecca Pearsey), who puts it in her purse and departs in anger. Frank then sallies off, arm-in-arm with his partner, Omar (Richard B. Shull), having just won the "cockfighter of the year" award. "She loves me," Frank says to Omar, breaking at last his silence.

What do we have here? A living affirmation of men among men? A two-lane testament to gendered dead ends? Corman didn't know, either. New World distributed the film as *Born to Kill*, for which Joe Dante edited in some car chases from *Night Call Nurses*. It has also been known as *Gamblin' Man*, and as *Wild Drifter*. The box for the *Born to Kill* videotape release reads: "The woods are scary . . . The people are worse!"

Cockfighter is the second and last film Hellman made with Laurie Bird; she's last seen in Monteland dressed entirely in coxcomb red, hauled out of the cockfighting pit slung over Harry Dean Stanton's shoulder. In two films, she made more of an impression, left more of a synaesthetic presence, then many actors do in a career. Look at her hair in *Two-Lane Blacktop*, the way a little sweat and a little wind and a few days sleeping in the back of a car culminate in the odor of an era; behold Laurie Bird's bell-bottomed ass and frumpled eyes, her moccasins and her scrape, her petulant voice—you can smell the sixties on her.

Only it wasn't the sixties anymore, and it never would be again.

Hong Kong Whorehouse

"They asked me to direct a scene in what I considered to be a racist way, so I quit," Hellman recalls of (*Call Him Mr.*) *Shatter*, a Hammer/Shaw Bros. coproduction, shot in Hong Kong, that may have been as close as the director ever got to the inside of Robbe-Grillet's *maison*. It is more or less awful: Whitman as some sort of world-weary punisher, sidesaddle with Ti Lung, stripped to the waist, two years after Bruce Lee died.

Michael Carreras gets the directing credit, but Monte gets the memories. On the commentary track of *Two-Lane Blacktop*'s laser disc release, you can hear Hellman snorting loudly as the trailer announces "the most ferocious martial arts thriller of them all." Asked how he felt, knowing that *Shatter* was about to be reissued, Hellman replied, "It makes me question the validity of the entire medium."

All Stuart Whitman remembers is working with "these little Chinese people—I didn't want to hurt them," and something about one of Hellman's girlfriends, now dead, and something about a screening of the film at Hugh Hefner's mansion. Tactless, crummy, but you can see what it might have been, maybe: "The leading character in *La Maison de rendezvous*, although he's called Sir Ralph, is also known as The American. He's really Humphrey Bogart in Hong Kong," Hellman explained once, pondering moves, West to East.

All one can really sense from the film is the *why?* of something, then the bitter termination of something. "In a low-budget film like this, what things are you aiming for?" the laser disc producer wants to know.

"What you're aiming for," the director informs him, "is to live through the experience. And there's the great sense that you're not going to make it."

The Last Woman on Earth

In 1978, Monte Hellman finished a film called *China 9, Liberty 37*. It starred Warren Oates, Jenny Agutter, and Fabio Testi, and in case you're wondering whether or not it's a Western, know only that Sam Peckinpah shows up, as a frontier tabloidist, long enough to murmur the lines, "I take the West to the East." All the way to the East: The film was shot in Spain, with Italian money. In Italy, it's sometimes known as *Love, Bullets and Frenzy*.

The videotape of *China 9, Liberty 37* sold by Video Search of Miami is marketed as "uncut," largely on the basis of its multiple nude exposures of Jenny Agutter. ("Remember the nude scene in the lake?" pants VSoM honcho Tom Weisser in his book on spaghetti Westerns.) That videotape, as it turns out, is not uncut. It omits the following line, spoken by Warren Oates: "Women. If they didn't have cunts, there'd be a bounty on 'em."

The film is an inversion of *Pat Garrett and Billy the Kid*, with the younger Testi riding into the young Agutter's britches and forgetting his job, to kill her husband, Oates, who's older and bearded and fresh out of fantasies. The nude scenes between Testi and Agutter are nauseatingly gauzy, string-sectioned, a fouled reminder of Laurie Bird's nude scenes by the lake, now lost from *Two-Lane Blacktop* but partially documented in an ancient issue of *Show* magazine. (Laurie Bird moved to New York, took a bit part in *Annie Hall*, and died of a Valium overdose in 1979.)

Oates glowers grimly throughout, wincing as Italian stuntmen warble "Red River Valley."

China 9, Liberty 37 just about seethes with hatred, and not all of it directed toward women. At time, it feels like an antidote to *Shatter*: In the beginning, Testi's in Jail in China (pop. 132), standing in for Monte, waiting to be hanged. "Tomorrow you'll be a big hunk of dead meat and a little headline," Testi's Jailer, who you wish was R. G. Armstrong, says. "Better than a big bag of shit everyday," Testi smiles (testifying on behalf of Monte's free-falling career?).

But, like Hellman's career, things don't end in China—they move toward liberty, toward cocaine and circuses, toward whores used as shields and brothers raping sisters, toward a final burning frame. Beyond sexuality and into psychosis, as in the joke Testi teaches Agutter when he teaches her to stay with Oates, teachers her to show him her nuts.

It's a rough road from China to Liberty, but everyone struggles to live and forgive. Sometimes they don't make it. Hellman dedicated the film to his father, and he named his dogs after the two destinations in the title.

He-God of Shark Reef

"He's back to the *Beast from Haunted Cave*," someone quipped to me at the American Cinematheque in 1996, recalling Hellman's 1959 directorial debut, after a screening of 1988 *Iguana*—in which a cheapo-Cubist lizard-man abducts a woman in answer to some biological and *ur*-sociological need. It's the last film Hellman made for which he feels any genuine regard; its dedication reads, "For Warren"—presumably the same

Warren who drove out of *Two-Lane Blacktop*, looking for a set of emotions that would stay with him.

Everett McGill—the titular reptile—already has a set; a face like a svelte Ben Grimm, bumps, boils, swirls, scales, and emotions to match: He's declared war against mankind. Surely Hellman's admitted it somewhere: The film's a remake of Carol Reed's *Outcast of the Islands*.

It was made with Italian and Spanish resources and "the participation of Fabio Testi," which means the Italian co-stars—co-stars in a way that reminds me of Franco Nero in Fassbinder's *Querelle*, maybe because *Iguana* might well have been called *Queequeg Overboard*.

McGill, the iguana, his name is Oberlus; he was a harpooner on a vessel called *The Old Lady* (hold that in your hand a minute), but he lowers himself into the sea and sets out to become the King of Hood Island. He builds his kingdom by enslaving castaways who happen to land upon his rock. Men first, kept in line by a series of castrations, and finally a woman, a Woman, not a Girl, not Destiny, but a monster in proportion to Oberlus—a sexual virago who prefers anything to indifference, and who, once raped by the King, fucks him to death.

Her name is Carmen (Maru Valdivielso)—it was Catherine in *China 9, Liberty 37*—and she repeatedly demands, of every man who beds her, her sexual freedom from the slavery of submission. She embraces the anarchy of individual desire, and her anarchy undoes Oberlus's tyranny. And there you have Monte's films: men, imprisoned by hideous flesh, lusting for nihilism, sideswiped by women they meant to possess. With a little Roger Corman thrown in: a cheaply executed beheading (Robert Ryan's son Tim), a quick trip to the haunted prop shop, a fistful of makeup that won't exactly stay put.

Iguana's about finding a ruthless, even altogether alienating, code of behavior, and sticking to it. The only film Hellman's directed since is one in which Santa Claus is an axe murderer: *Silent Night, Deadly Night 3*, a genre flick in which the blind lead the bland. There is no hero in it, save Monte, but there is a sightless heroine, a slasher with an exposed brain, and a bit of cockfighting rapport between Robert Culp and Richard Beymer. It's funny in parts, and sad in parts, but it mainly suggests that, *pace* Kenneth Anger, the gift of filmmaking is sometimes placed beneath a burning Christmas tree.

But *Iguana* and the Santa Claus film end floating on lullabies, lost among crags where women and their complications find no purchase, and where men are only free enough to fly into fury, drink to their cocks, and wander off who knows where, Warren Oates was the only warm spot on Hellman's battle-scarred planet, and once he was dead, everything else was cast adrift on a churning, spleen-darkened sea.

Epitaph

"I realized my hero had become miserable, stubborn and out of touch," Vincent Gallo complained of Monte Hellman, ten years later, in the summer of 1998, upon the abortion of a collaboration. It wasn't 1966 anymore, but Monte Hellman was holding firm. A man and a little person, maybe it was a child. In Gallo's puny circle of words hides the highest praise.

23

Stuart Klawans

The Not-Too-Long Discourses of Chantal Akerman

CURSED BY EARLY SUCCESS ALMOST as irrevocably as Orson Welles, who also premiered his defining masterpiece at age twenty-six, Chantal Akerman has spent the past decades making a body of work that is large, varied, and too readily summarized. Minimalist, feminist, lesbian: The tags that were stuck on her upon the debut of her first feature, *Je, tu, il, elle* (1974), became fixed with her second, the epoch-making *Jeanne Dielman, 23 Quai du Commerce, 1080 Bruxelles* (1976). Today, thirty years on, the labels still won't peel loose, no matter how much they obscure the artist and her films.

I say obscure, rather than misrepresent, because of course there's a lot of truth in these names. In her choice of style, Akerman remains one of the outstanding practitioners of the cinema of the blank stare, favoring meticulous compositions, distanced camera placements and lengthy takes. The theme of love between women, which she explored (in her own naked person) in *Je, tu, il, elle*, has been a regular feature of her work, up through *Demain on déménage (Tomorrow We Move)* (2004); and so, too, has her concern with the social and emotional constraints on women's lives. With her portrait of the relentlessly ordered, miserly, unemotive Jeanne Dielman, Akerman challenged audiences to detect the exact spot where a tightly regulated character went haywire, and in so doing to find where male domination shades into female self-denial. The impossibility of your marking those lines—despite Akerman's rigorously observational style, which promised to show you everything—made *Jeanne Dielman* curiously mute and teasing, even while it was overwhelming you with its cumulative power. Were you watching a polemic on women's suppressed rage, a case study drawn from Belgium's lower-middle-class or a very, very attenuated sex-and-violence thriller? The easiest answer (and an effective one) was simply to call *Jeanne Dielman* a feminist landmark.

And so it was. The scholar Ivone Margulies was surely right when she wrote in her 1996 monograph *Nothing Happens* that it is useless to cut down the meaning of Akerman's films to a program. All the same, look at the fierceness, the aggression, the protracted lovemaking that concludes and concludes and concludes *Je, tu, il, elle*; and then think of the similarly insistent feelings that seethe below the surface of *Jeanne Dielman*, until they break loose. You can't reduce *Jeanne Dielman* to a headline; but many people did so in the 1970s, and they weren't entirely wrong in their choice: "Woman's Fury Erupts at Last."

The problem, I think, is that the headline is wrong today—wrong for a contemporary viewing of *Jeanne Dielman* and also wrong for the many films that followed. The tags of minimalist, lesbian, feminist that back then identified Akerman as a rebel now threaten to rob her of her independence. Instead of joining her to an artistic and social movement, those labels today would conform her to an orthodoxy.

So I propose, as an experiment, to liberate Chantal Akerman from her own reputation by making matters worse. I want to go back to the beginning and look for a real orthodoxy running through her films—a Jewish orthodoxy.

> The Rabbis once said to Rabbi Abba ben Zabda, "Take a wife and beget children," and he answered them, "Had I been worthy I would have had them from my first wife!"—There he was merely evading the Rabbis; for, in fact, Rabbi Abba ben Zabda became impotent through the long discourses of Rabbi Huna.
>
> Rabbi Giddal became impotent through the discourses of Rabbi Huna; Rabbi Chelbo became impotent through the discourses of Rabbi Huna, and Rabbi Shesheth became impotent through the discourses of Rabbi Huna. . . .
>
> Rabbi Acha ben Jacob stated: "We were a group of sixty scholars, and all became impotent through the long discourses of Rabbi Huna . . ."
>
> —Talmud Yebamoth 64b (trans. Isidore Epstein)

I pursue my project under the heading of an orthodox text, which says nothing of a woman and her many artistic creations but instead addresses the sexual incapacity of a large group of men. Whether this story may be relevant to Akerman's films remains to be tested. All I will say for now is that this snatch of 1,600-year-old faculty gossip, though patently ridiculous, is also dreadful and absurd. To the Talmudic mind, the study of the Law is an absolute good, from which only blessings can flow. More study yields more blessings—and yet, because Rabbi Huna's students waited for him to finish expounding the Law, sixty scholars could not carry out the commandment to procreate. This should have been impossible.

Akerman's career, by contrast, is just highly unlikely.

She started from a quadruply marginal position in society: Belgian, female, lesbian, Jewish. Had she been smart, rather than a genius, she would have improved her professional chances by going to film school, securing an apprenticeship, and learning to do things right. Instead she dropped out, got her hands on a camera, and taught herself to make movies. What made her feel she could?

Her age at the time, and the era, suggest the beginnings of an answer. Akerman was eighteen years old in a year of upheaval, 1968, and had fallen under the influence of a rabbi named Jean-Luc Godard, who said that "Everything still remains to be done" and whose films made you believe it. But Akerman may have also needed another factor in order to invent herself as a filmmaker: an unwillingness to listen to the end of somebody else's long discourses. As you may sense by watching her earliest pictures, she was impatient and defiant.

Surely the defiance contributed to her success. A certain *je-m'en-foutisme* mattered a lot to that period's moviegoers, especially those who were in the feminist orbit. Nevertheless—in Talmudic discourse, there is always a "nevertheless"—I would argue that the more important trait for her has been impatience. The defiance has long since drained out of her work, as one might have hoped. (To quote John Waters, "If you're still a rebel at 50, it's pathetic.") The impatience remains. Now as at the beginning, Akerman's pictures stretch your sense of time and demand more patience than you'd give to an ordinary film—even though they're also direct to the point of brusqueness.

What types of impatience do you find in her work? First, there's the impatience of the characters, starting with the young girl whom Akerman played in her first picture, a little vaudeville skit called *Saute Ma Ville*, or *Blow Up My Town*. Maybe a better English title would be *Boom Town*. Anyway—the kid was in a big, comic hurry to get to her kitchen, do some cooking, and then (too quickly) light the stove. For people who think of Akerman as a dry and somber filmmaker, the mere existence of this slapstick short should prompt a reassessment—especially because Akerman again played a character in a hurry in *Je, tu, il, elle*: someone who couldn't wait to get to her lover, though waiting was what she had to do for most of the picture. Next, with *Jeanne Dielman*, Akerman made a film about a woman who was so impatient that she double-scheduled her tasks. Catastrophe had to strike before Jeanne would sit quietly with nothing to do.

And then there were the impatient characters in the films beyond *Jeanne Dielman*. *Nuit et Jour (Night and Day)* (1991) was a portrait of Julie, who scheduled two shifts of lovers, rather than wait for one of them to come home from work. *Demain on déménage* told the story of Charlotte, who let her widowed mother move in with her and then couldn't wait to sell the apartment and move elsewhere. I should also mention the clinching exception: the character played by Sami Frey in the short *Le Déménagement*, or *Moving In* (1993). During the course of a forty-minute monologue, this man told about a long, delicious moment of hesitation he had once experienced, when he had been caught up in the lives of three young women and couldn't decide which of them was the most delightful. Imagine it: the ability to savor being in suspense. In Akerman's cinema, that would be true happiness—which of course can't last forever.

I've already spoken of Akerman's own impatience—her rush to get her hands on a camera and start making movies, her direct, head-on style of filming, which reads like the visual equivalent of "Let's just get on with it." There's also an impatience in her choice of subject matter. Akerman has spoken of the urgency she felt in making her great 1993 documentary of post-Soviet life in Eastern Europe, *D'Est*—her assumption, which turned out to be warranted, that the places she wanted to film were disappearing, so she had to hurry up and see them now.

These places, as Akerman said, were the sites of an alternative life, that she might have led if history had not driven her family from Eastern Europe. This commentary on *D'Est* names another aspect of her impatience: the sense of loss that haunts Akerman's work. Her concern with absent scenes and phantom companions goes back as far as *Je, tu, il, elle*—or, to take a more explicit example, *News From Home* (1977), her meditation on living as a foreigner in America. While Akerman's eyes, or her camera, are in one place, experiencing the slow unfolding of the here and now, her thoughts pull her elsewhere.

This particular kind of impatience figures centrally in *La Captive* (2000), her modern-dress reinterpretation of Marcel Proust's *La Prisonnière*. You might say there are several inaccessible elsewheres in this picture, the first of which is the world of Proust's novel. His wealthy young protagonist, living a century ago, could own his live-in lover in a way that might still be possible today but is no longer credible. With every intrusion of a matter-of-fact, contemporary detail (such as the presence of workmen in the apartment), Akerman reminds you that her Simon (Stanislas Merhar) and Ariane (Sylvie Testud) are figures from a vanished Paris, which a filmmaker can't present directly.

But then, even the things that a filmmaker can put before her camera will turn out to be elusive. When we first see Simon, he is watching home-movie footage of Ariane at the beach. Rapt before her image, he begins to say "Je vous aime bien"—the words a would-be lover might use in declaring his feelings—but gets caught up in stammering "Je, vous, je, vous." He seems to be baffled by the distance between self and other, or between his three-dimensional world and the adored picture on the screen.

Most inaccessible of all, most impossible to attain through an image, are the thoughts and feelings of Ariane. To the extent that it's a story (which is to say, barely), *La Captive* is the tale of Simon's endless failure to penetrate Ariane: sexually, emotionally, mentally. He follows her through the city, much as James Stewart followed Kim Novak in *Vertigo*, but there is no discovery to be made, no tension to be built up (even when the soundtrack music swells, to accompany an image where nothing much happens). This is a different kind of suspense film. You wait, agonized with impatience, for Simon to accept what he already knows, which is that this woman is beyond him. More than that, you wait for some slight sign of impatience in Ariane—the least hint that she has a will of her own and isn't a mere projection of Simon's desires. If you didn't know that Simon and Ariane, as movie characters, are just so many colored lights, you'd want to shake them both by the shoulders. Or maybe you wouldn't; they provide such a juicy peep show that you want them to go on.

It's easy enough to see the fusion of feminist, lesbian, and formalist themes in *La Captive*. But what's Jewish in Akerman's project? For an answer, we might turn to her next feature, *Demain on déménage*, a spiritual slapstick comedy.

Once again Sylvie Testud stars, this time as a woman whose desires are very much in evidence, though also elaborately and hilariously thwarted. To cope with her mother, make a little space for herself, finish a potboiler novel, and maybe find love, Charlotte goes through an increasingly intricate set of activities, almost ritualized in their performance, which result in her apartment's filling up uncontrollably with boisterous, unruly, entertaining life. The humor in this outcome, and the irony, is that the apartment was already full, but with the ghosts of Europe's Jews.

Like Akerman herself, Charlotte is the daughter of Jews who lived through World War II. Charlotte does not speak of this history, but its traces are everywhere: in the attic where she sleeps, like Anne Frank hiding behind the trap door; in the black smoke that billows from the house vacuum cleaner, like soot from the chimneys of Auschwitz; in a suitcase that Charlotte inherited from her father (along with the items with which it was perpetually packed); in a vacant apartment's scent of bug spray, which reminds characters unavoidably of the gas chambers. The background of *Demain on déménage* is literally suffused with Jewish suffering.

The foreground, meanwhile, bustles with livelier markers of Jewish identity. Charlotte may be a nervous chain-smoker, always distracted, always badly in need of sleep and peace—in other words, an impatient Akerman heroine—but on the positive side she writes pornography, delivers sales spiels for real estate, and knows absolutely no one who can't play the piano. Despite herself, she manages to have some fun being a rootless cosmopolitan—even though, at the end of the film, she winds up not with a lover but with a baby in her lap . . .

Which takes me back to my orthodox text. Like all passages in the Talmud (a text devoted exclusively to matters that are in doubt), this one from Yebamoth is built upon an anxiety. The teacher must take care to remember the needs of the students—and the students must dare, if necessary, to walk away from the teacher, or else discourse on the Law may result in sterility.

Does an analogous anxiety run through Akerman's films? Like Rabbi Huna, she has tried people's patience by running on past all expectations. If the effect is misjudged, then viewers become bored, or provoked in the wrong way—a possibility that Akerman surely understands. She knowingly adopted a high-risk strategy at the start of her career, and she's had the nerve to maintain it up till now, knowing that if she succeeds in stretching time in the right way, the gamble will pay off. By making a film discourse that is almost too long, but not quite, she can break through the barriers of impatience and achieve her own kind of cinematic fecundity: an abundance of the emotional, the spiritual, the real.

That, for me, is what's really at stake in Akerman's films. Yes, her most famous picture deals with the weight of time and of grubby, everyday things. A lot of her other pictures deal with those elements as well. But at heart, the not-too-long discourses of Chantal Akerman feel closer to those of Chekhov and Joyce than to Andy Warhol or even Michael Snow—which is to say, her brusque, rigorous, convention-defying approach directs you straight to the thought that our lives matter.

Even when we're drifting aimlessly through the streets, humming to ourselves, like Julie in *Night and Day*, our lives matter. Even when we're standing around like all those people in *D'Est*, waiting for a tram that never seems to come, our lives matter. If time sometimes stops dead in its tracks—if the objects around us feel as heavy and limp as the cloth *Jeanne Dielman* uses to scrub her bathtub—it's because we're full of desires, and that's why we're impatient and angry and funny and heartbroken.

The reason I love Akerman's cinema is because it takes me straight into those feelings. And, although I have nothing but admiration for Michael Snow and don't want to praise Akerman at his expense, I will also tell you why, ultimately, I like her work a little better. It's because, when she in effect remade *Wavelength* as *Le Déménagement*—when she, too, did a film that in formal terms amounted to a single long zoom forward—the shot that finally filled her screen was not an inanimate object but rather the face of a man who was starting to weep.

As the rabbis said, "You are not expected to finish the work—but neither are you permitted to abandon it."

Contributors

GEOFF ANDREW is Senior Film Editor of *Time Out London*, programmer of the National Film Theatre, London, and the author of numerous books on the cinema, including studies of Kiarostami's *Ten*, Kieslowski's *Three Colors Trilogy*, and the films of Nicholas Ray.

MICHAEL ATKINSON was a writer and critic for *The Village Voice* for thirteen years, and his books include *Ghosts in the Machine*: *Speculating on the Dark Heart of Pop Cinema* (Limelight Eds.) and a debut volume of poetry, *One Hundred Children Waiting for a Train* (Word Works), which won the 2001 Washington Prize. He has written about film and culture for scores of publications, including *Sight & Sound*, *The Guardian* (London), *The Believer*, *Film Comment*, *SPiN*, *The Progressive*, *Cinema Scope*, *In These Times*, *Details*, *Interview*, and *The American Prospect*.

PATRICIA AUFDERHEIDE is a professor in the School of Communication at American University in Washington, D.C., and directs the Center for Social Media there (centerforsocialmedia.org). She serves on the board of directors of the Independent Television Service and on the advisory boards of several academic journals and academic book series. A prolific critic of independent and documentary film, she has written for *Cineaste*, *In These Times*, *The Nation*, *International Documentary*, *The Independent*, *Dox*, and other journals as well as newspapers such as the *Washington Post*, *Boston Globe*, and *Los Angeles Times*.

GODFREY CHESHIRE has worked for more than twenty-five years as a film critic, with long tenures at *The Spectator* (Raleigh), *New York Press*, and *The Independent Weekly* (Durham). He's also written for *The New York Times*, *Film Comment*, *The Village Voice*, *Variety*, *The American Scholar*,

Cineaste, *Newsweek*, *Interview*, and other publications. In 1998, he served as the chairman of the New York Film Critics Circle; in 2000, the Museum of Modern Art and the Sundance Film Festival both presented special discussions of his writings about the issues surrounding digitization. A member of the National Society of Film Critics, Cheshire is working on a book about Iranian cinema.

JOSHUA CLOVER is the author of two books of poetry, *The Totality for Kids* (University of California Press) and *Madonna anno domini* (Louisiana State University Press) and contributed a volume on *The Matrix* to the *Modern Classics* series for the British Film Institute. He writes on music, literature, and film for *The Village Voice* and *The New York Times*. His critical blog site is janedark.com.

GRAHAM FULLER, previously an editor for *Interview* and for *The New York Daily News*, is also the editor of Faber and Faber's *Potter on Potter* and *Loach on Loach*, and has written on film for *Sight & Sound*, *Film Comment*, *The New York Times*, *The Guardian*, and many other publications.

ED HALTER is frequent contributor to *The Village Voice*, has been an organizer of the New York Underground Film Festival for more than a decade, and has written for *New York Press*, *Cinema Scope*, *Filmmaker*, *Net Art News*, *Kunstforum*, *Vice*, and elsewhere. He teaches at Bard College and is currently finishing a book of essays on war and videogames for Thunder's Mouth Press. His Web site is edhalter.com.

HOWARD HAMPTON has written about Asian cinema, among other things, for *Artforum* and *Film Comment*. His book *Born in Flames: Termite Dreams, Dialectical Fairy Tales, and Pop Apocalypses* was published in 2006 by Harvard University Press.

B. KITE lives in Brooklyn and has written for *The Village Voice*, *Cinema Scope*, and *The Believer.*

STUART KLAWANS has been the film critic for *The Nation* since 1988. He is the author of the books *Film Follies: The Cinema Out of Order* (Cassell) and *Left in the Dark: Film Reviews and Essays 1988–2001* (Nation Books), and is at work on a critical study of Preston Sturges, for which he received a Guggenheim fellowship.

DENNIS LIM was the film editor at *The Village Voice* from 1999 to 2006, and is a contributing editor to *Cinema Scope* and a member of the New

York Film Critics Circle. He edited *The Village Voice Film Guide: 50 Years of Movies from Classics to Cult Hits* (Wiley, 2006).

GUY MADDIN, an utterly unique and yet internationally beloved and respected filmmaker, also writes about cinema, his own and others', for *Film Comment*, *The Village Voice*, *Cinema Scope* and *Montage*. His scores of films, both short and feature-length, include *Tales from the Gimli Hospital* (1988), *Archangel* (1991), *Careful* (1992), *Odilon Redon, or The Eye Like a Strange Balloon Mounts Toward Infinity* (1995), *The Heart of the World* (2000), *Dracula: Pages from a Virgin's Diary* (2002), *Cowards Bend the Knee* (2003), and *The Saddest Music in the World* (2003).

MAITLAND MCDONAGH has been writing about movies for more than twenty years, speaks on radio, television, and at film festivals and panels and abroad, and has appeared in many film-related documentaries, most recently Bravo's *100 Scariest Moments in Horror*. She has written three books: *Broken Mirrors Broken Minds: The Dark Dreams of Dario Argento*, *Filmmaking on the Fringe: The Good, the Bad and the Deviant Directors*, and *The Fifty Most Erotic Films of All Time* (all from Carol Publications). Her articles and reviews have appeared in *Time Out New York*, *Film Comment*, *The New York Times*, *Maxim*, *Paper*, and *Fangoria*, and she has taught film history, theory, and criticism at the City University of New York. She is currently the Senior Movies Editor of TVGuide.com.

ED PARK has served as a senior editor and writer for *The Village Voice*, is a founding co-editor of *The Believer*, and a writer for *Cinema Scope*. He blogs at thedizzies.blogspot.com and publishes *The New-York Ghost*.

MARK PERANSON has been the publisher and editor of *Cinema Scope* (www.cinema-scope.com) since its inception in 1999, and is also a programmer for the Vancouver International Film Festival. His criticism has appeared in *The Village Voice*, *The Globe and Mail*, *eyeWeekly*, *City Pages* (Minneapolis/St. Paul), *De Filmkrant*, *Indiewire*, *Cineaste*, and elsewhere.

JONATHAN ROMNEY is a film writer for *The Independent*, *The Guardian*, *The New Statesman*, *Sight & Sound*, *The Village Voice*, *Film Comment*, *Screen International*, *ArtForum*, and elsewhere. He is the author of *Short Orders: Film Writing* (Serpent's Tail), and co-editor of *Celluloid Jukebox: Popular Music and the Movies Since the 1950s* (British Film Institute, 1995). He's served on the jury at the Cannes Film Festival and as an editor of *Sight & Sound*.

JONATHAN ROSENBAUM is the chief film critic for *Chicago Reader*, and the author of many books, including *Moving Places* (University of California Press), *Movies as Politics* (University of California Press), *Movie Wars: How Hollywood and the Media Conspire to Limit What Films We Can See* (A Capella), *Movie Mutations: The Changing Face of World Cinephilia*, co-edited with Adrian Martin (British Film Institute), and *Essential Cinema: On the Necessity of Film Canons* (Johns Hopkins University Press). His writing on films has appeared in scores of publications, including *Film Comment*, *Sight & Sound*, *Trafic*, *Cineaste*, *Senses of Cinema*, *The Guardian*, and elsewhere.

LAURA SINAGRA has been an editor and writer for *The Village Voice*, *Rolling Stone*, *SPiN*, *Salon*, *The New York Times*, *Entertainment Weekly*, *City Pages* (Minneapolis/St. Paul), *Orange County Weekly*, *TracksMusic.com*, *Alternative Press*, and *Seattle Weekly*.

CHUCK STEPHENS, a contributing editor to *Film Comment*, has written about cinema for *The Village Voice*, *L.A. Weekly*, *San Francisco Bay Guardian*, *Cinema Scope*, *The Guardian*, *City Pages* (Minneapolis/St. Paul), *Filmmaker*, *Pulp*, *Kinema Jumpo*, *Indiewire*, *Monterey County Weekly*, and elsewhere. He lives and works in Nashville.

DAVID STERRITT, longtime film critic of *The Christian Science Monitor*, is chairman of the National Society of Film Critics and co-chair of the Columbia University Seminar on Cinema and Interdisciplinary Interpretation. His writing has appeared in *The New York Times*, *Cahiers du Cinema*, *The Journal of Aesthetics*, and *Art Criticism*, and many other publications. His latest of many books, *Guiltless Pleasures: A David Sterritt Reader*, is published by University Press of Mississippi (2005).

DAVID THOMPSON worked in film distribution and exhibition before joining BBC Television as a film programmer, after which he became a producer/director of numerous documentaries on arts subjects, including artists Mark Rothko and Henri Matisse, writer Anthony Burgess, composers Aaron Copland and Karlheinz Stockhausen, and such film directors as Jean Renoir, Quentin Tarantino, Milos Forman, Paul Verhoeven, Busby Berkeley, and Robert Altman. Recently he made a film for the *Arena* series on Alec Guinness, *Musicals Great Musicals* (the story of the Arthur Freed Unit on MGM), and a behind-the-scenes look at Bertolucci's *The Dreamers*. He has also programmed seasons at the National Film Theatre, was co-editor of *Scorsese on Scorsese*, and is editor of *Altman on Altman* (both from Faber & Faber).

GEORGE TOLES is the Chair of Film Studies at the University of Manitoba. He is the author of *A House Made of Light: Essays on the Art of Film* (Wayne State University Press) and has been a screenwriter for many of Guy Maddin's films. He has recently supervised a feature-length student film project entitled *Dizzy Spell*, and is currently working on a screen adaptation of a George DuMaurier novel.

JESSICA WINTER has been a contributor at *The Village Voice*, *Minneapolis City Pages*, *OC Weekly* and *Time Out London*, and also writes about film for *Sight & Sound* and *The Guardian*. She is an associate editor at *Cinema Scope*. Her latest book is *The Rough Guide to American Independent Film* (Rough Guides, 2006).

Index